The Seduction of Culture
IN GERMAN HISTORY

The Seduction of Culture
IN GERMAN HISTORY

Wolf Lepenies

Princeton University Press ❧ *Princeton & Oxford*

© 2006 by Princeton University Press
Published by Princeton University Press, 41 William Street,
Princeton, New Jersey 08540
In the United Kingdom: Princeton University Press, 3 Market Place,
Woodstock, Oxfordshire OX20 1SY

LIBRARY OF CONGRESS CATALOGING-IN-PUBLICATION DATA

Lepenies, Wolf.
The seduction of culture in German history / Wolf Lepenies.
p.   cm.
Includes bibliographical references and index.
ISBN-13: 978-0-691-12131-4 (alk. paper)
ISBN-10: 0-691-12131-1 (alk. paper)
1. Politics and culture—Germany—History—18th century. 2. Germany—
History—Philosophy. 3. Politics and culture—Germany—History—19th
century. 4. Politics and culture—Germany—History—20th century.
5. Germany—Intellectual life—18th century. 6. Germany—Intellectual life—
19th century. 7. Germany—Intellectual life—20th century. 8. Germany—
Cultural policy. 9. National socialism—Moral and ethical aspects.
10. Germany—Historiography. I. Title.
DD97.L47   2006
943—dc22   2005048907

British Library Cataloging-in-Publication Data is available

This book has been composed in Adobe Caslon

Printed on acid-free paper. ∞

pup.princeton.edu

Printed in the United States of America

1 3 5 7 9 10 8 6 4 2

To
The School of Social Science
Institute for Advanced Study,
Princeton, New Jersey

CONTENTS

The Seduction of Culture
in German History

INTRODUCTION

~

Bombs over Dresden
and the *Rosenkavalier* in the Skies

On February 13, 1945, a young mother, with a baby in her arms, and her sister, holding a small boy by the hand, missed the overcrowded train to Dresden. Instead they had to spend the night in a nearby village. The farm where they found shelter was on elevated ground, and among the images the boy could later recall from his childhood was a stroll in the open on the night that Dresden burned. Quietly but with a definite feeling of triumph, he occasionally spoke of this night—as if there were personal merit in having survived the disaster. When the refugees returned to their quarters, the grownups stayed up for a long time. The boy was put to bed, but the door was left open a crack, letting in light. So he could see above him a lamp with strings of glass beads that softly clinked back and forth. Could any German artillery or flak have remained to shake the ground and make the lamp move? Sleep came swiftly.

The boy could not have known that, at the same time, his father was only two kilometers away—two thousand meters up in the sky above Dresden, to be exact—as one of the few German fighter pilots who had scrambled to attack the Allied bomber fleet. That night, most of the pilots had rushed from flash to flash and had finally had to land without ever making contact with the enemy. German air defenses were having increasing difficulty figuring out the course and destination of the English and American bomber squadrons. Often the fighter pilots had to use incidental clues from the ground to guess where they should fly.

When the boy's father took off with his squadron on the evening of February 13, the men initially flew toward Strasbourg in a waiting pattern, circling there to receive destination orders from the ground. The orders, however, never came. The crew included a pilot, an observer, a gunner, and a radio man. When the ground spotting station suddenly rebroadcast a radio program with Richard Strauss's waltz sequences from his opera *Der Rosenkavalier*, the educated men on board—two crew members had doctorates—thought they knew where they should fly: Vienna. So they headed toward the city that provides the setting for the *Rosenkavalier*. Yet the longer they flew, the more they doubted that Vienna was really the target of the Allied attack. Then the gunner remembered the city where the opera had had its world premiere on January 26, 1911, and so they turned back toward Dresden to prevent what could no longer be prevented.

All this is hard to believe, but this is the story my father told much later, when he felt able to talk about what he had done and what had happened to him during the war. The music of Richard Strauss remained, in a curious way, a basso continuo to the ongoing work of the destruction of German cities, "an absolutely devastating exterminating attack by very heavy bombers," as Churchill described it to Lord Beaverbrook. Among the reminiscences the writer W. G. Sebald has assembled about the air raids on Germany is the narrative of a man who listened, as he said, "on the radio to some songs from the sensuous Rococo world of Strauss's magical music" immediately before the devastating raid on Darmstadt.[1] Shortly after the First World War, Walter Hasenclever had written a poem directed against the bellicose German military, which ended with the refrain "The murderers sit in the *Rosenkavalier*."

Bombs over Dresden and the *Rosenkavalier* in the skies create a disturbing image that suggests itself to me as a symbol of the close connection that war and culture, education and destruction, politics and poetry, and spirit and violence had entered into in Germany.[2] When the news that Dresden had been destroyed reached the Nazi leadership, Robert Ley, head of the German Labor Front, reacted as if a heavy burden had been lifted from his shoulders: "We [can] almost heave a sigh of relief. It is over. Now we will no longer be distracted by the monuments of German culture!"[3] Three years earlier, Goebbels had reacted in a similar manner after a British bomber attack on the city of Rostock. He did not mention human casualties at all, but spoke only of the necessity to answer terror with terror and to flatten English "centers of culture" after German centers had been destroyed by the Royal

Air Force.[4] It was well known in Nazi Germany that the loss of great works of art hit Hitler much harder than the destruction of large residential districts.[5] German propagandists allowed this to be known, convinced that Hitler's reaction would be seen as a sign not of his brutal disregard for human suffering but of his artistic sensibility that the war had not been able to destroy.

But not only Hitler and his consorts saw the Allied bomber attacks as above all an attempt to destroy German culture. In May 1942, German-Jewish émigrés in the United States planned a large fund-raising campaign that would enable them to donate a bomber, to be called "Loyalty," to the U.S. Air Force. They tried to enlist Thomas Mann to chair their campaign's West Coast committee. Mann was furious. He would have agreed to collect money for the Red Cross or to buy war bonds, but he found it impossible to support the air raids that were, though by necessity, destroying German cities: "I do not want, after my death, that Germans who read my books—or don't read them—think of myself as chairman of a committee responsible for the destruction of German monuments of culture."[6] Mann was probably right in anticipating the German mind-set: people knew about the thirty thousand casualties the air raid on Dresden cost, but the city also became a symbol, maybe even more well known, of the destruction of cultural treasures, above all the Frauenkirche now rebuilt.

When Ian Buruma reviewed works by the historian Jörg Friedrich on Germany's suffering during the bombing war, he pointed out that Friedrich's book *Der Brand* ended "with a long lament for the destruction of German books kept in libraries and archives. The lament is justified, but its placement at the end of a 592-page book is curious, as though the loss of books, in the end, is even worse than the loss of people—which, from a particular long-term perspective, may actually be true; but that does not make it morally attractive. . . . The real calamity, as it is presented in Friedrich's book, is the destruction of beautiful old cities, of ancient churches, rococo palaces, baroque town halls, and medieval streets."[7] Buruma is certainly right in interpreting *Der Brand* (The fire) as an attempt to correct a "collective turning away from German history and culture," but I am not sure that Friedrich's diagnosis is correct. Writers and historians, perhaps, have not paid enough attention to cultural losses. In the collective memory of the Germans, how-

ever, names like Dresden are reminders as much of the loss of monuments of culture as of human life. The attitude of my father, who could
not speak of the burning of Dresden without mentioning the *Rosenkavalier*, was, among his generation, more the rule than the exception.

As Norbert Elias wrote in his book *The Germans*, "embedded in the
meaning of the German term 'culture' was a non-political and perhaps
even an anti-political bias symptomatic of the recurrent feeling among
the German middle-class elites that politics and the affairs of the state
represented the area of their humiliation and lack of freedom, while
culture represented the sphere of their freedom and their pride. During
the eighteenth and part of the nineteenth centuries, the anti-political
bias of the middle-class concept of 'culture' was directed against the
politics of autocratic princes. . . . At a later stage, this anti-political bias
was turned against the parliamentary politics of a democratic state."[8]
Elias here describes the role of culture in German "domestic policy"; its
role in "foreign policy" was characterized, says Elias in *The Civilizing
Process*, by the German obsession with distinguishing between civilization and culture: "In German usage, *Zivilisation* means something
which is indeed useful, but nevertheless only a value of the second rank,
comprising only the outer appearance of human beings, the surface of
human existence. The word through which Germans interpret themselves, which more than any other expresses their pride in their own
achievement and their own being, is *Kultur*." Whereas the French as
well as the English concept of culture can also refer to politics and to
economics, to technology and to sports, to moral and to social facts,
"the German concept of *Kultur* refers essentially to intellectual, artistic,
and religious facts, and has a tendency to draw a sharp dividing line
between facts of this sort, on the one side, and political, economic, and
social facts, on the other."[9]

Ultimately not only the German middle classes but Germany as a
whole has distinguished itself by its cultural achievements and aspirations. The domestic appeal of culture, accompanied by a mandarin-like
scorn for everyday politics, has been based on the assertion of the deeply
apolitical nature of the "German soul"—an assertion that eventually
nurtured Germany's claim, as a *Kulturnation*, to superiority vis-à-vis
the merely "civilized" West. This peculiar role of culture in German

domestic as well as foreign policy is the theme of this book. I deal with the "German seduction," the tendency to see in culture a noble substitute for politics, if not a better politics altogether.

Describing the antipolitical bias in the German notion of "culture," Elias found it astonishing "to see the persistence with which specific patterns of thinking, acting and feeling recur, with characteristic adaptations to new developments, in one and the same society over many generations. It is almost certain that the meaning of certain key-words and particularly the emotional undertones embedded in them, which are handed on from one generation to another unexamined and often unchanged, plays a part in the flexible continuity of what one otherwise conceptualizes as 'national character.' "[10] Analyzing the German usage of "culture" as an antipolitical key word, I, however, prefer to speak not of a national character but of a national attitude. A national character resembles a body's skin, which may be stretched—"flexible continuity"—but which the body cannot get rid of. An attitude, in contrast, is characterized by a certain looseness; it resembles a favorite item of clothing that one can put on and off and that one can change when one's own mood or fad and fashion require it. "National character" is a serious term, whereas "attitude" has a touch of irony in it—as in the term "Anglo-Saxon attitudes," whose ironic undertone was apparent when Lewis Carroll coined it in *Through the Looking Glass* in 1871 and became even more visible when Angus Wilson used it as the title of his 1956 novel.[11] Irony was a counterweight against the confidence with which the British believed in their own civilization and wanted it to be acknowledged as superior by the rest of the world. The triumphant tone with which the Germans speak of "culture," which only they possess, while the rest must make do with "civilization," needs an equally, if not stronger, ironic distance.

This book examines the German attitude of regarding culture as a substitute for politics and of vilifying politics, understood above all as parliamentary politics, as nothing but an arena of narrow-minded, interest-group bargaining and compromise. But this work is not a debate on the *Sonderweg* (special path) in disguise, asserting that the aversion to politics and the idealist and romantic veneration of culture were the main reason why Germany departed from the "normal" Western course of development and steered into the disaster of Nazism. I do not describe an attitude that is a uniquely German phenomenon. Still, I argue that an overestimation of cultural achievements and a "strange indifference to politics" (G.P. Gooch) nowhere played a greater role than in Germany and have nowhere else survived to the same degree. Seeing culture as a substitute for politics has remained a prevailing attitude throughout German history—from the glorious days of eighteenth- and nineteenth-century Weimar through, though now in considerably weaker form, the reunification of the two Germanys after the fall of communism. Peter Gay, Georg Mosse, Fritz Ringer, Fritz Stern, Peter Viereck, and others have explored this specific German attitude toward culture and politics. I am revisiting their arguments and try to offer new insights into an old problem.

In the area of "domestic policy," I follow a roughly chronological pattern, beginning with the view of culture as a "noble" substitute for politics that originated in the heyday of Weimar classicism. This distance toward parliamentary politics in the name of culture was one reason why the Weimar Republic did not secure the broad-based acceptance and emotional support of its citizens that could have prevented it from falling prey to the Nazis. I regard the aesthetic appeal first of fascism and then of National Socialism not as a superficial phenomenon of the most sinister period in German history, but as an important element in the attempt to explain the attractiveness of Nazi ideology for a large segment of the German bourgeoisie and many German writers, artists, and intellectuals. And even for members of the intelligentsia in exile, the attitude of playing off culture against politics remained. After the Second World War, staying aloof from parliamentary politics on cultural grounds made less and less sense with the integration of the Federal Republic and eventually of a reunited Germany into the mainstream of Western democracies. Still, the tension between old cultural aspirations and new political realities helps to explain developments first in both German states and then, finally, in a country that no longer had to resign itself, as a consequence of a self-inflicted political catastrophe, to remaining solely a cultural nation, but found itself bestowed with the gift of a political reunion.

In the area of "foreign policy," I have concentrated on two case studies—along with a brief glance at Central Europe, where the various revolutions that did away with communism were hailed, at least for a while, as a victory of culture over politics. The first case study deals with the "culture wars"—a term, as far as I can tell, invented in France—that have been so important, throughout history, in shaping French-German relations. The second case study addresses the interplay between German cultural legacies and American political traditions. The chapter on European and American cultural patriotism is a coda to the German-American case study, an example of how loudly the debate over the relationship between culture and politics reverberates down to the European-American rift witnessed in the recent past.

My account does not seek to compete with the well-established approaches of political and social history, and I have not tried to tell a continuous narrative in which the different periods of German history are neatly interwoven with one another. I am aware of the limitations of my history-of-ideas approach. The wish to secure Germany's dominance on the European continent led Bismarck to found the Reich after Prussia's victory over France in 1871; the transformation of the cultural nation into a cultural state was a welcome consequence, but not the primary intention, of Bismarck's strategy. The skepticism of Germany's poet-seers toward parliamentary politics was one factor that led to the demise of the Weimar Republic, but it was not the decisive one, compared with the specter of Versailles, the shock of inflation, huge unemployment, and the revival of nationalist and racist ideologies. The Nazis were brought to power not so much by the aesthetic appeal of their rituals as by their pledge to restore German pride, their promise to limit the power of big corporations and to create jobs, and their appeal to widespread anti-Semitic feelings, among other reasons. After the war, the inner developments in the German Democratic Republic were also characterized by the cultural policy of its elites, but this policy depended on the continuous strategic interest of the Soviet Union in profiting from East Germany as a political and military glacis against the capitalist West. Political apathy and cultural excitement prevailed in postwar West Germany, at least for most intellectual observers, yet the country's quick political and economic recovery was fueled by pragmatically oriented political leaders, who knew how to run a trade union, organize a party, and administer a pension fund.

In short, intellectual history is an addition, but no alternative, to social and political history. Intellectual history is, to a considerable degree, the history of a small group only, the history of intellectuals. Only intellectuals themselves take the impact of intellectuals on the course of events for granted; the question whether and how their ideas were transmitted to a larger audience and what kind of influence they may eventually have exerted must often remain unanswered. One might see in intellectual history or the history of ideas not much more than an ornament on the building of social and political history that could easily be removed from it. After removing it, though, the building would certainly not collapse but it would not be the same building anymore. Intellectual history is not a superficial but a useful adornment of political and social history, reminding us that human societies are characterized not just by what people do, but also by what people say and think they are doing. History is not only about what is happening, history is also about making sense.

An attitude is an act of interpretation: it is a comment about what is happening or should happen in a society. This book describes an intellectual attitude that can be observed throughout German history: the overrating of culture at the expense of politics, especially in the sense of parliamentary politics. Rather than telling a grand narrative, I will take my reader on a tour and draw her attention to a series of vignettes or "constellations" in which this attitude comes to the fore in different historical circumstances. I hope the tour will take on coherence through the kaleidoscopic recurrence of problems and themes, leitmotifs and authors that play a role in several of these constellations. At some points on this tour I will follow a guide in whose life and letters the "German attitude" toward culture and politics, in different facets and variations, miscues and paradoxes, has found its most eloquent, often painfully honest and always ironic expression: Thomas Mann.

This is a book on the history of ideas. One cannot understand German history by talking solely about German intellectual life, but one can understand German history more fully by taking intellectual life into account.

1

Culture: A Noble Substitute

Lessons in Diminished Particularity

If there is anything that can be called a specific German ideology, it consists in playing off romanticism against the Enlightenment, the Middle Ages against the modern world, culture against civilization, and *Gemeinschaft* against *Gesellschaft*. Based on cultural aspirations and achievements, the belief that Germany was traveling a special path, a *Sonderweg*, was always a point of pride in the land of poets and thinkers. The inward realm established by German idealism, the classic literature of Weimar, and the Classical and Romantic styles in music preceded the founding of the political nation by more than a hundred years. Henceforth, they gave a special dignity to the withdrawal of the individual from politics into the sphere of culture and private life. Culture was seen as a noble substitute for politics.

Having thus described the German ideology in my first book *Melancholy and Society* (1969), I was pleased when Hans Magnus Enzensberger quoted my argument in one of his essays. Pleasure turned into perplexity, though, when I realized that he had used my own words to characterize the modern history of—Spain. Thus I was taught an ironic lesson: German history is not nearly as exceptional as the Germans are inclined to believe. Culture has been seen as a substitute for politics at many times and in many places. In Spain, the writers and intellectuals of the "Generation of 1898" were convinced that only a cultural renaissance (*renovación estética*) could rejuvenate their homeland (*la regeneración de España*) after the last significant Spanish colonies overseas had been lost in the war against the United States. In France, writing entries for the *Encyclopédie* and performing plays like Beaumarchais' *Barber of Seville* became a substitute for politics at the time of the Enlightenment, when domestic political action was barred; after the French had been defeated by the Prussians in 1871, political and military revenge had to be postponed and were preceded instead by a "culture war." In Russia, the life and letters of Pushkin were described as an example of how art could serve as an alternative to politics, whereas later literature—the pamphlets and novels, plays, and poems of the intelligentsia—paved the way for the overthrow of the tsarist regime. In Ireland, W. B. Yeats treated the literary renaissance of the 1890s "as a case of culture filling a political vacuum, after the death of Parnell in 1891 and the failure of Westminster to deliver Home Rule in 1893. . . . Young people, disillusioned with politics, were turning to culture to express a national identity and achieve a measure of intellectual freedom."[1] The preeminence given to culture in Germany, and its use—and abuse—as a substitute for politics, seems to be just one case among others.

In recent decades, this lesson in diminished particularity has been convincingly taught in attempts to show the persistence of the ancien régime in all of modern Europe; in the examination of the interconnectedness of Europe's societies and their politics in the decade after the First World War; in the reconstruction of a cycle of German national doctrines whose ideological transitions, rather than ideological persistence, are seen as characteristic; and in the assurance that cultural pessimism was not a German specialty, but rather a feature of bourgeois societies in general.[2]

These attempts, persuasive in different ways, yet convergent in counteracting "the chronic overstatement of the unfolding and ultimate triumph of modernity," have done much to reinsert Germany's peculiar past into a broader context of European history.[3] At the same time, they have reflected a climate of opinion that has enticed revisionist historians to insist on the imitative character of National Socialism, whose ideology, they claim, was modeled on the original fascisms of Latin Europe, and whose atrocities only mirrored the earlier crimes of Stalinism. One might remind these historians of Thorstein Veblen's remark that, as a rule, the Nordic races improve considerably what they borrow. Using chronology not only as an explanation but also, equally falsely, as an excuse, the revisionists have sought to reduce German particularity to a European normality.[4] The Holocaust, in this view, was not much else than a dreadful accident on a road where careless and ideology-intoxicated driving was not the exception but the rule. The historian's search for "normality" in writing about the Nazi regime and the Holocaust may easily lead to understanding and understanding may eventually lead to oblivion and to forgiveness: *Tout comprendre c'est tout pardonner.*

A Strange Indifference to Politics

It remains a challenge for historians to understand the rise of National Socialism and the nightmarish consequences of the Nazi regime without resorting too easily to the viewpoint that Germany was on a special path throughout its history or at least since Bismarck founded the empire after the Prussian victory over France in the war of 1870–71. Many philosophers in ensuing decades were convinced that only philosophy could come up with an explanation for such developments that, at first glance, eluded historical understanding. This was the argument in John Dewey's *German Philosophy and Politics* as well as in George Santayana's *Egotism in German Philosophy,* published in 1915 and 1916, respectively.

Dewey's book had its origin in lectures given at the University of North Carolina in 1915. He singled out Kant's doctrine of the two realms—"one outer, physical and necessary, the other inner, ideal and free . . . primacy always [lying] with the inner"—as the most important element for understanding German national life;[5] and George Santayana did the same when he described transcendental philosophy as the Germans' preferred "method of looking for reality in one's own breast"—adding "that the German breast was no longer that anatomical region which Locke had intended to probe, but a purely metaphysical point of departure."[6] For Santayana, Germany's political actions were nothing but a consequence of German thought characterized above all by a perverse inwardness, glorifying an egotism that other nations regarded as an impediment to be gotten rid of as quickly as possible. For Dewey, a "supreme regard for the inner meaning of things . . . in disregard of external consequences of advantage or disadvantage" distinguished the German spirit from the worldliness of the Latin mind-set or the utilitarianism of the Anglo-Saxon nations. Even German authors ridiculed the "German spirit." In 1933, the year the Nazis came to power, Oswald Spengler described the Germans as a people poor and pitiful who dreamed of an empire in the clouds and called it German idealism. The land of poets and thinkers was in danger of becoming a province of babblers and demagogues (*Hetzer und Schwätzer*).[7] Yet some critics, Dewey among them, also admired the pervasiveness of the transcendental method, which had made Germany the only country in the world where even cavalry generals employed metaphysics to bring home practical lessons. Other observers hated metaphysics for exactly this reason, Flaubert called the Prussian soldiers who were bombarding Paris "Hegel's compatriots."

At the beginning of and during the Second World War, both Dewey and Santayana republished books they had written in the middle of the First World War. They reprinted them without any alteration, for apparently Germany had not changed at all. "Culture" had remained the catchword by which the Germans tried to distinguish themselves from the rest of the civilized world, but "culture is a thing seldom mentioned by those who have it," as Santayana remarked.[8] Whenever he taught German metaphysics at Harvard during the First World War, he felt that "under its obscure and fluctuating tenets [was] . . . something sinister at work, something at once hollow and aggressive"[9]—a statement of inspired vagueness sharpened, during the Second World War, by Dewey, who spoke of the "underlying strains of continuity connecting the creed of Hitler with the classic philosophic tradition of Germany."[10] Such claims of continuity—which were often stretched to claims of causality—were reinforced by the Holocaust, the singular collective crime that doomed Germany and seemed to seal its separation from the mainstream of Western civilization once and for all. Yet attempts to construe causal links between the sphere of politics and the spiritual realm have not been convincing—regardless of whether individuals like Luther, Kant, Schelling, and Nietzsche or intellectual movements like idealism or romanticism were seen as the beginning of a road that inevitably, with Hitler, turned out to be a dead end. Whether one calls it introspection or inwardness, emotional individualism or philosophical egotism—none of these traits belongs exclusively to the German national character.

How could Germany become a modern economy without fostering modern social values and political institutions at the same time? This question is usually answered by referring to the preponderance of the state, which gave from above what, in other countries, the bourgeoisie had to fight for and acquire through its own efforts. Modern Germany, it has been argued, "thought primarily in terms of the might and majesty of the state, modern England primarily in terms of the rights and liberties of the citizen."[11] In this view, Germany, land of obedience, as Herder and others had called it, is contrasted with the land of the free— England. Although this distinction is rather crude, one can hardly deny that idolization of the state has shaped the contours of German society and the course of German history to a large extent.

A look into Matthew Arnold's *Culture and Anarchy* (1869) helps to point out the peculiarities of the confrontation of culture with politics in Germany.[12] Arnold's essay in political and social criticism was an answer to the attack on the chatter about culture that Frederic Harrison had called "perhaps the very silliest cant of the day." Harrison, an English follower of Auguste Comte's positivism, accepted "culture" as the required quality of a literary critic or a belletrist, but he rejected any role for culture in politics, where it necessarily would lead to "indecision in action." Therefore men of culture were perhaps "the only class of responsible beings in the community who cannot with safety be entrusted with power."[13] Arnold made it clear that for him the word "culture" designated much more than just the quality of a good literary critic, yet he emphasized that he did not aim to turn men of culture into politicians. The reason for his reluctance, however, was not that men of culture were unfit for political action. Rather, the deficiency of the current political system had to be deplored because it did not yet permit the intrusion of culture into the world of power. Culture was "a study of perfection," a passion for doing good that in many ways resembled religion. In this respect the modern world was in desperate need of culture, not least in England, where most people believed that the greatness of their country consisted above all in coal and iron.

Those who mocked the "religion of culture" were, to a large extent, members of the middle class, representatives of trade and religious dissent whose maxim "everyman for himself in business, everyman for himself in religion" was responsible, said Arnold, for a dangerous weakening of the moral fabric of English society and a reckless contempt for the state. Arnold sounded rather un-English when he praised the notion of the state that had been so familiar to antiquity and was still familiar on the Continent. For him, the state represented "the nation in its collective and corporate character, entrusted with stringent powers for the general advantage, and controlling individual wills in the name of an interest wider than that of individuals."[14] The English national idea, however, was as remote from this notion of the state as one could possibly imagine. In England, it was Everyman's deep conviction that he had the right to do as he liked. The national idea fostered the "relaxed habits of government" and eventually tended to anarchy. Culture was the necessary antidote—but it needed the support of the state to survive and, if possible, to be strengthened.

Arnold reminded his English readers that Wilhelm von Humboldt, who had made a strong plea for individual self-perfection and the restraint of state activity in his book *The Sphere and Duties of Government*, was nevertheless convinced that the action of the state would still be needed for a long time to come. Arnold also quoted the French liberal Ernest Renan's warning that modern societies would be in jeopardy if the state withdrew its engagement in public matters too soon.[15] Arnold's praise of the strong state sounded "German" or at least "Continental," and his recommendation to the English to apply a more "inward operation" to their own culture must have appeared equally "German" to them.

Matthew Arnold's thoughts, however, were not the reflections of an apolitical man. He was aware that in England people cherished the idea of country as a sentiment; what he wanted to put forward in addition was the idea of the state as a "working power." Culture was needed above all to achieve this goal, not as a compensation for politics, but as the most effective means to change politics as it had been exercised in England over a long period of time. Arnold stressed that he was pursuing a social idea; he insisted that men of culture were the "true apostles of equality," since they wanted culture to be made efficient outside the "clique of the cultivated and learned."[16] Using culture as the most effective weapon in his fight against anarchy, Arnold was anything but indifferent to politics. The *Daily Telegraph* was misled when it took him to task for his supposed indifference to political action by calling him an "elegant Jeremiah." Regardless of whether the prophet Jeremiah was not more of a politician than the *Daily Telegraph* wanted its readers to believe, *Culture and Anarchy* certainly was a powerful piece of political and social criticism and therefore constituted a political action at the same time.

To outsiders it has often seemed that Germans have been obsessed with claiming the uniqueness of their culture and its superiority over Western civilization. But it has not always been understood that this pride was also the result of political disappointments. It was a poet, Gotthold Ephraim Lessing, who led Germany toward unification—not because he gave poetry priority over politics, but because unification was not yet a political option in his time. The Germans had no choice: they had to establish a national theater before they were able to become a nation. As long as the bourgeois was denied political participation and thus did not become a citizen, he had to use the theater to play virtual politics. But even Lessing's idea of creating a national theater in Hamburg was a dream that only lasted two years. Schiller dreamed the same dream and was convinced that Germany would inevitably become a nation once a national theater was established.

In Germany, culture was not least compensation. When the many small German states could not find common ground in politics, Goethe's admiration was even greater for Lessing, who succeeded with his moral comedy *Minna von Barnhelm*, "a specifically north-German product, . . . in delighting the whole of Germany, uniting all Germans in conscious sympathy."[17] When, once again, the Vienna Congress in 1815 failed to unite the many German states, "those Germans who wanted unity looked increasingly to the formation of a cultural cohesion among their people, rather than to a political unity which seemed far distant."[18] Shortly before the outbreak of the Franco-Prussian War, Richard Wagner, in his essay on German art and politics, still had to evoke Lessing and Schiller when he wanted to talk about German experiences of achievement.[19] Indifference to or disappointment with politics had less to do with German mentality than with German history. Indifference toward politics—understood as the collective will of the citizens to participate in the affairs of the *polis*—became a mark of distinction for many who saw themselves as representatives of German culture. At times, it even seemed as if the German state was a state without politics, that is, a state with vassals but without citizens. Yet it never aimed at being a state without culture. In Germany, both nationalism and antinationalism could be characterized by a preponderance of cultural achievements. The finale of *The Mastersingers of*

Nuremberg was proof of "the intellectuality of Wagner's nationalism and its remoteness from the political sphere; . . . a complete anarchistic indifference to the state, so long as the spiritually German, the '*Deutsche Kunst*' survives."[20]

As Fritz Stern has argued, the deliberate withdrawal from politics can be largely explained by the high premium placed on cultural preeminence and on the illiberal elitism that had prevailed in Germany since the time of Weimar classicism. Culture was the arena of the absolute, a realm without compromise. Its exaltation nourished the illusion that culture could be a substitute for power and therefore a substitute for politics.[21] A considerable weakening of politics and of the public sphere was the result. Unlike "civilization," "culture" has remained to this day a term that, in the German language, is almost naturally distant from, if not contrary to, politics. The connotation of "culture" is as positive, warm, and promising as that of "politics" is ambivalent, cold, and suspicious. Today the term "Weimar Republic" still suffers from linguistic bruises, whereas "Weimar Culture" is nostalgically remembered as a great promise that has remained largely unfulfilled. "Bonn is not Weimar" was the battle cry of the second German republic in the fifties, a political promise to do everything possible to fight political radicalism and ensure the stability of the democratic regime. Yet Berlin always felt flattered when the city was seen, decades after the end of the Second World War, as the place where elements of Weimar Culture had survived.

The distance between Potsdam, a symbol of Prussia's military might, and Weimar, the symbol of German culture, is not great. Looking at Germany's past and present confronted foreigners with a paradox. It was "the co-existence through the centuries of a community almost slavishly docile to constituted authority and of a rich, critical, creative cultural life."[22]

The German Spirit and the German Reich

On October 4, 1914, ninety-three well-known, highly respected German intellectuals, scientists, writers, and artists—"mandarins" is the generic term Fritz Ringer has applied to them—published a manifesto addressed "An die Kulturwelt" (To the civilized world) in which they defended the actions of the Reich against criticism from abroad. The text of the manifesto had been drafted by a Jewish poet, Ludwig Fulda, who would commit suicide in 1939. The manifesto was, as Fritz Stern has described it, a moral declaration of war, a document of autistic arrogance. Germany was a peace-loving nation; the war had been imposed upon it. Germany had not violated the neutrality of Belgium; rather, the German army had anticipated and prevented Belgium's violation by French and English troops. Germany had not broken the rules of international law; on the contrary, it suffered much from the atrocities of its adversaries to the east and west. Most important, though, was the claim that the war against Germany was not, as the foreign propaganda would have it, a war against German militarism. It was above all a war against German culture—preposterously justified by the Liberal government in England as a war for civilization. The fight between British "civilization" and German "Kultur" became even more furious because there had been intellectual concord between Liberal Britain and prewar Germany.[23]

What was not understood abroad was that German militarism and German culture could not be separated from each other: "Without German militarism German culture would already have disappeared from the soil of the earth." Statements like this were signed by the painter Max Liebermann, the liberal politician Friedrich Naumann, the professor of Romance languages Karl Vossler, and the psychologist Wilhelm Wundt, among many other unlikely names. The classicist Ulrich von Wilamowitz-Mollendorf even went so far as to declare that the fate not only of German but of European culture depended on the victory of German militarism. The signatories of the manifesto vowed that they would fight the war as members of a cultural people (*Kulturvolk*) for whom the legacy of Goethe, Beethoven, and Kant was as sacred as German soil.[24] T. S. Eliot was appalled that the Germans insisted that they were fighting a culture war; the "normal" war interested him much less and was no reason to get angry. He would fight not against German crimes but against German civilization, "all this system of officers and professors."[25] Eliot's letter, however, was not only ambiguous because he spoke of German civilization and not of German culture. After announcing that he would protest German civilization as represented by the system of officers and professors, he closed his letter with the ominous remark: "But very useful to the world if kept in its place."

Most of Germany's adversaries, however, declared they were fighting not the country of Goethe, Hölderlin, and the brothers Humboldt, but a nation that was led by the Kaiser, Hindenburg, and Ludendorff. Yet it was not easy to separate the two Germanys. True, a German tradition that saw culture as naturally detached from politics lent itself to such a split. But this view had changed after the transition from a cultural to a political nationalism in the first half of the nineteenth century. Now politics was seen in Germany as the guarantor of culture, and culture provided politics with additional legitimacy. The French especially could not help but envy the coalition between the professor and the officer that had been victorious at Sedan in 1870. After the lost battles of Jena and Auerstedt in 1806, Prussia was the first European state to introduce compulsory military service as well as compulsory education. German soldiers had been able to defeat the French because they were disciplined and educated at the same time. There was nothing enigmatic about Germany's success: its source was the coalition between culture and politics. For Paul Valéry, discipline was the most efficient German weapon. German intellectuals were as methodical as German generals.[26]

Ironically enough, it was the founding of the German Empire that led Friedrich Nietzsche to insist on the split between politics and culture—for the sake of culture. At the start of the Franco-Prussian War, Nietzsche asked the University of Basel, where he had been appointed associate professor at the age of twenty-four a year earlier, for leave so that he could join the Prussian army. He enlisted as a medical assistant in August 1870. On July 19, Nietzsche had written to his mother that the French tiger was attacking German culture. To fight the tiger was worth any sacrifice. On the same day, however, Nietzsche struck a quite different note in a letter to the classicist Erwin Rhode in which he prophesied that the war would reveal how shaky the foundations of German culture really were. And in December 1870, again in a letter to his mother and sister, he admitted that his sympathies for the German war of conquest were rapidly dwindling. The French tiger was no longer threatening the survival of German culture. German culture was threatened above all by the coming Prussian victory.[27]

Germany's unity had been achieved not by politics but by culture. For a long time, the Germans were content to remain a *Kulturvolk* whose self-esteem could not be lowered by the absence of a unified German state. For this self-sufficiency, they were admired not least by the French. With the Napoleonic conquests and the war of liberation, however, all this changed. Proud of officers like Blücher, Gneisenau, and Scharnhorst, the Germans became aware that culture had not been enough to defeat Napoleon. "After 1815 the *Kulturvolk* of Germany had to recognize that it could only compete in the harsh world of modern politics if it had the protection of a powerful state: if, from a *Kulturvolk*, it became a *Kulturstaat*," as Hugh Trevor-Roper has put it. Similarly, Georg G. Iggers has described the transformation of German historical thought "from Herder's cosmopolitan culture-oriented nationalism to the state-centered exclusive nationalism of the wars of liberation."[28] The notion of a cultural state was as strange to the historian Jacob Burckhardt as it was to his colleague Friedrich Nietzsche. Burckhardt stubbornly refused to identify state and culture. "Power, he believed, was separate from culture, could be hostile to it, had a momentum of its own, and was, in itself, evil." When the Franco-Prussian War broke out in 1870, Burckhardt predicted that culture would be the victim.[29]

Nietzsche did the same. When the war of 1870–71 was won, he opposed the popular belief that, with the Prussian army, German culture had been victorious at Sedan. It was a dangerous delusion that would inevitably turn victory into the defeat, "if not the extirpation, of the German spirit for the benefit of the 'German Reich.' "[30] From then on, the intricate relation between political success and cultural failure remained a leitmotif for Nietzsche. After the founding of the Reich, the Germans had become bored with the spirit: "Politics swallows up all seriousness about really spiritual things.—*Deutschland, Deutschland über alles*: I'm afraid that was the end of German philosophy." For Nietzsche, no true philosopher or poet could be found in Germany anymore but only a single outstanding individual whose political success had destroyed culture and had therefore, as an ironic compensation, turned politics into a work of art: Bismarck. His admirers called him a political sculptor and architect, or the Rembrandt of German politics.[31] Nietzsche also came to despise Richard Wagner because Wagner had seen, at least for a while, the resurrection of the German empire as the prerequisite for the progress of German culture. Nietzsche anticipated a veneration of Bismarck that would survive well into the Weimar Republic, based above all on the delicate brutality with which the chancellor of the Reich was able to achieve his political goals. From the middle of the nineteenth century, German political thought was characterized by a conflict between idealism and realism, between a romantic yearning for morality in the public sphere and the deliberate refusal to let ethics enter the realm of politics. In Bismarck, these diverging attitudes were brought together: the Iron Chancellor was regarded as the model of the shrewd German politician in whom romantic sensibility became brutal, and whose cynicism was tempered with spirituality. Max Weber said as much, with his characteristic common sense, when he saw no divergence between Bismarck's eminent intellectuality and his excelling in *Realpolitik*.[32]

Nietzsche's remark that he was the last apolitical German meant distancing himself from the union between politics and culture that Bismarck had achieved. The term "apolitical" (*unpolitisch*) is somewhat misleading here; Nietzsche rather wanted to express his "antipolitical" reaction to Germany's political triumphalism. As for Burckhardt, culture and the state remained antagonists for him. Any attempt at creating a union between them was doomed to fail: "You can't ultimately spend more than you have—that's true of individuals, it's true of peoples. If you spend yourself on power, on grandiose politics, on economics, world trade, parliaments, military interests—if you give away in *this* direction the quantity of understanding, seriousness, will and self-overcoming that you *are*, then this quantity isn't available in the other direction."[33] The cultural state, Nietzsche believed, was a chimera of modern times that would never become a reality. In truth, one always had to choose between politics and culture: "One lives off the other, one prospers at the expense of the other. All the great ages of culture are ages of decline, politically speaking: what is great in the cultural sense has been unpolitical, even *anti-political*." Emerson should not have been surprised that Goethe, "the head and body of the German nation," to whom he devoted one of his lectures on "Representative Men," lived in a defeated state.[34] For Nietzsche, it could not have been otherwise. After the Prussian victory over France, German culture no longer counted. Its future resurrection required political defeat: "A nation usually rejuvenates itself on the political sickbed and rediscovers its spirit, which it gradually lost in its seeking for and assertion of power. Culture owes this above all to the ages of political weakness."[35] George Sand echoed Nietzsche's view when she wrote to Flaubert, in 1876, that Germany's moral decay would begin with Germany's military victory. It was the contrast between culture and power that led Nietzsche, in an aphorism in *Human, All Too Human* (1878/1886) to the warning that "the teachers and promoters of culture destroy themselves when they desire to go about in arms and through precautions, night watches and evil dreams transform the tranquillity of their house and calling into an uncanny lack of tranquillity."[36] The aphorism was entitled "Do not be a warrior of culture if you do not need to be."

Nietzsche thus bequeathed to the German intelligentsia a dangerous gift. He had not only taken the split between culture and politics seriously by using it to understand recent German history. He had made a vicious attack on patriotism in the guise of a political prophecy: for its renaissance, German culture would need nothing less than a political and military disaster. After the Franco-Prussian War, Nietzsche's bitter sarcasm could be easily swallowed because Germany had been victorious, the Reich had finally been founded, and the country was on its way to becoming one of the world powers, both militarily and economically. On the eve of the First World War, however, German intellectuals were forced to distance themselves from Nietzsche's ironic forecast. They had to proclaim the inner unity not just of politics and culture but also of culture and Prussian militarism. Only in skeptical realists like Max Weber could one hear an echo of Nietzsche's voice. Weber was convinced that a nation's political prestige enhanced the prestige of its cultural achievements. Yet he doubted that German culture would profit from the increase in political power that Germany enjoyed after its victory over France in 1871.

The industrialist and politician Walther Rathenau was equally skeptical. In retrospect, he felt ashamed of the hypocrisy of the self-satisfied German intellectuals and professors who claimed that theirs was the only country in which culture reigned supreme, while the other European nations had nothing but civilization. In a text written in 1918 and pointedly labeled "the last essay before the revolution," Rathenau called the patriotic fervor that led into the First World War the low tide of the German spirit. In the past, this spirit had been magnificently engaged in all kinds of idealist endeavors but had remained aloof from politics—now it had given up its ideals and had deteriorated into an instrument of propaganda. In the future, the German spirit would have to be idealistic and realistic at the same time.[37] During the war, however, only a few intellectuals had the courage to distance themselves from the new wave of cultural patriotism or to suggest, as Rathenau did, that the word "culture" should be eliminated from the German vocabulary. Among them were Hugo Preuß, the jurist and co-founder of the German Democratic Party, who would later write the first draft of the Weimar constitution, and the historian Ernst Troeltsch, who had the courage to call idealist nonsense the pathetic claim that the First World War was a culture war. In truth, he said, it was nothing but a power struggle that was basically fought not by the intellectual elite but by the military and business, by technicians, chemists, and workers. Eventually Troeltsch joined his colleagues who spoke of the First World War as a "war of spirit and character," but he continued to insist that this culture war was totally alien to the Germans. The German people had great trouble finding the "formula and the ideas" with which to fight a spiritual struggle.[38]

When political and military defeat came in 1918, German historians were well prepared, as at the war's outbreak four years earlier, to reject the claim that the Allies had fought a war against German militarism only, but not against German culture. The underlying distinction between politics and culture did not make sense, because the two could not be separated in a country whose people would forever remain poets and philosophers—and fight as brave soldiers at the same time. Germany had been dragged into a culture war for which it was not at all prepared. Worse than bombs and mortars were the literary attacks that its adversaries mounted against Goethe's homeland.

German historians were proud to admit that their country had departed from the mainstream of European political thought between 1770 and 1840, but they flatly rejected the claim that Germany had, at the same time, turned to inwardness as its apolitical ideal. They would have been appalled at the insinuation that Germany's greatest achievement was its culture and politics by far its greatest failure. They saw high treason in Nietzsche's remark that he did not care much about the political reunification of his country since he was only interested in the unity of German life and spirit. It was above all Friedrich Meinecke who took upon himself the task of telling the story of how, in the history of Germany, culture had by necessity turned into politics. The former separation of culture from politics, in his view, had nothing to do with the German national character. It was a distinction that had been inflicted upon the German people from the outside. Robbed of their political independence after the collapse of the Holy Roman Empire in 1805 and Prussia's defeat by Napoleon a year later, their intellectual creativity might seem to have nothing to do with the war or with politics. Meinecke was ready to admit, like Nietzsche before him, that the cultural creativity of a nation does not depend on a powerful nation-state. Against Nietzsche, however, he insisted that a society that was eager to maintain its creativity through generations could not do so without a robust body politic. Arguably the greatest achievement of the Prussian reform period had been that "culture and intellect freely joined the state, and springs were tapped that irrigated all of German life, far beyond the immediate goal of liberating the country." Nevertheless, culture and politics could not be seen on the same level, as Meinecke, perhaps inadvertently, made clear when he argued that the German spirit, "by *descending* to the state, . . . not only preserved its own endangered existence as well as that of the state, it secured a reservoir of moral and psychological wealth, a wellspring of creative power for later generations."[39]

Things had been quite different before France's triumph in 1806. In the time preceding the Napoleonic Wars, the Prussians lived in an old territorial state and in a new military monarchy at the same time. The educated classes inhabited yet another world, "a wholly new realm, untouched by the state, where the individual shed his political and social cloak and man himself stood revealed as the origin, measure and end of all values." Theirs was a literate and artistic society where what happened on earth to ordinary human beings "reached them only as an echo." The Prussian state maintained a division of duties that suited the purveyors of culture marvelously well. What they thought and wrote and quarreled about did not matter much in the realm of politics. As a reward they were left completely untouched by the outside world: "Many of them praised their condition and saw it as the epitome of civilization."[40]

Meinecke detected deep historical wisdom in the early separation of culture and politics. Had the German educated classes at this time not been able to distance themselves from ordinary political life, they might have been forced to sacrifice art and literature, music and philosophy for the sake of the state. The classical decade from 1795 to 1805 might not have come into existence at all. A long period of incubation was needed before the military state of the eighteenth century could become the cultural state of the era of reform and the nineteenth century. Thus the delay in the development of political consciousness was seen as a precondition for the blossoming of philosophy, literature, and the arts. This formulation was a typically German way of coming to terms with the tension between culture and politics. France offered the counterexample. On the one hand, in the seventeenth century, the works of classical authors like Molière, Corneille, and Racine could hardly be understood without seeing them in conjunction with the national splendor that the court of Louis XIV displayed. On the other hand, it would have been wrong to assume that the apolitical if not antipolitical character of German classicism necessarily led to world-weariness or to provincial attitudes. Cosmopolitanism quite often became a refuge for those who could not but stay aloof from national politics. The idea of a "World Literature" was hatched not in a metropolis like London or Paris, but in a small town like Weimar.

In France, the middle classes and men of letters had joined forces to create the national idea—in Germany, this idea had been created by men of letters alone, as Meinecke insisted, not intentionally but as a by-product of their poetic achievements and their philosophical thought. It was only too understandable, therefore, that Wilhelm von Humboldt could write, in a letter to Goethe from Paris on March 18, 1799, that "whoever occupies himself with philosophy and art belongs to his fatherland more intimately than others" or that Schiller, in a prose synopsis of a poem written after the peace of Lunéville (1801) with the title "German Greatness," claimed that German dignity "resides in the culture and in the character of the nation that are both independent of her political vicissitudes. . . . While the political Empire has tottered, the spiritual realm has become all the firmer and richer."[41]

These were not antipolitical statements. They pointed, on the contrary, to a specific period of German history in which the political consciousness of the nation developed first in the arts, literature, music, and philosophy. When Novalis boldly claimed that all culture had its origin in the relationship between the individual and the state, he did not contradict Wilhelm von Humboldt or Schiller. Novalis rather expressed the same convictions as they had, now couched in other words, because the circumstances of political life had changed with the new ruling couple in Prussia, Friedrich Wilhelm III and Queen Luise. Novalis also demonstrated how false it would have been to identify romanticism with inwardness.[42] Only as a consequence of the Prussian victory over Napoleon in 1813 could Germany turn into a cultural state. German spirit and Prussian politics could no longer be separated. Culture and power now subsisted side by side; *Machtstaat* and *Kulturstaat* were one. From now on, Prussia was cast in a providential role in the history of Germany.

Why, then, did the tension between politics and culture not only survive well into the Weimar Republic but also eventually contribute to its downfall by playing into the hands of the Nazis? After the Napoleonic Wars, freedom from foreign occupation did not bring political freedom to the German people. During the Restoration period that followed, a coalition between culture and a specific kind of politics was sealed in Germany. Politics meant the submission of civil society to the state, the surrender of the individual to the community, and the propagation of national values and racial pride rather than the pursuit of universal ideals. It kindled a romantic revolt against modernity and rejected "civilization" for the sake of "culture." In this sense, German politics was not an example of a liberalism *manqué*; it was the deliberate rejection of the liberal ideas that played such a crucial role in the development of Western democracy.

Democrats and liberals were not absent from Germany. Yet many of them, like Georg Forster, who fought for the French Republic, and Heinrich Heine, who mocked German authoritarianism, were forced to leave their homeland and died in exile. They remained outsiders. There was a widespread consensus among the German cultural elite that the democratic form of government was as alien to the German spirit as was the view that politics should be regarded as the art of the possible. To accept compromise as an outcome of political conflict was seen as a sign of decadence. The "Ideas of 1914," as the German sociologist Johannes Plenge had called them, were opposed to the "Ideas of 1789" that shaped the development of the West. Many therefore regarded the Weimar Republic, the attempt to establish a democratic regime in Germany for the first time, as a betrayal of German political ideals. Attempts to reconcile culture with parliamentary democracy were stigmatized as attacks on the German spirit. Even Meinecke, who had turned into a "republican through reason" (*Vernunftrepublikaner*)— that is, one who came to accept the Weimar Republic less than wholeheartedly and more by cool reasoning—and had, though somewhat grudgingly, accepted the new democracy and defended the Republic, bitterly complained that in Germany the hero had left the political stage. Only shopkeepers remained. Meinecke still favored the attempt to create a cultural state in Germany—but he did it in a mood of political resignation, not of political enthusiasm. One is reminded of the 1918 party program of the German Democratic Party, which, by suggesting the creation of a *Kulturstaat*, read as if it "were written by a committee of frustrated metaphysicians rather than by one composed of politicians."[43] An attitude of self-destroying prophecy prevailed, the feeling that nothing could be done to reconcile parliamentary politics and culture.

Nietzsche's prophecy from 1870 now served as a weapon against unpatriotic activities in the field of culture. A cultural renaissance that was enhanced by democratic ideals and liberal values could be vilified as profiting from the military disaster of the First World War and the political collapse of the Reich. It was this tension between politics and culture that would contribute to the rise of National Socialism and the fall of the Weimar Republic. As Peter Gay wrote at the beginning of his book on Weimar Culture, "to found a country in the city of Goethe did not guarantee a country in Goethe's image. It did not even guarantee its survival."[44]

2

From the Republic into Exile

Reflections of a Political Thomas Mann

When Thomas Mann heard the news of the mobilization of the German army, he wrote to his brother Heinrich on July 30, 1914, that he felt "shaken and confounded by the terrible weight of reality."[1] Some months later he published a patriotic polemic in honor of Frederick the Great with an introduction titled "Thoughts in War"—thereby following his character Gustav Aschenbach, the doomed hero of *Death in Venice*, who was the author of a "lucid and vigorous prose epic on the life of Frederick the Great." In 1918, when the war came to an end, Mann's *Reflections of a Nonpolitical Man* appeared, a true "monument," as the author himself called it with his typical modesty. National-conservative readers could feast on Mann's Frederick essay as well as on his *Reflections*. In both of them, not only patriotism but also militarism prevailed. It would be utterly wrong, though, to read them as nothing but conservative manifestos that made it difficult for Mann, once he had turned into a republican through reason, to distance himself from his earlier writings. In truth, he later cut a few pages from the *Reflections*, but he always saw this book as a necessary step on his way to an honest yet painful acceptance of the Republic and of the democratic creed.

The democratic spirit, Mann wrote in his "Thoughts in War," was totally alien to the Germans, who were morally, but not politically, inclined. Interested in metaphysics, poetry, and music but not in voting rights or the proper procedures of the parliamentary system, for them Kant's *Critique of Pure Reason* was a more radical act than the proclamation of the rights of man. German militarism and German mores could not be separated from each other. Mann had not signed the manifesto

"To the Civilized World," but he could rightfully be regarded as its ninety-fourth author. For him, a defeated Germany would entail the demoralization not only of a great European nation, but of Europe as a whole. German thought was an indispensable element of the European spirit, precisely because it differed so much from values and ideals that were pertinent for countries like England and France. The Germans insisted on the unbridgeable difference between culture and civilization. German tradition was "culture, soul, freedom, art and *not* civilization, society, voting rights, and literature." Mann was therefore deeply convinced "that the German people will never be able to love political democracy simply because they cannot love politics itself, and that the much decried 'authoritarian state' is and remains the one that is proper and becoming to the German people, and the one they basically want."[2]

What Mann wrote was not new. The ninety-three signatories of the manifesto from 1914 could also have expressed the same sentiments. In all likelihood, however, they would not have expressed them as well. The reason Mann's patriotic manifesto "Frederick and the Great Coalition" from 1914 and his nonpolitical reflections from 1918 had such an impact on German and European public opinion, beyond their stylistic brio, was that their author had not been previously regarded as a dyed-in-the-wool conservative. The majority of superficial readers thus saw in both texts documents of a great and painful conversion. These texts have remained alive, however, for a different reason: the manifesto and the book still appeal to us today because they are full of a timeless ambivalence.

Had Mann accepted a precursor to his own thought, it would undoubtedly have been Friedrich Nietzsche. And as was the case with Nietzsche, Bismarck too played a crucial role in the development of Mann's thinking. Yet this influence led him to views that were finally opposed to those of Nietzsche. The *Reflections of a Nonpolitical Man* were also written to rebut the view that power and intellect could not be reconciled in Germany, "that blossoming of the state and blossoming of culture seem to exclude one another . . . that a politically powerful Germany would necessarily be opposed to intellect and culture."[3] This prejudice was often exercised by playing off Goethe against Bismarck. Mann, however, regarded it as foolish not to recognize the one in the other. Bismarckian traits could undoubtedly be found in Goethe and that "Bismarckian power politics and the 'German idea' came together to the most remarkable degree around 1860" was nothing less than the realization of a utopian dream. Bismarck's politics and Richard Wagner's music conquered Europe. Both represented the romantic hegemony of the German spirit.[4]

This was not at all what Nietzsche had thought of Bismarck and the founding of the Reich after the Prussian victory over France in 1871. When, in a distinctly ironical mood, Nietzsche had called Bismarck the only poet and philosopher left in Germany, his words were not a praise of Prussian politics but a complaint about German culture. The triumph of politics, even a dismal one, necessarily led to intellectual impoverishment. During the First World War, Mann discarded this Nietzschean view. He adopted it again only much later, at the end of the Second World War. When he gave a speech at the Library of Congress with the title "Germany and the Germans" after the Nazi regime had collapsed, he called the German Reich a cultural disappointment: "No intellectual greatness came from Germany that had once been the teacher of the world. It was only strong."[5]

Throughout the *Reflections*, Thomas Mann reserved his ironical wit for others, especially for his brother Heinrich, who had finished, shortly before the beginning of the war, the satirical novel *Der Untertan* (Man of straw), the "bible of the Wilhelminian epoch."[6] Heinrich Mann was the "literary prophet of civilization" against whom his brother's book had largely been written.[7] At the end of the *Reflections*, however, the supreme form of irony prevailed, that is, self-irony. Thomas Mann concluded the book with an extraordinary chapter, "Irony and Radicalism," that was nothing less than a prophecy of things to come in Germany. He talked of "ironic politics," for which Kant and the conservative romantic philosopher Adam Müller, among others, served him as examples. The term "ironic politics" was thereby synonymous with "conservative irony." Friedrich Gentz, the close collaborator of Metternich and sympathetic translator of Edmund Burke's *Reflections on the Revolution in France*, had provided the best example: "I was always aware that in spite of all the majesty and the strength of my principals, and in spite of all the individual victories that they achieved, the spirit of the times would finally be more powerful than we. . . . *But this was no reason* for me not to follow faithfully and patiently the task that had befallen me; only a bad soldier deserts his flag when fortune seems to be becoming unfavorable."[8] At the end of the First World War, Thomas Mann behaved as "a soldier, and brave." He was fighting for a lost cause—and he knew it.[9]

Conservatism, said Thomas Mann, can be a simple and strong attitude, bereft of wit and melancholy. Being proud and robust, it is indistinguishable from a "happy-go-lucky progressiveness." But this was not the conservatism that Mann claimed for himself. In a rather casual remark at the beginning of the *Reflections*, he said that he might have contributed in a limited way to the Europeanization of the German prose story. In a book written to uphold German exceptionalism against the despised normalcy of the European democracies, this claim was rather strange and even dangerous. Only at the end of the *Reflections* did it become obvious how well aware Mann must have been that he might have contributed—as much as Nietzsche alone did before him— not only to the Europeanization of German prose but also to the Europeanization of the German spirit. Conservatism, he explained, "only becomes witty and melancholy when international intellectual emphasis joins national emotional emphasis; when a bit of democracy, of literature, complicates its essence. Irony is a form of intellectualism, and ironic conservatism is intellectual conservatism. In it, being and effect contradict one another to a certain extent, and it is possible that it may promote democracy and progress in the way it fights them."[10]

When the Weimar Republic had been destroyed, Thomas Mann wrote to his children that they had all been, to a certain degree, responsible for its destruction. Yet he had also been responsible, in his own ironic way, for the German special path's turning into the road to democracy and international understanding. In a moving essay, "Portrait of Our Father," Thomas Mann's children Erika and Klaus described why the *Reflections* must be seen not as a relic of Mann's conservatism but, rather, as a turning point that would lead him first to the acceptance of and then to support for the Weimar Republic. With this "pamphlet in the grand style, written with passion and grief against the spirit of the Entente Cordiale, the spirit of the democracies with which the Germany of Luther and Bismarck was at war," Thomas Mann was taking a political stance and bidding farewell to inwardness: "The creative spirit had quitted his tragic, ironic isolation to enter a community. Suddenly the man who till then had held aloof from life, half quizzically, half sadly, participated directly in life with his whole heart, struggling and suffering."[11] The decisive step in Thomas Mann's conversion was not the shift from conservatism to republicanism but the substitution of political interest for inwardness. In 1924 Mann characterized Oswald Spengler as a conservative thinker who only seemingly distanced himself from civilization; in truth Spengler was affirming it not just with words but with his being as well.[12] With these words, Mann painted his own self-portrait. Defending German culture against Western civilization, art against literature, and the intellect against democracy, the author of the *Reflections of a Nonpolitical Man* helped to reconcile German culture and Western politics.

Reconciliation did not come easily. It was accompanied by Thomas Mann's first reluctant and then rather enthusiastic embrace of his own European heritage. This eventual adoption was helped by the author's ironic insight that his prose might always have been more European than his political beliefs. The distance to Heinrich Mann's beloved France remained, however, for quite a while and was eventually overcome only by personal acquaintanceships with French colleagues and the high critical acclaim of Parisian critics for his own work. Later, being awarded the Legion of Honor was a welcome accolade. For England, Thomas Mann always felt a kind of affinity, and when he browsed through *Royal Highness*, the English translation of his novel *Königliche Hoheit*, for the first time in 1920—it had been published in 1916—he was struck by the fact that his own book read as if it could only have been written in English. Mann admonished himself that he must not have been nearly as nationalistic as he had portrayed himself up to that point. At one time he had wondered why Nietzsche decided to read Schopenhauer only in French after a good translation of the philosopher's writings had been published in Paris. Now Mann could very well imagine reading his own novel only in English.[13]

Thomas Mann, the European writer, eventually accepted the political and the social as indispensable parts of humanity. It was a lesson that he taught himself and that he then felt compelled to teach others. The essay "The German Republic," written as a tribute to Gerhart Hauptmann on the occasion of his sixtieth birthday, was given, in the presence of the poet, as a lecture in the Beethoven-Saal in Berlin on an October evening in 1922. On June 24th of the same year, Walther Rathenau had been murdered by a right-wing death squad. When the English translation of the essay was published in the United States in 1937, Mann recalled that his speech had met with considerable opposition from the German youth to whom it was addressed. Revered for his patriotic *Reflections*, Thomas Mann was seen by many as a somewhat unlikely mentor to reconcile the Germans with the new Republic: "The voice of traditional culture sought to speak out on the side and in favour of the new necessities; to give democracy a gloss of the familiar by linking it with German romanticism."[14] Such words were a bit too much for those who remembered that Mann had argued, only four years earlier, that democracy and the German spirit were incompatible and that German culture and German militarism were simply two sides of the same coin.[15] Now he declared that war was a lie and stripped of all honor and that the Republic—defined by him as the union of the state and culture—was not a nightmare for his country but its destiny. When he remembered the occasion of his speech in his American exile, Thomas Mann became aware of the contradictions to which he had exposed an audience that was well acquainted with his former views. It must have been difficult for his public to acknowledge that the speaker, rather than looking back and trying to come to terms with his own intellectual past, was attacking a postwar nationalism that threatened not only the Republic but the country as a whole.

Out of necessity and almost overwhelmed by the Herculean task of establishing a bond between the Republic, the idea of democracy, and the German romantic movement, Thomas Mann got carried away with the enthusiasm he had imposed upon himself. At the end of his speech he asked his audience to lend its "still stiff and unaccustomed tongues" to the battle cry: "Long live the Republic!" This rather un-German ending must have pleased someone for whom this cry, familiar to the French, had been painfully absent from German political life: Heinrich Mann. He now acquired a special and indispensable position among the German writers. Unheard of in Germany so far, Heinrich Mann wrote with a social and political impulse that connected German literature with the Western democracies and particularly with the Latin parts of Europe. The apology Thomas Mann certainly owed his brother almost turned into an apotheosis when he commended Heinrich Mann for having proved that "society elevates and gives meaning to poetry and poetry lends soul and humanity to society."[16] Six years later, in 1928, Thomas Mann delivered an address in honor of his brother at the celebration of Heinrich Mann's sixtieth birthday in the Prussian Academy of Arts in Berlin, in which he called him a "classical representative of the Germanic-Mediterranean artistic genius."[17]

In the tributes to the Republic and to his brother, Thomas Mann obeyed the Kantian maxim that man must not so much follow his inclinations as fulfill his duty. As is so often the case, however, Mann sought rather to convince the public that he was following his own convictions. Thus his tribute and praise became excessive. They sounded sincere, but they had obviously been crafted a bit too cunningly, as Mann himself was well aware. Repeatedly he spoke of the contrast between aesthetic charm and ethical responsibility that had never been greater than in the years after the First World War when the Republic was founded and desperately tried to survive. Thomas Mann did not belittle this contrast. It haunted him and yet it was a welcome artistic challenge. It was a splendid source of irony.

In the elections for the Reichstag in September 1930, the National Socialist Party (NSDAP) increased its share of the vote from 2.6 percent in 1928 to 18.3 percent, making it the second-largest party after the Social Democrats. These elections marked the beginning of the end of the Republic: in 1932 the Nazis received 37.3 percent of the vote and became the strongest party in parliament. At a moment when reason was dealt a terrible blow, Thomas Mann rose to the occasion. In 1930, once again in the Beethoven-Saal in Berlin, where he had greeted the old Gerhart Hauptmann and the young Republic in 1922, he gave a speech called "An Appeal to Reason" that even some of his foes could not help but admire. When Mann affirmed that he did not want to play the *praeceptor patriae* or become a new Fichte, what he really wanted to say was the opposite. The Weimar Republic suffered from a lack of political legitimacy. After politics had failed, the time had come for the poet, the writer, the artist to act. Thomas Mann, a nonpolitical man no more, assumed the role of the poet and seer who utters his ominous warning. He proclaimed that form, "be it never so playful, is akin to the spirit, to that which leads one on to social betterment; and art is the sphere wherein is resolved the conflict between the social and the ideal."[18] Culture had to come to the rescue of the Republic. But culture was helpless, as it turned out before long. Four years after Thomas Mann had spoken of art as the sphere in which the great conflicts of the times could be solved, books were burned in Berlin.

"An Appeal to Reason" was a poet's speech, admirable not least because it was as concrete as the speech of a politician could possibly have been. Mann mentioned the Nazis as a threat not only to the Weimar Republic but to the German spirit, and he added that the Nazi movement was considerably helped by intellectual elements, "a certain ideology, a Nordic creed, a Germanistic romanticism, from philological, academic, professorial spheres." For Mann, the conclusion was clear: the German citizen who wanted to save his country had to side with the Social Democratic Party. And yet even in this, perhaps his most convincing and certainly his most courageous speech in support of the Republic, Thomas Mann could not conceal his doubts as to whether the Republic could find a home in Germany. He not only admitted how difficult it was for most voters to come up with a rational decision in times of economic turmoil. He expressed his doubts "whether the parliamentary system of western Europe, which Germany took over as being in a way ready to her hand after the collapse of the feudal system, is after all quite suited to her case; whether it does not in some sense and to some extent warp and do violence to her political ethic."[19]

In almost the same words, Hugo Preuß had asked this question in 1915.[20] To ask it again in 1930 was a sign of deep skepticism in times when an enthusiastic belief in the survival of the Republic was badly needed. Mann was skeptical because the "German question" had not yet found an answer: was the country able to invent a new and original political vision, or would it be left with the alternative of either preserving a tradition that separated it from the Western democracies or imitating a political philosophy and political institutions that were alien to its inner substance? That he left this question open was even more surprising, because only two years earlier Mann had answered the question whether it was possible and desirable to transform "the German cultural idea in a world-reconciling, democratic sense" with an astounding yes.[21] The tension between the spirit and material reality that had always haunted German thinkers and poets was considerably relieved in "German socialism, the invention of a Jewish social theorist brought up in western Europe." Whereas in the *Reflections of a Nonpolitical Man* Thomas Mann had refused the social to enter the sphere of humanity, he now deplored that not only the social but also the "socialistic ingredient" had been absent from German intellectual life: "The translation of the folk idea into politics, the transposition of the community conception into the social and socialistic, will mean the real, inward and spiritual democratisation of Germany." The "German problem" could be solved by a new alliance between Greece and Moscow. Germany would be well "as soon as Karl Marx shall have read Friedrich Hölderlin."[22] In order to save the German Republic, the reconciliation of culture and politics was not enough. What was needed was an alliance between culture and socialism that had already become a political reality in the Soviet Union. This vision, a kind of spiritual Rapallo Pact, must have come as a surprise to Thomas Mann's readers—not least because it had been his brother's lifelong dream. Socialism had to come to the rescue in order to bridge the gap between culture and politics, between the artist and the democratic state. It was also the only political idea that could redeem Richard Wagner, not as a nationalist or a narrow-minded patriot, but as "a Socialist, a believer in a cultural utopia," for a future democratic Germany.[23]

At the end of the First World War, Thomas Mann had forced himself to jump over a brook. At the end of the Weimar Republic he found himself on the other bank of a river. Only irony could make such a tremendous leap possible. The First World War had been lost. The Republic was in jeopardy. Hitler's dictatorship was looming on the horizon. And yet Thomas Mann could only continue to write and to argue in a mood of sustained ambiguity. Mann's writings in the time of the Weimar Republic resemble a palimpsest. Hidden beneath the most fervent speeches in defense of the Republic, the early skepticism of the nonpolitical man who had regarded the German nation as naturally opposed to democracy still shines through. Mann's sentences sound as if we were listening to Richard Wagner's *Tannhäuser* overture: in the end, the Pilgrim's chorus must ostensibly triumph over worldly love and lust, and yet we overhear, until the last tone, the lusciously seductive motifs from the Venusberg prevail behind the pious score.

The Aesthetic Appeal of Fascism

In the First World War, when his section of the front was quiet, the
corporal Adolf Hitler spent his days drawing and reading. While he
was sketching a courtyard gate and a church in the fall of 1915, a British
officer was painting the ruins of a farmyard just across the front line. His
name was Winston Churchill. Nazi folklore has it that Hitler admired
Churchill as an artist and that the British prime minister was the only
enemy leader who would not have been jailed after a Nazi victory.
"Churchill will live comfortably in a fortress where I shall make it possible for him to write his memoirs and paint," Hitler promised.[24] Allegedly, the "Führer" respected Churchill the artist because he wanted to
be seen as an artist himself.

Shortly after their escape from Germany—their "escape to life"—
Thomas Mann's children Erika and Klaus saw not only individual writers, artists, and intellectuals but "the true German culture" as the victim
of Nazi fanaticism. When Theodor Adorno was asked what National
Socialism had done to the arts, he replied that the Hitler gang's dictatorship had been one of the most terrifying anticultural phenomena of
modern times. Today we are still inclined to think of National Socialism
and culture as a contradiction in terms. Watching Hitler and his com-
panions at the Munich exhibition of "degenerate art" in 1937, poking
fun at some of the greatest paintings of the century, is enough to
strengthen our belief that the Nazis could not but destroy the cultural
state that had, for centuries, been the idol of German self-understanding and national pride. Yet many Nazi leaders—among them Hitler
the painter, Goebbels the novelist, and Albert Speer the architect—still
carried the artistic ambitions of their youth around with them after they
seized power, sometimes turning meetings of the inner circle of the
National Socialist Party's leadership into a quixotic *salon des refusés*. Aggressive political rhetoric also concealed a feeling of cultural failure—
not least in Hitler, who, as a young painter, had been rejected by the
Vienna Academy of Fine Arts in 1907.

Yet today we can only laugh or shake our head in disbelief when we
read about Hitler telling Sir Nevile Henderson, the British ambassador
in Berlin, that he was tired of politics and longed to return to oil paint-

ing, "as soon as I have carried out my program for Germany. . . . I feel
that I have it in my soul to become one of the great artists of the age
and that future historians will remember me, not for what I have done
for Germany, but for my art." Hitler sounded like Bismarck, the born
artist, who had forsaken "any contact with art in order to victoriously
complete his own work."[25] Hitler's remarks were reported in an article
in *Time* on September 11, 1939. The Second World War that had just
begun was called a "Painters' War," alluding to the fact that the Polish
commander-in-chief, Marshal Edward Smigly-Rydz, was "an able if
academic landscapist." While *Time* could poke fun at the artistic ambitions of the Führer, Goebbels had to take these ambitions seriously. In
doing so he unwittingly revealed the truth about the perverted, inhu-
man nature of the Nazi regime: "I then talked with the Fuehrer about
many matters of general interest. He yearns for the day when he can
end this war. . . . We want then again to devote our energies chiefly to
the fine arts, the theater, the films, literature, and music. We want to
begin again to be human beings."[26] Twenty years after the end of the
Second World War, admirers of Hitler would still claim that he must
have been a moral person deep down in his heart because he had had
an artistic vein.[27]

In an article in *Foreign Affairs* published in April 1940, Dorothy
Thompson called Germany the problem child of Europe, pointing out
that many of Hitler's character traits resembled those of a sick society
that eventually brought a sick person to power: "What frustrations must
be in this man, one thought—so sensitive, so cruel, so weak, and so
aggressive! And those characters around him—perverts and adventur-
ers, frustrated intellectuals who could not hold a job in any good
newspaper or get their plays produced or their books published." In
Hitler she saw a man who, after the common adventure of the First
World War, took refuge in a dream world, "a man whom nobody 'understood,' full of envy, furtive hatred, frustrated creative power."[28]
Thompson not only detected traits of the typical *homo germanicus* in
the Nazi regime; she also took the regime as an example of the possible
aberrations of a decaying middle-class society in the middle of the
twentieth century. That she had hit close to home became obvious when
an angry Goebbels called her insane and a foolish wench whose brains
consisted only of straw.[29]

As early as 1929, the jurist and political scientist Hermann Heller had predicted that an ethics of violence that reigned with the help of aesthetic means would, over time, not be stable enough to sustain a modern European state.[30] Any such state would isolate itself before long. On October 22, 1933, the *Neue Zürcher Zeitung* published a lead article with the title *Einsames Deutschland*, "Germany Alone." Three days before, Germany had left the League of Nations. The author of the article was Max Rychner, a Swiss citizen and one of the great literary critics and essayists of the twentieth century. He had been dismissed from his post as cultural editor of the *Kölnische Zeitung* when the Nazis seized power, whereupon he became a correspondent for the Zurich paper.

Ethically dignified and aesthetically appealing, solitude (*Einsamkeit*) had always been a preferred German state of mind. Nazi politics wanted Germany to reign over the world and remain solitary at the same time. In a plebiscite held along with the Reichstag elections on November 12, 1933, 95 percent of German voters supported the government's withdrawal from the League of Nations. This result may have been rigged. In any event, international isolation undoubtedly helped the Nazis to consolidate their power domestically. Many Germans must have shared in Oswald Spengler's mocking dismissal of the League as "a pack of summer holiday-makers idling on the shores of Lake Geneva."

This sinister and overt contempt for the community of nations had one of its root causes in the politics of the United States, Rychner argued. After the First World War, virtually chiliastic hopes were placed in the plans of President Woodrow Wilson, the "Messiah from Washington." The dashing of those hopes sowed the seeds in Germany for the coming catastrophe. For it is part of German character, Rychner wrote, "to weave politics into something utopian and to base it on an all-embracing doctrine of salvation." It was much more the Nazis' worldview than their political program that seduced the voters. The Germans were incapable of viewing politics as a necessary struggle of interests and as the art of balancing those interests. Santayana and Dewey would have supported Rychner's observation that in Germany every diplomatic note had to contain between the lines its nugget of metaphysics. Politics was not a human enterprise, but "a stroke of fate and act of providence." How could a mere committee like the League of Nations stir the souls of Germans, when they demanded the laying out, step by step, of the basic principles of a world order by which every nation, even the mightiest, would have to abide?

Added to this, Germany—unlike France—did not live by a separation of church and state. The Protestant churches, Rychner observed, had instead voluntarily fallen into line with the Third Reich. This cowardice reinforced to a fateful degree the German penchant for an eschatological interpretation of history. The psychological bridges to other peoples were cut off. Germany retreated into itself: "in every corpuscle of the blood courses the feeling of one's singularity and the fullness of one's promise." Refusing to negotiate its politics in international organizations, the country proudly held itself aloof in its solitary fate. In a national rapture, politics in Germany became the aggressive art of the impossible. The impetus behind this movement was so strong that it brooked no further thoughts of realistic obstacles to its goals. The imagination of German politicians came "without precise images of future difficulties." Providence obviated any need to be provident. Prophecies replaced prognoses.

The German sense of self after the 1933 "revolution" took on ecstatic forms, culminating in a drama of cultist self-apotheosis. The more passionate Germany became, the more it isolated itself. In addition, according to Rychner's diagnosis, there was a shortage of psychologists among the European statesmen who could lead Germany back to appropriate sobriety. The other nations did not understand Germany— and Germany felt itself misunderstood by all. "Germany," concluded Rychner, "has for some time now chosen an exaggerated solitude. It has turned away from the world in all its avowed imperfection in favor of its own Weltanschauung, which it calls that of the twentieth century." It was a worldview that saw history as drama and politics as ritual.

After 1933 German politics was molded into an operatic form, but it was the form of dictatorship, not of democracy. As early as 1938, Hermann Rauschning, an early apostate, called National Socialism an opera in which inflated words and shrill banners were more important than the musical score. Hitler's attempt to transform the world into a Wagner opera led to the creation of a strangely illuminated no man's land where art and politics could no longer be separated, as Joachim Fest has convincingly argued. To fully understand Hitler, who boasted that he had listened to the *Mastersingers of Nuremberg* a hundred times, one had to see him in a Wagnerian context. When Count Harry Kessler met Heinrich Brüning, the former German chancellor, in Paris in July 1935, he compared Hitler's politics to the maneuvers of Richard III. The former chancellor replied: "Much worse, because the theatrical, sentimentally romantic, Wagnerian element enters into it."[31] Hitler always insisted that he had become a politician and the Führer of the German Reich only by necessity. He wanted to be taken seriously as an artist-politician who was above all poised to turn Germany into a cultural state. It was not by chance that the House of German Art in Munich became the first great new building of the Nazi era. It came as no surprise that Hitler, while visiting the conquered Paris for a few hours, spent considerable time in the Opéra Garnier and was accompanied by a sculptor (Breker) and an architect (Speer), not by politicians or generals. Even in his last days in the *Führerbunker* in Berlin, shortly before he killed himself, Hitler made sure to stage his exit from the world as operatically as possible.

After Hitler, much of German history looked as if it had been staged in Bayreuth. When he regarded Wagner's operas as a mold into which he would cast German culture and German politics, Hitler was not inventing a tradition, but following one. In a speech given in Karlsruhe on December 6, 1914, Ernst Troeltsch had attacked Arthur Balfour, the former British prime minister, for misrepresenting Germany and its political goals. After all, Balfour had been a regular visitor to Bayreuth. He should have known better![32] In all likelihood, though, Balfour had not misrepresented German politics—precisely *because* he had been to Bayreuth. Addressing the German youth in the summer of 1918, Walther Rathenau voiced a scathing critique of German foreign policy that he saw as characterized by its operatic features.[33] Today it sounds like a rhetorical question when Saul Bellow's Ravelstein, alias Allan Bloom, asks whether Hindenburg was nothing but the bass and Ludendorff nothing but the fat tenor of a third-rate Wagnerian opera.

In one respect, Hitler was a kind of Anti-Nietzsche: for him, art could only flourish in a strong state, and political decline must inevitably lead to artistic decadence. This view, by necessity, also became that of his coterie. Goebbels, in his dispute with the conductor Wilhelm Furtwängler, who had asked that the Nazis tolerate excellent Jewish artists in Germany, insisted that he as a politician did not need any lessons from an artist, since National Socialist politics, that is, modern politics par excellence, also represented the highest form of art. Goebbels was almost quoting himself, for these sentences could already be found in his novel *Michael, or a German Destiny*, which had been published in 1929. In Nazi Germany, statecraft and stagecraft could no longer be separated.[34] Thanks to Hitler, Goebbels said, politics, which had been performed by professionals on the distant stage of parliament for too long, had become a popular drama again. In a letter written on August 31, 1932, the writer Ernst Jünger thanked jurist Carl Schmitt, who had helped legitimize the Nazi regime, for having rekindled his interest in politics by helping to turn it once more into drama and play.[35]

To succumb to the artful staging of Nazi politics, however, did not necessarily entail an enthusiasm for Nazi art. Works of art that were merely icons of Nazi ideology fared less well with the German population than the party leadership had hoped for. In a letter from Princeton, the first station in his American exile, Thomas Mann triumphantly wrote to Franz Werfel that the books of prize-winning Nazi writers were no longer read in Germany, whereas translations of foreign authors were in high demand. In its campaign against German intellectuals, *Das Schwarze Korps*, the weekly newspaper of the SS, had attacked German booksellers, "declaring that if it were up to them nothing but exile literature would be sold." Mann remarked: "On this point we have every reason to believe the *Schwarzes Korps*."[36] In a similarly sarcastic vein, Theodor Adorno noted that the Germans were quite willing to die for Hitler in his wars, but that they would rather have been killed than listened to his operas, had he written any.

In his Spandau diaries, Albert Speer wrote that he was never interested in power; he would have been satisfied to become a second Schinkel, arguably Germany's greatest architect so far. In the Third Reich, this dream seemed to turn into reality. After the war had been lost, Hitler's master builder insisted that there was no specific Nazi ideology to be found in the buildings of the Third Reich. All that was required was monumentality. The Nazis failed in their attempt to create an aesthetic of their own; only for a short moment did a "Nordic Modernism" seem to survive in the Third Reich.[37] In the absence of a monolithic power structure, the regime did not come up with a unified aesthetic. Goebbels, for instance, would rather have tried to win over modernism, or at least parts of it, for the Nazi movement; Alfred Rosenberg, founder, in 1929, of the League for German Culture (Kampfbund für Deutsche Kultur), and others vehemently opposed it. These conflicts were not confined to the inner circle of the Nazi leaders, but became openly visible. Antagonistic trends and personalities were engaged in a bitter running fight. In the end, the regime did not have to worry too much about the lack of worthy Nazi works of art. When the Wehrmacht invaded Russia, Hitler promised the German people that after the war he would give them the best and most beautiful art in German history.

It was more through ritual than through belief that German fascism was able to cast a powerful aesthetic spell. The reactions to the Nuremberg party rallies by Germans and visitors from abroad were strikingly similar. They all fell prey to what they regarded as a specific Nazi style—impressed much more by the mise-en-scène of political leadership and loyalty than by the cultural addresses (*Kulturreden*) Hitler used to deliver at Nuremberg.[38] Pierre Drieu la Rochelle, one of the founding fathers of French fascism, wrote that the emotional impact of the rallies on him could only be compared to the effect of Russian ballets. In 1937 the British ambassador Nevile Henderson went to Nuremberg for the first time and reacted in exactly the same way: "The effect, which was both solemn and beautiful, was like being inside a cathedral of ice. . . . I had spent six years in St. Petersburg before the war in the best days of the old Russian ballet, but in grandiose beauty I have never seen a ballet to compare with it."[39] That Henderson was also an apostle of appeasement probably helped his fascination by fascist choreography but was not a prerequisite for it.

Intellectuals were enthralled when they saw to what a large degree politics could be shaped by aesthetics. Seduced by the idea that politics was the highest form of art and the state was an artwork, they could also bring themselves to see the Führer as an artist. Wyndham Lewis was not the only one who—in his book on the Hitler cult published after the outbreak of the Second World War—originally saw in Hitler a politician with a muse, though he added immediately, as if shocked by his own words, that if Hitler were a poet, he would be "one of the most boring poets."[40] For many observers, fascism was the equivalent of *l'art pour l'art* in politics. It seemed only natural that any modern politician who dreamed of being a poet must become a fascist in his country—as Léon Degrelle in Belgium, Mussolini in Italy, Hitler in Germany, and Codreanu in Romania did. During his first visit, Robert Brasillach had found Nazi Germany a strange country. Later he came to admire what he called the aesthetic sensibilities of Hitler as an individual and of National Socialism as a political movement. Better than anyone else, Brasillach wrote, Hitler had understood that to become attractive for the masses, a nationalist movement had to display poetic qualities.[41]

The aesthetic underpinnings of fascist politics led to a rivalry between politicians that matched the petty jealousies of second-rate artists. Fascist Italian writers admired Mussolini because his political ambitions resembled those of a ruthless literary hero, like Balzac's Rastignac. They loved to quote Rilke, who had seen in Mussolini above all a man of poetic qualities. For a fascist, it was only natural that, as late as 1938, Drieu la Rochelle found it important, in his portrait of the Duce, to mention that Mussolini read a lot.[42] In Germany, the Nazis reacted with suspicion to this praise of the poet Mussolini. Their leadership had always insisted that National Socialism, not least in its grip on culture and in its fostering of cultural achievements, was much more successful than the fascist movement in Italy had ever been. Goebbels went even further. After he had seen *The Tragedy of Love*, a movie with Benjamino Gigli, on February 6, 1942, "the artistic level of which is so far below the normal that it really ought to be prohibited," he complained that "the Italians are not only not doing anything about the war effort, but . . . are hardly producing anything worthwhile in the realm of arts." The creative life of the Italian people, said Goebbels, had been destroyed by the fascist movement. Whereas National Socialism went deep down to the roots of culture, Italian fascism had remained a superficial thing: "That is regrettable, but one must recognize it clearly."[43]

In France, members of the political Far Right envied Germany because National Socialism was seen as the legitimate heir to the fascist movements that had their origin in the Latin countries of Europe. Only National Socialism would be able to transform the "demoliberal century," as Mussolini had called it. While fascism had become sclerotic and hesitant in both Italy and France, in Germany it had been vigorously transformed into a political art form and thus survived. National Socialism, originally a kind of political bohemia, had preserved the anarchistic and artistic attitudes characteristic of early fascism: a youthful disrespect for established authority and the general will to *épater le bourgeois*, especially since the bourgeoisie was, to a large extent, identified with Jewish culture. After National Socialism had been defeated, it was accused by some of its French sympathizers of excessive "Germanic pride" that had prevented it from winning over the fascism-inclined European nations once and for all. The Nazis had overplayed the concept of race and had not paid enough attention to creating a common culture that might have united the European nations under the fascist banner.[44]

Many French *hommes de lettres* who were skeptics when they set out to attend the rallies of the National Socialist Party in Nuremberg returned as fanatics. They admired Nazi Germany not because it was so familiar, but because it was so strange to them, primitive, devoted to myth, ordered through ritual, and deeply mistrustful of reason. The French fascists returned to Paris not so much convinced as emotionally overwhelmed. "Oui, Hitler est bon" was Alphonse de Chateaubriant's conclusion in 1937, whereby a strange aesthetic fascination was turned into a moral judgment; for the French writer, Hitler's strength was his sincerity.[45] It must be said, however, that there were other, less emotion-driven ways for a French intellectual to express his sympathy with the Nazi movement. Whereas Pierre Drieu la Rochelle and André Breton, for instance, admired Chateaubriant's book *La gerbe des forces*, Brasillach hated it for its confused and false ideas: "I am distressed to see such a serious, such a vital problem as the relations between France and Germany, treated with such puerility. That is the only word one can use for this book, in which the author kneels lower on each page, with religious respect, before all that Germany and Hitlerism represent. I have rarely seen such a ghastly spectacle."[46]

European writers and intellectuals, without necessarily becoming unmitigated admirers of the Nazis and certainly not of Germany, helped to create a context of empathy and understanding that made collaboration not only possible but honorable and even necessary. Alphonse de Chateaubriant justified his collaboration with Nazi Germany as a confession of faith in a unified Europe. The German fascists had long despised the idea. But it became an important tool for the Nazi propaganda machine once German aggression turned into an internecine war. Now the German Reich was hailed as the only bastion able to defend Fortress Europe. Destruction and genocide were transfigured into the last and decisive crusade of the West. These propaganda slogans did not fail to produce their effects. The SS division Charlemagne, which consisted of French and francophone volunteers, was among the last troops who fiercely defended Hitler's Chancellery in Berlin against the Red Army. Fired by anticommunist feelings and the deeply ingrained anti-Americanism of the French Right of the thirties, these soldiers, who knew that they were doomed to die, believed they were fighting a culture war in which European values had to be defended against Asiatic Bolshevism and American materialism.[47]

Art and Morality

In 1939 an extraordinary portrait of Hitler was published in *Esquire*. Its title alone was shocking: "That Man Is My Brother." The author of the portrait was Thomas Mann, who had written it on his first visit to Beverly Hills, California, in 1938. Not only was Hitler more representative of his country than the world had originally thought. Not only did even a likable observer come to detect, in the dreadful Nazi physiognomy, familiar German features. With Thomas Mann, a great artist took Hitler's artistic claims seriously: "The ineffable disgust this man has always inspired in me is here held in check by an ironic approach which seems to me to bring the little study closest to the artist sphere."[48]

The disappointed bohemian painter who passed unopposed from one political triumph to the other was a catastrophe, a miserable phenomenon, and yet one could not help viewing him with a certain shuddering admiration: "Must I not, however much it hurts, regard the man as an artist-phenomenon? Mortifyingly enough, it is all there: the difficulty, the laziness, the pathetic formlessness in youth. . . . The lazy, vegetating existence in the depths of a moral and mental bohemia; the fundamental arrogance which thinks itself too good for any sensible and honourable activity, on the ground of its vague intuition that it is reserved for something else. . . . A brother—a rather unpleasant and mortifying brother.

He makes me nervous, the relationship is painful to a degree. But I will not disclaim it."[49]

Mann's confession was convincing because here an artist made things difficult for himself by admitting, painful though it was to do so, that he found a certain aesthetic appeal in Hitler and in National Socialism. Given his admiration for Richard Wagner, one of the great German masters, Thomas Mann must indeed have hesitated to bring Hitler and Wagner together at all. Yet he saw the predicament of German culture exactly in the fact that it had produced both Wagner and Hitler.[50] He could therefore qualify Hitler's ideas as "a distorted phase of Wagnerism" and permit himself to call Hitler's reverence for the musician-artist well founded, if rather illegitimate. The hours when he hated Hitler the miserable, Thomas Mann said, were not his best hours. He was able to cope with him only when he overcame his hatred and used the device he recognized as the prerogative and prerequisite of all creative writing: irony.

"That Man Is My Brother" is a literary masterpiece. The intellectual courage and honesty of its author become even more obvious when compared, to give but one example, with Ernst Cassirer's assertion that Hitler was an error and had nothing to do with German history.[51] The essay points to the limits of art and literature. Caught in irony, Thomas Mann the artist was in the end unable to come to terms with a phenomenon like Hitler, since "the moral sphere . . . is really not altogether the artist's concern." It was the moral distance inherent in the arts and in literature that, in European history, had led many to regard the great man, the genius, as usually an aesthetic, not an ethical phenomenon. So, whether one liked it or not, Hitler—in part an aesthetic phenomenon in which madness was tempered with discretion—also had to be called a genius.

Thomas Mann recognized the moral limits of artistic aspiration and aesthetic judgment. He did not fall prey to the illusion or hope that there is a natural affinity between artistic modernism and democratic beliefs. Almost the opposite seems to be true when one realizes how many of the great modern writers and artists belonged to the "antidemocratic intelligentsia." Henry James acted as spokesman for this intelligentsia when he deplored the "incurable democratic suspicion of the selective and comparative principles" that tried to secure a "democratic use" for almost any book. The democratic principle that could, if just barely, be accepted in politics threatened to invade culture and would thus lead to a decline in literary and artistic standards.[52]

Among the great German painters whom Hitler and his comrades publicly despised, quite a few, including Emil Nolde, who had joined the National Socialist Party in the early 1920s, would have been only too glad to be accepted by this third-rate draftsman, because they felt close to his ideas. In calling Hitler his brother, Thomas Mann helped bring an uncomfortable truth to light. At its core, artistic modernism was by no means genuinely democratic; rather, it overtly displayed a propensity for authoritarian, if not totalitarian, views. As an aesthetic program, modernism could not be condemned on moral grounds. To avoid censorship, it had to be contained, as it were, in a social context in which moral considerations permeated politics and public life. To a considerable degree, such containment existed in those Western democracies from which Germany consistently distanced itself.

But the illusionary overrating of culture thus played a particularly dangerous role in German history. When culture was accepted as a substitute for politics, the absence of morality in the public sphere was easily accepted as well. The aesthetic appeal first of fascism and later of National Socialism was not a superficial phenomenon. Addressing it must be a core aspect of any attempt to explain the attractiveness of Nazi ideology for a large segment of the German bourgeoisie and many German artists and intellectuals. When members of the London Institute of Sociology predicted during the Second World War that Germany would be able to survive Nazism only if its core cultural values, represented by Goethe, were restored, it fell prey to the grand German illusion: culture came first, politics followed. The contrary was true. To survive the rupture of civilization it had inflicted upon Europe, Germany would have to give up the most German of all ideologies: the illusion that culture can compensate for politics. But this process took a long time. The Holocaust, the great divide of Western civilization, should have marked the point of no return, after which the exaltation of culture over politics was no longer possible in Germany. This is what Adorno wanted to say when he called barbarous any attempt to write a poem after Auschwitz. Yet the poems Paul Celan wrote after Auschwitz were anything but barbarous—because his poetry reflected the helplessness, not the power, of culture. The Holocaust was not only a political crime; it was also a moral failure of a magnitude that could no longer be compensated for by any artistic achievement. And yet the grand German illusion that culture could be a substitute for politics survived the war well into the second German republic. It survived exile and emigration.

The Blurring of Exile and Emigration

Walter Benjamin was the first to make the now commonplace distinction between the politicization of culture, which was characteristic of communist regimes, and the aestheticization of politics, which was part of fascist ideology. In Germany, the aestheticization of politics had unforeseen consequences. Authors like Oswald Spengler and Stefan George, in whom one might have suspected potential followers of the Nazis, dissociated themselves from the regime. Mindful of artistic quackery, they were not willing to accept impostors like Goebbels and the ideologist Alfred Rosenberg as either their mentors or their students. Even Leni Riefenstahl, who was an enthusiastic admirer of the "Führer," began to doubt Hitler's political wisdom when he denounced Goya and her favorite painter, van Gogh.

Yet it remains true that, much more than racist propaganda and anti-Semitism, the aesthetic appeal and the seduction by ritual turned members of the German intelligentsia, Ernst Jünger and Gottfried Benn among them, into followers of the Nazi regime—at least for a while. Bystanders watched the rise of the Nazi movement as if it were a play. One did not bother to find reasons for it; it just happened. The sympathies of many fellow travelers dwindled only when, on June 30, 1934, dissidents within the National Socialist Party and suspected enemies of the state were executed without trial in the so-called Röhm massacres. Intellectuals who had sympathized with the Nazis reacted in disgust. It was more the lack of taste, however, than the absence of proper legal procedure that they found intolerable in the behavior of the Nazi death squads, which had finished off the danger of a "second revolution." For these fellow travelers, form was more important than content.[53] The Nazi crimes left them not morally appalled, but aesthetically disappointed.

Rather unwittingly, the poet Gottfried Benn made this clear when he wrote to his friend, the writer Ina Seidel, on August 27, 1934, "I live with my lips pressed tightly together, inwardly and outwardly. I can't go along with this anymore. Certain events have pushed me over the brink. What a horrible tragedy. The whole thing begins to look to me like a third-rate theater that constantly announces a performance of *Faust* when the cast hardly qualifies for a potboiler like [the operetta] *Hussar Fever*. How great seemed the beginning, and how dirty it all looks today."[54] How dazzled must he and others have been to believe that the Nazis would ever be able to play *Faust*! Yet this was the dream of much of the cultural elite: that Germany would become a state in which politics and culture were no longer separated. It was the fascist dream of a theatrical state.[55] When the dream turned out to be an illusion, it was disappointment, not distance or opposition, that followed. After 1934, many German intellectuals would have gladly remained fascists—if only the Nazis had only tolerated it.

Lips pressed tightly together—this was to become a prominent feature of Germany's intellectual physiognomy during the Nazi period. One could still think but hardly speak and certainly not speak up. After 1934, many intellectuals who stayed on went into what they called their "inner exile." "On January 1, 1935," Benn wrote, again to Ina Seidel, "I am going to leave my apartment, my practice, my whole life here in Berlin and I am going back into the army. . . . I don't know what place they will send me. My future is uncertain. . . . But morally and economically I cannot go on living like this, I have to cut myself loose from all my ties here. It is an aristocratic form of emigration."[56] The old German illusion thus survived: the belief that while politics took its murderous turns, the better part of Germany, the cultural state, would remain unharmed. When the Third Reich had vanished, these intellectuals did not for a moment think of themselves as fellow travelers who had, though indirectly and with a certain degree of reluctance, added legitimacy to the Nazi regime and prolonged its criminal life span. Having felt aesthetically averse to the Nazis was enough to foster, in retrospect, the self-delusion that they had also been contemptuous of Nazi politics.

They had lived in exile. They had resisted—deep down in their hearts, so deep that no one else could possibly have realized it.

This strange yet powerful self-delusion was enhanced by a curious fact. There was one institution in Germany that withstood the Nazi seduction without compromise: the German language. Unlike France, where the literary quality of the *Nouvelle revue française,* for instance, hardly declined when a fascist like Pierre Drieu la Rochelle took over its editorship from Jean Paulhan and where many *collabos* wrote as well as members of the Resistance, the German language put up decided resistance—admittedly, against the majority of its speakers and writers.[57] These authors' artistic sensibility had not prevented them from falling prey to a crude political ideology. Once they had succumbed to it, however, literary finesse and aesthetic intelligence disappeared from their work. When Gottfried Benn, who in his earlier work had been able to test the German language to the extreme, seemingly surrendered to Hitler and to the Nazi ideology, his poetic abilities collapsed instantly, as Carl Zuckmayer remarked in a dossier on German artists and intellectuals that he prepared for the American administration. Only in the clandestine texts that Benn wrote during the Third Reich but could not publish and in his private letters did he regain the sovereign command over the German language for which he had once been famous. There is no National Socialist literature of high rank. Thomas Mann insisted that the "totally false German" the Nazis used sufficed to prove the antihuman character of their politics. The resistance of the German language, however, eventually led to a blurring of the notion of political resistance. The German intellectuals who wrote in "inner exile," with no chance for publication or public esteem, later believed that they had also lived in political opposition.

When Benn was asked after the war why he had remained in Germany even after 1934, he replied that the idea of emigrating had never occurred to him. First of all, there was no pressure to leave the country. More important still: to go into exile was not a viable intellectual option, because it had no tradition in Germany. True, Marx and Engels lived in London to wait for times to change, and in recent years Spanish intellectuals had fled their country to escape persecution there. However, the notion of "emigration," which would only later acquire its entire ethical weight, allegedly did not yet exist. When members of his generation left Germany, Benn said, they were not taking the political action of emigration, they were just trying to escape personal hardships and unpleasant circumstances by traveling elsewhere. This was a curious statement and a cynical one indeed. It seemed as if Benn, for instance, had never heard of Heinrich Heine's Parisian exile—though he quoted Heine's poem "The Grenadiers" only a few sentences later. There was an unmistakable anti-Semitic tone in the rejection of emigration and exile: how could a German possibly adopt what had been the fate of the Jewish people for centuries?

One may be inclined not to take Benn's argument too seriously. After all, it did not explain anything; it merely served as an excuse. The case of Thomas Mann, however, shows how difficult it was for a non-Jewish German intellectual to accept the idea of emigration and of exile. In February 1933, Thomas Mann left Germany for Amsterdam, Brussels, and Paris, where he was scheduled to talk about Richard Wagner, whose worldview, as Mann was eager to remind his audiences at home and abroad, was the epitome of German culture insofar as it displayed a complete indifference to politics as long as German art survived. A vacation in Arosa, Switzerland, was to follow. There his children convinced him not to return to Germany. In the beginning, Thomas Mann tried to see the necessity of exile as spiritually beneficial and as a welcome opportunity "to throw off those obligations I had assumed in the course of the years out of social considerations [and] to concentrate hereafter on my own life."[58] A more German reaction to the exile forced upon him is hardly imaginable: no political outburst, no cry for revenge, just a quiet retreat into inwardness.

For quite a while, Thomas Mann hesitated to attack the Nazi regime publicly. He thought it foolish to sever his ties with Germany as long as there was a chance to keep the family villa in Munich and to redeem half of the Nobel Prize money that was still deposited in a German bank. Most important, however, it was his wish that S. Fischer in Berlin should publish *The Stories of Jacob*, the first novel of the tetralogy *Joseph and His Brothers*. Many years thereafter, when he recalled in the United States that the larger part of the third volume, *Joseph in Egypt*, was a work born in exile, Mann bemoaned "the break in my outward existence . . . , the trip from which I could not return, the sudden loss of my life's basis."[59] Yet Switzerland offered some comfort in exile because it allowed him to live in "German spheres" when the Joseph novel would appear. The German cultural soil was indispensable for Mann if he wanted to go on with his writing. Eventually, the furniture from their Munich residence arrived in Küsnacht, the Swiss village where the Mann family was by then living. After having slept the first night under his old comforter made all of lace and after having dozed for the first time in his beloved Empire chair, the longing to return to his homeland almost overwhelmed Thomas Mann.

Although it became obvious that he would have to live the life of an émigré, Mann used the word "emigration" with apparent disdain. He hated the climate of resentment that the émigrés were indulging in and insisted on remaining an outsider to their circle. Himself he regarded not as a refugee, but as a German citizen who was forced to live abroad for a while. The thought of returning to Germany remained alive, as it did in so many writers and artists who were abroad when Hitler came to power. When Erika and Klaus Mann asked Max Beckmann in April 1933 in Paris whether he would go back to Frankfurt, he answered: "Why not? Of course I'm going home. What has changed? What have I to do with politics? I am an artist. I can paint my women or acrobats or landscapes whether the government is in the hands of Hitler or the Communists or the Great Mogul."[60] It was also Thomas Mann's wish, hardly understandable in hindsight, to go back to Germany at that time and live there in a kind of inner emigration whose aristocratic character might have resembled that of Gottfried Benn: "One would not have to behave like [Gerhart] Hauptmann or [Richard] Strauss, but one could try to preserve a noble attitude and refrain from any public appearance."[61] In a letter to the German Ministry of the Interior, dated April 1934, Mann asked for a renewal of his German passport and the restitution of his home, his library, and his property. It was a courageous letter in which Mann declared once more how deep his resentment vis-à-vis the Nazi regime was and that it would not change. And yet he promised, should he be allowed to return to his fatherland, to accept the verdict of history, tolerate the Nazi regime, and remain absolutely silent politically.

As was the case with many German intellectuals, the point of no return was reached for Thomas Mann with the Röhm massacres. Until then he had withstood pressure from his children and his friends to react publicly to what was happening in Germany. Eventually he yielded. He felt relieved, because now he could no longer hesitate to distance himself for good from what was happening in Germany, "the outrageous contempt of reason, the vicious violation of the truth, the cheap, filthy backstairs mythology, the criminal degradation and confusion of standards; the abuse, corruption and blackmail of all that was good, genuine, trusting and trustworthy in our old Germany."[62] Emigration now became a viable and accepted form of existence. Throughout his diary, Thomas Mann mentions the political statement or manifesto that he must now write. As so often, art and life become indistinguishable for him: more and more he resembles Joseph the Dreamer, who turns into a responsible political being in exile.

The final decision to act politically came with an artistic farewell. When Mann was forced into exile, he was on a speaking tour abroad in praise of a German master, Richard Wagner. When he reached the conclusion that he must accept exile and bid farewell to Nazi Germany, it was Wagner again who accompanied his verdict. On August 9, 1934, Thomas Mann wrote in his diary: "The whole day nothing but rain and thunderstorms, so that one cannot go out. I made excerpts for my political statement. . . . In the evening I browsed through my diaries and noted passages of political importance. . . . Katia and the children were listening to the radio, which was broadcasting the 'Twilight of the Gods' from Bayreuth, which was constantly disturbed by the thunderstorm. I resisted listening to it, I do not want to hear anything from Germany anymore. . . . It's nothing but cultural propaganda. My toothache is coming back."[63]

Even after this farewell, however, Mann was still puzzled by what was happening in Germany. He had always taken the interest the Nazis expressed in cultural matters quite seriously, even though he found it appalling. On September 8, 1933, he read a Franconian newspaper "that was sent to me for some mysterious reason, containing a speech by the 'Führer' about culture. Astounding. This man, a typical product of the lower middle class, with a limited education and an acquired taste for philosophizing, is truly a curious phenomenon. No doubt at all that for him, in contrast to types like Göring and Röhm, the main concern is not war but 'German culture.' . . . Never before have the men of power, the men of action in world affairs, set themselves up in this way as the preceptors of their people, even of mankind. Neither Napoleon nor Bismarck did so. . . . They took political measures to promote what aspects of . . . cultural life seemed useful to them, rigorously suppressing what went against them. But never would they have spoken *ex cathedra* to proclaim a cultural theory for the nation or to outline a cultural program. . . . To be sure, they had as yet had no notion of the 'totalitarian state,' which provides not only a power base but a base for everything and even dominates culture—culture above all."[64] Thomas Mann despised the cultural ambitions of the Nazis, and yet there was a seductive power in their totalitarian attempt to give politics a cultural base. Even in exile, he had to say to himself that Germany remained a "tremendous country."

The primacy accorded to culture so uniquely in Germany did not cease casting its spell on Mann—even when this idea was shrouded in something as dreadful and despicable as the Nazi ideology and the crimes that were justified with it. Even though he had once declared himself to be above all suspicion of wanting to become a new Fichte, a *praeceptor patriae*, Mann often toyed with the idea and almost burst into tears when he came to realize that the decision to remain in exile had made it impossible for him to play this role for many years to come. On March 14, 1934, a visitor from Germany quoted a remark by Gottfried Benn: "Do you know Thomas Mann's house in Munich? There is truly something Goethean about it." Thomas Mann felt tormented: "The fact that I was driven away from that existence is a serious flaw in the destined pattern of my life, one with which I am attempting—in vain, it appears—to come to terms, and the impossibility of setting it right and reestablishing that existence impresses itself upon me again and again, no matter how I look at it, and it gnaws at my heart."[65] This attitude was the reason why Gottfried Benn could praise Thomas Mann for having played an almost singular role in trying to save the Weimar Republic while it was still alive. When literati of the inner emigration attacked Mann, Benn refused to join their ranks. Even in exile, Benn said, Thomas Mann had remained a German and had to be regarded as such. Without Mann, German culture would only have been represented by second-rate authors.[66] Thomas Mann could dream of becoming a new Fichte only because he had not yet given up the wish for culture to teach politics a lesson, as Goethe had been able to do. Goethe had once exclaimed: "What do the Germans want? Have they not me?"[67] This was the poet's and also Mann's wish: not just to be readmitted to the city, but to become a teacher to its citizens.

At the beginning of his exile, it seemed for a while as if Mann had forgotten the lesson that he had taught himself after the First World War: that the cultural and the social could not be separated from each other. Politics was a sphere in its own right, the art of the possible, the realm of compromise that should not be confounded with the realm of the spirit and of the arts, where the absolute reigned. Memory came back however, when in 1936 the Frederick William University of the Rhine in Bonn, in a pitiful move, decided to revoke the honorary doctorate it had awarded him in the year 1919—whereupon Mann had dedicated a collection of essays, *Rede und Antwort*, to it. In a noble, if melancholy, letter to the dean of the philosophical faculty, Mann recalled that he had tried for quite a while not to meddle with recent German politics and to live apart from it to avoid jeopardizing his ties with German culture and, above all, his German readers. It was not possible. The terrible things that were happening in his fatherland forced him to speak out. He could no longer retreat into a solitary cultural existence. If the Nazi regime had taught him a lesson, it was the insight that culture could no longer be separated from politics and that the social and the spiritual belonged together. Thomas Mann's letter, written in Küsnacht on New Year's Eve 1937, is a document of pride and sadness. Its beginning is triumphant, however. Thomas Mann reports to the dean that he is still able to call himself a *Doctor philosophiae honoris causa*, since the title that Bonn revoked had been given to him once more by Harvard University. The United States would become the country where he was welcome both as a writer and as a democrat.

Novalis and Walt Whitman:
German Romanticism and American
Democracy

A Country without an Opera

Hitler impressed his followers with the time and energy he devoted to questions of culture, especially architecture. He was enchanted by the *palazzi* of Italy: each of them surpassed Windsor Castle by far. If the English bombers were to destroy Florence or Rome, it would be a crime against humanity. If they were to destroy Moscow, nothing would be lost—and the same, alas, would be true of Berlin. The Duce was a great man, a real imperator, but he disappointed the Führer because he could not see more than three paintings in succession. All this was said in the midst of the war in Hitler's military headquarters, the East Prussian *Wolfsschanze*, and mostly at night when the sleepless Hitler forced his drowsy vassals to simulate interest in everything he said.

When he flew to Paris after the victory over France in June 1940, Hitler first paid a visit to the Opéra Garnier. He remarked how little the splendor of the building corresponded to the mediocre quality of the operas performed there. Later Hitler would sketch plans for a new opera house in Munich, three times as big as the opera in Paris. Still, he commended the French because more French than English visitors could be seen in Bayreuth. The English loved music, but she did not love them. Neither their operas nor their theaters could compare with those in Germany. Worse still, nowhere were Shakespeare's plays performed as badly as in England. And yet, Hitler predicted hopefully, England would later become the nation with which Germany would ally itself.[1]

Hitler often bragged about culture and the arts to justify alliances and acts of aggression. During the short interval of the German-Soviet pact, Bolshevist Russia was praised for its theaters, but it was denied any cultural achievement whatsoever after the pact had been broken. The war against the United States was seen as a culture war—unlike the war against France and England, whose cultures were criticized but basically accepted. In one of his monologues, delivered at the *Wolfsschanze* on January 7, 1942, Hitler declared that he found "an Englishman a thousand times preferable to an American. . . . I feel the deepest hatred and repulsion towards anything American. In its whole outlook America is a half-Jewish, half-Negroid society." Worst of all, said Hitler, who saw himself as the reincarnation of Rienzi, the hero of Wagner's early opera *Rienzi*, the German Reich had "270 opera houses and a richer cultural life than is known there. Basically Americans live like pigs in a well-tiled sty."[2] On April 22 he came back to the same topic. The United States, Hitler predicted, was about to face a breakdown of culture. There was an ominous sign pointing to this: the closing of the Metropolitan Opera in New York. The reasons for its closing, he said, were not solely financial. The Americans simply lacked the artists who could adequately perform in an opera. All great operas were of German, Italian, or French origin. Now that European singers could no longer travel across the Atlantic, the cultural poverty of the United States had become painfully apparent. Hitler urged the German press to give due attention to this "fact." It was a clear indication that American culture was about to collapse; military and political defeat would surely follow.[3]

Obediently, Joseph Goebbels, minister for "public enlightenment and propaganda," echoed Hitler's view in his diary on April 23, 1942: "I have the impression . . . that the Americans participate in a European war every quarter century in order to be able to take for themselves as cheaply and easily as possible whatever cultural work has been done in Europe. The American continent is hardly in a position to bring forth anything of its own in the cultural realm. It is dependent upon imports from Europe, and since the Americans are so crazy about money they naturally like to take possession of the results of our creative and inventive labors as far as possible without paying for them." Goebbels also saw the closing of the Met as a verdict on the inferiority of American culture: "The Metropolitan Opera has been closed. And that happens in a country that has only a single opera and whose leadership is insolent enough to wage war on behalf of a European culture allegedly threatened by us! It surely is a crazy world in which we are living."[4] But Hitler and Goebbels were wrong: the Metropolitan Opera was never closed at any time during the Second World War.[5]

Hitler could not know and certainly would not have liked to be informed about an incident that had happened to Ralph Ellison, a black writer, in New York City at the end of the 1930s. Ellison described the incident in his essay "The Little Man at Chehaw Station." As a member of the New York Writers' Project, Ellison was trying to get people to sign "a petition in support of some now long-forgotten social issue that I regarded as indispensable to the public good." Behind a door in the basement of a building "in San Juan Hill, a Negro district that disappeared with the coming of Lincoln Center," Ellison overhears voices, "raised in violent argument" over which of two Metropolitan Opera divas was the better soprano: "The language was profane, the style of speech a southern idiomatic vernacular such as was spoken by formally uneducated Afro-American workingmen." Ellison, disturbed that his knowledge of his own people is obviously deficient, knocks at the door, enters the room, and meets four black coal heavers who, asked where they learned so much about grand opera, tell him, to his astonishment, that they work as extras at the Met. "At the Metropolitan Opera, just like I told you," one of the men says. "Strip us fellows down and give us some costumes and we make about the finest dumn bunch of Egyptians you ever seen. Hell, we been down there wearing leopard skins and carrying spears or waving things like palm leafs and ostrich-tail fans for *years!*" With the shock of recognition, Ellison joins them "in appreciation of the hilarious American joke that centered on the incongruities of race, economic status, and culture." Black workingmen as opera buffs: "Seen in the clear, pluralistic, melting-pot light of American cultural possibility there was no contradiction." Hitler would have found this "cultural possibility" a disgrace—but even a decent European might have seen it as a bit unusual, given that in Europe there were fewer such possibilities in the sense of opening culture to a wider public.[6]

In December 1941, the *New Yorker* published two witty and well-informed articles on Thomas Mann by Janet Flanner under the title "Goethe in Hollywood." Poking some fun, if reverentially, at a master of self-stylization, Flanner described America's cultural scene with a considerable degree of irony. To a modern Goethe, the United States must look like a cultural desert, where symphonies and serious literature had been abandoned in favor of movies and musicals. Did Thomas Mann not feel as if he had traveled from Weimar to Hollywood? The contrary was true. For Mann, the United States would become a land of spiritual redemption where the gulf between culture and politics was bridged. Goethe played a crucial role. In March 1932, the last year of the ailing Republic, Mann gave a lecture in Weimar on "Goethe's Career as a Man of Letters." In the *Reflections*, he had once called art, like religion, the truly human sphere: "Politics disappears before it like mist before the sun."[7] One hundred years after Goethe's death, Mann now spoke of the Olympian as a human being, a citizen and a man of letters who had stubbornly resisted the two main tendencies of his epoch, the nationalistic and the democratic. Less with outspoken self-righteousness than with a grin of inner satisfaction, Thomas Mann seemed to ask: what have I done in the *Reflections of a Nonpolitical Man* but point to a truth that Goethe had already found one hundred years ago? "Goethe's conception of the German people, as an unpolitical, intellectual nation, centred upon human values, receiving from all and teaching all, will it not always have its profound justification, even in times of violent over-compensation and national self-correction?"[8] As late as 1938, when he talked about Goethe's *Faust* before students at Princeton University, Mann did not forget to mention, with a tinge of nostalgia in his voice, how shrewdly Goethe had always distinguished between the social and the intellectual sphere. This distinction, however, which Mann himself had upheld throughout the First World War but had rejected a few years later in his defense of the Republic, was about to vanish in his American years to come.

In 1940 Mann toured the United States with a lecture on "War and Democracy," in which he characterized the idea of humanism as uniting both art and politics—a leitmotif of everything he would say or write in America in his role as a public moralist. His friend and supporter Agnes E. Meyer disapproved of his meddling with politics. As early as 1937, she had reminded Mann in his Swiss exile that he was a *Kulturmensch*, not a political leader.[9] Now Mann angrily replied that their viewpoints could not differ more sharply. His friend talked of "mere politics" and wanted to see him *au-dessus de la mêlée*, whereas for him politics had become a necessary part of his life and consequently also of his literary work. After 1918 Mann had spoken of war as "the archfoe of culture and thought." Now, however, he himself was entering a war. To fight for democracy had become a moral duty that Thomas Mann did not want to eschew: "Je fais la guerre."[10]

Joseph in America

On January 16, 1942, the Library of Congress appointed Thomas Mann Consultant in Germanic Literature. As Librarian of Congress, Archibald MacLeish had been instrumental in inviting European émigrés, among them Saint John-Perse, to the library and had inaugurated a lecture series, "Poet in a Democracy." The consultancy was a sinecure for Thomas Mann that was financed by Agnes Meyer, a trustee of the library and co-owner, together with her husband, Eugene Meyer, of the *Washington Post*. Agnes Meyer had read *The Magic Mountain* and *Joseph in Egypt* in the Wyoming mountains and had fallen in love with Thomas Mann's style—"while squirrels, mink and various birds circled around me, curious as to why I lay so still hour after hour"[11]—before almost falling in love with the author. Mann held his post at the Library of Congress for three years and remained associated with it as a Fellow in Germanic Literature until his death in 1955. Proudly introducing himself as a member of its staff, Thomas Mann gave five lectures at the library between 1942 and 1949. They were tokens of appreciation for a country that fortified his own conviction, reluctantly acquired during the Weimar Republic, that politics and culture must not be separated and that the spirit may feel at home in a democracy.

On November 17, 1942, Thomas Mann delivered his first address, "The Theme of the Joseph Novels," in the library's Coolidge Auditorium. Vice President Henry Wallace introduced the speaker. The Joseph novels seemed to be, as Mann said, a remote and rather out-of-the-way subject. Unbeknownst to his audience, however, Mann had tied his work unabashedly to his own ego and to his recent experiences in the United States. The character Tamar, for instance, he had modeled after Agnes Meyer, who was proud to have thus become part of a German tradition and who would later ask herself: "Did Tamar love Jacob, as he loved her? Probably not, since he was the older and wiser of the two, but more than enough to become a troubling and enduring problem for the rest of her life."[12] In Joseph, the seriousness of the man of action was combined with the playful irony of the artist; politics and culture came together. Talking about the Joseph novels, Mann turned his lecture into a moving appeal for the unification of European and American traditions, in culture as well as in politics.

As a boy, Johann Wolfgang Goethe had once dictated the Joseph story to a friend. He had found it too short, though, and had toyed with the plan of retelling the story by adding details that were missing from the Bible. What Goethe had only dared to think of, Mann felt courageous enough to do in his four Joseph novels. While he was writing the third, he was abroad and could not return to Germany; while he was writing the fourth, *Joseph the Provider*, he was forced to leave Europe. Thomas Mann had for a long time been convinced that, to write the Joseph novels, he must live in Germany or at least, as he called it, in "German spheres." Now an American exile offered a surprising and magnificent compensation to the refugee. The last Joseph novel came into being "largely under the serene, Egyptian-like sky of California"—in the display of an unexpected and therefore even more rewarding affinity between the Old World and the New.[13] It was not by accident that in the Joseph novels an artistic ego eventually found its way into the social world while their creator was living and writing in a democracy. Joseph's Egyptian reforms resembled the New Deal, and Roosevelt was about to become the provider of the democratic world. How much the American experience meant to Thomas Mann became obvious in a short yet telling side remark and in the sweeping political statement with which he ended his address.

The empire of the Nile, Mann told his American audience, had been familiar to him since boyhood—as it obviously had been familiar to the young Goethe. The twelve-year-old Thomas Mann knew more about the subject than his teacher in school. One day when the class was asked for the name of the holy steer of the ancient Egyptians, Thomas volunteered the answer: "Chapi." The teacher reproached the boy; the right answer, in his opinion, should have been "Apis." That, however, was only the Latinized or Hellenized form of the authentic Egyptian name: "I knew better than the good man, but discipline did not allow me to enlighten him about it. I kept silent—and all my life I have not forgiven myself for this silence before false authority. An American boy would certainly have spoken up."[14]

Writing in America, Mann brought the last Joseph novel into close contact with the American myth. It was the myth of "pioneer-like optimism and hearty faith in man" that Goethe had cherished in his old age. It was the myth that had spurred the early emigration to America, as depicted in Goethe's novel *Wilhelm Meister*. Now German and European intellectuals profited from contact with this myth in exile. It led them to the experience of a new humanism and to the insight that it was not enough to ask for the unification of Europe. At the end of his address, quoting Goethe, Mann sounded like he was quoting Woodrow Wilson when he spoke about the necessity to form a "coalescence of the hemispheres, of the unification of the earth."

On October 13, 1943, Thomas Mann delivered a lecture entitled "The War and the Future." The author of the *Reflections of a Nonpolitical Man* found himself once more in his preferred state of mind—irony—when he heard himself talk in America on his belief in democracy and the liberal tradition. After all, he was still a German author who came from a country that, as he reminded his audience, was rather indifferent to social and political questions. As a German intellectual faced with new realities, he had had to learn not to shy away from a confession of faith in which politics mattered. At the same time, Mann still betrayed a typical German attitude when he told a bewildered Washington audience that the future belonged to communism. In a typical German twist, shyness almost turned into arrogance, as the student of Western democracy instantly promoted himself to the rank of teacher and prophet who knew better than the Americans themselves what the political future of the United States should be.

Immediately after the end of the Second World War, on May 29, 1945, Mann gave his address on "Germany and the Germans." It could have been a tempting occasion for him, having been an American citizen for over a year, to distance himself from his German past. He did the opposite. He talked about Germany's seclusiveness and melancholy unfitness for the world, he reminded his audience of how inwardness and the romantic counterrevolution had led to the disastrous separation of the speculative from the sociopolitical sphere that made the Germans unfit for modern democracy—and he acknowledged at the same time that these German attitudes, together with a late love of democracy, would always remain a part of his own existence and a prerequisite for his work as a writer. There were not two Germanys that could be neatly separated. The good and the bad belonged together. The Germans were the most provincial folk on earth and at the same time they were cosmopolitans, citizens of the world. It was this blurring of ideas and convictions, the endurance of contradictions that could not possibly be resolved, that made Thomas Mann declare that his type of Germanism was "most suitably at home in the hospitable Panopolis, the racial and national universe called America."[15] Never before, Mann said, had he felt so much in harmony with his own German past than as an American citizen who had been sworn in under the presidency of the much-admired Franklin Delano Roosevelt.

German Democratic Vistas

The audience must have understood Mann's pledge of allegiance as the fruit of his experience in American exile, and this is perhaps how the speaker understood his own words. Talking about Germany and the Germans, Thomas Mann praised Americans and the United States. It was a moving, heartfelt expression of sympathy. His declaration of love for America, however, he had already delivered much earlier, in 1922, in Berlin, in his speech "The German Republic."

Four years earlier, in the *Reflections of a Nonpolitical Man*, under the spell of German romanticism, Thomas Mann had fired a salvo against the "Roman West" and democracy at home "across the Ocean where the new Capitol stands."[16] Now in 1922 Mann, the late convert, set himself the daunting task of winning an authoritarian German youth, both among his Berlin audience and in the country at large, to the cause of the Weimar Republic and of German democracy. It did not suffice to remind his audience that his own hometown, Lübeck, had been a "republican federated state of the Reich" or to claim that "it is possible for democracy to be more German than imperial grand opera."[17] The new-born republican found a better way to stabilize his own republicanism and to make it attractive to his youthful audience. He had to bring German, if not Germanic, ideas together with the political ideals of the United States of America.

Mann knew that it would be impossible to win German youth to the side of the Republic, "to the side of what is called democracy, and what I call humanity," if he asked the younger generation to part with a distinctly German element of its emotional and intellectual heritage, romanticism. The Weimar Republic had a chance for survival only if it could be shown that romanticism was not alien to the ideas of democracy. Looking back at Germany's past, republicanism had to be found at the core of the romantic worldview. By recalling "the wonderful intellectual sphere" to which Friedrich von Hardenberg, alias Novalis, belonged, Thomas Mann described German romanticism as a movement in which nationalism and universalism dwelt side by side and patriotism and love of the Republic were one and the same thing. Whoever had read Novalis—who was falsely denounced as the reactionary of romanticism—knew that one could be a royalist and a democrat at the same time. The Republic was unavoidable; it was, Mann said, Germany's *amor fati*, its unavoidable love. At the same time, the Republic was Germany's future. It was, as Novalis had written, "the *fluidum deferens* of youth. Where young people are, there is a republic."[18]

Looking back at the romantic movement with the fresh view of a republican, the expression "German democracy," which at first sounded strange and uncomfortable, appeared suddenly as correct and respectable as the familiar notion of "the German people." It would not have been sufficient, however, to make a plea for the Republic merely by invoking the republican element in romanticism. Romantic traces in republicanism also had to be found. Novalis needed a counterpart. Mann called to his support an American who had become familiar with the poetry of Novalis, especially his *Hymns to the Night*, through Carlyle's essay on Novalis: Walt Whitman. Mann told his audience that he had conceived his speech as "a lecture upon this extraordinary pair, upon Novalis and Whitman."

Two volumes of Whitman's writings had just been published in Germany. Mann had read them with growing enthusiasm. For him Goethe and Whitman were like two "fathers," resembling each other in the importance each gave to the sensual side of humanity. Mann celebrated the coming together of humanity and democracy in the "Manhattan thunderer" and hailed Whitman as a spiritual compatriot of Goethe.[19] By aligning Whitman's emotionally charged Americanism with the ideas of Novalis, that "highly intellectual dreamer," he hoped to convince German youth of the ideals of the Republic: "If I could succeed in establishing a relation between republic, democracy, and the German romantic movement, should I not at the same time be making the former more acceptable to the sticklers and bickerers among my countrymen?"[20] This question showed Mann's cleverness: he could assure his young and skeptical listeners that he did not have to convert them to the Republic—unbeknownst to the German youth that had gone to war in 1914, they were already fighting in a republican spirit.

Mann, who went on to dig out the roots of republicanism in Novalis's writings, did so perhaps more thoroughly than his audience cared for. At the same time he drew its attention to the romantic core of American democratic ideals as represented in the life and letters of Walt Whitman. Did the singer of Manhattan not sound like a German poet when he declared, in his prose collection *Democratic Vistas*, that political tactics, procedures of suffrage, and legislation were not enough to vivify democracy but that "men's hearts, emotions and belief" must be touched by it? In the *Reflections*, Thomas Mann had distanced himself from democracy, whose inherent feminine character he said inevitably attracted the French; in the "Thoughts in War," his sympathy for Frederick the Great may have been sustained by the homosexuality of the Prussian king. Now Walt Whitman touched the emotions of Thomas Mann, who could finally embrace the idea of democracy—and thereby admit, ever so delicately, his own homoerotic inclinations.[21]

Rather than for democracy, allegedly alien to the Germans' innermost soul, Germany had always longed for autocratic regimes whose backbones were male societies. These male societies turned out to be the fiercest enemies of the Weimar Republic; the murderers of both the left-wing official Matthias Erzberger and Walther Rathenau were members of such all-male groups. To win over the conservative German youth for the Republic, Thomas Mann had to convince himself that homosexuality and democracy need not be seen in contrast to each other. This objective made Walt Whitman a welcome ally. He was not only the poet of democracy; he was the poetic thinker who hailed the homoerotic bond as indispensable for the functioning of a democratic nation. In *Democratic Vistas*, Walt Whitman had talked about the necessity for a nation to be led by what he called a "soul." In a democracy like the United States, this soul was literature. Immediately after having bestowed a soul-like quality upon literature, Walt Whitman talked about the male bond that would be so important for the future of the United States: "Intense and loving comradeship, the personal and passionate attachment of man to man—which, hard to define, underlies the lessons and ideals of the profound saviours of every land and age, and which seems to promise, when thoroughly develop'd, cultivated and recognized in manners and literature, the most substantial hope and safety of the future of these States, will then be fully express'd."[22]

It would be difficult to find, in Thomas Mann's work, expressions of greater enthusiasm than in this speech, delivered in 1922, in which he called Walt Whitman to the rescue in his attempt to reconcile homosexuality and democracy. True, German society had begun to look more calmly at "that zone of eroticism . . . where what we see linked in passionate communion is like with like, maturer masculinity with admiring youth," and Mann could rely on, among others, Goethe and Schopenhauer for the blessing of his own inner feelings. Yet the homosexual bond so far had been above all the "secret cement of the monarchist leagues": it had been mainly associated with war and death, with destruction, aggressiveness, and terror. "Democrats" like Harmodios and Aristogeiton, the Greek lovers who killed the tyrant Hipparch in 514 B.C., had lived too long ago to make the homosexual acceptable to democracy. Thomas Mann needed the poet of the Calamus songs, Walt Whitman, to persuade his audience that reviving the old idea of seeing Eros as statesman did not lead back to a monarchist restoration. It led forward to the idea of a republic, which for Mann was nothing else but the unity of state and culture.[23]

In the end, Whitman became even more important for Mann's republican conversion than Novalis: "Whitman's worship of boys, since in his case it forms but one fine province of the all-embracing realm of his phallically healthy, phallically brimming inspiration, was certainly something more healthy than poor Novalis with his love for the pale Sophia." Never before and never again did Thomas Mann express a deeper sympathy for an American author. Walt Whitman made it possible for him, in praising the German Republic, to passionately admit his own sexual feelings and describe them with an almost graphic fervor. And yet not only did Mann not refer to these passages of his early American eulogy in his lecture in the Library of Congress in May 1945, but, three years earlier, he had made sure that they were omitted from the English translation of his Berlin speech when it was included in *Order of the Day*, the collection of political essays that Knopf published in 1942. Thomas Mann's praise of Whitman was translated into English, in its entirety, for the first time in 2003.

His friend Agnes Meyer had urged him to cleanse his speech, probably thinking, as others did, of American readers as a "high-toned, censorious, prudish lot."[24] Mann thanked his friend for her considerate censorship in a letter written in Pacific Palisades on May 26, 1942. Obviously he did not want to remind himself that Walt Whitman's praise of the male bond had once enabled him, in the presence of nationalist and autocratic German youth, to embrace democracy and the idea of a republic. To even think that the male bond could still play a political role, Mann obediently wrote to Agnes Meyer, would be nothing than bad romanticism. His early speech had also to be cleansed, because mentioning the relationship between homosexuality and democracy would have deeply disturbed a puritan American audience at a time "when a standard trope of anti-Nazi propaganda had been the alleged sexual perversity of Hitler and his followers."[25] To avoid hurting the pure feelings of Americans, Thomas Mann, in 1942, became his own censor and banished the pages on which he had, twenty years earlier, expressed his deepest feelings for an American and for American democracy, for the poet whom Hart Crane called the "Meistersinger of America": Walt Whitman.

While Mann had given Whitman's poetry an enthusiastic yet still cursory reading, *Democratic Vistas* had won his full attention and admi-

ration. Whitman and Novalis were connected by the social eroticism
with which the one looked at the state and the other at democracy.
Both saw individualism and universalism as nothing but two sides of
the same coin—"One's Self I sing, a simple separate person, / Yet utter
the word Democratic, the word En-Masse." Both aimed at uniting intellectual life and service for the nation and wanted to preserve religion
as a core element of democracy.[26] Whoever read Novalis again after
becoming acquainted with the work of Whitman could not but make
out, underneath a German romantic vocabulary, the voice of democratic
pluralism at home in America. The German romantic's voice was freed
from metaphysical air and suddenly displayed "an almost American
freshness," not least because Novalis went so far as to call the spirit of
commerce the spirit of culture: "Gentlemen, there is no denying it, that
is democracy," was Thomas Mann's summary statement.[27] And Walt
Whitman, who had helped him "to give democracy a gloss of the familiar by linking it with German romanticism," let him finish his speech
with the most un-German of all possible endings, with the battle cry:
"Long live the Republic!"

   These mentions were not the end of Thomas Mann's unexpected
reading of Novalis as a precursor and foreseer of the German Republic.
Walt Whitman had anticipated a law that would bind all nations, all
men into a brotherhood, one family: "It is the old, yet ever modern
dream of earth, out of her eldest and her youngest, her fond philosophers and poets." Among those fond philosophers was Immanuel Kant,
who had written about eternal peace. Among those poets was Novalis,
who had spoken not only of a "State of States" that would unite Europe
but also of universal law-giving activities that would eventually lead
to a universal state.[28] This was not only democracy; this was political
enlightenment, as Thomas Mann said. Such enlightenment was even
more remarkable both in Walt Whitman and in Novalis because it was
based not just on reasoning but on an all-embracing sensuality that also
touched the body politic. Whitman's political sensuality brought him
into close contact not only with Novalis but with Goethe and Nietzsche
as well. In Whitman's verses, Mann said, Hellas was born anew out of
the spirit of American democracy. Now democracy and aestheticism
could be reconciled.

   It was an American lesson that helped Mann in 1922 to come to the
vigorous defense of the young German Republic. Reading Whitman

must have been a relief and a revelation for a writer who wanted not only to praise the Republic but to embrace it. Thomas Mann was poised to instill enthusiasm for democracy in young men who had been told by many, and once upon a time also by him, that the idea of democracy was alien to the German spirit. Born out of the Lutheran protest against the Catholic Church and the defeat of Napoleon in the Prussian wars of liberation, German nationalism had always been directed against someone else, had always made the country look as if it had to fight against the rest of the world. Inwardness and an aggressive nationalism went together. Both made Germany a solitary nation. Nationalism was not at all absent from the poems and prose of Walt Whitman, but his was a nationalism that was characterized more by pride than by aggressiveness. By calling the United States the greatest poem, Whitman did not deride other nations as prosaic but encouraged American writers to live up to the expectations of a truly poetic country.

Whitman expected much from poetry and literature. America was the country where, more than anywhere else, poets would influence politics—a prophesy alluded to, though probably inadvertently, when Herbert Hoover, during the Depression, declared, "What this country needs is a great poem. Something to lift people out of fear and selfishness." When Whitman praised the United States, "with veins full of poetical stuff," as the nation where not presidents but poets were the "common referee," a German author could nurture the illusion of feeling at home.[29] It was an illusion, though, because the great psalm of the Republic could only be sung under the conditions of political liberty and with a striving for democratic egalitarianism. The United States was a country of "unrhymed poetry," not least because here the people did not take off their hats to the president, but the president did take off his hat to them. When a poet like Stefan George was adored by large parts of German youth and called a seer in the Weimar Republic, the praise for him was also a rebuke of the nation's political elite. When Walt Whitman spoke of the American poet as a seer, his praise was also a battle hymn for the Republic. "Resist much, obey little" would have been a strange motto both for German poetry and for German politics. In the United States, where the largeness of nature corresponded to the largesse of the citizens' spirit, it was a motto that brought politics and culture together.[30]

Twelve years after *Leaves of Grass*, Walt Whitman published his *Democratic Vistas*, from which Mann quoted at length in his Berlin speech. *Leaves of Grass* is an exuberant and visionary text, including the introduction that Whitman wrote for it. *Democratic Vistas* is, in parts at least, a somber description of reality during the overwhelming materialism of the Gilded Age. Here Whitman took neither America's athletic democracy nor its poetry of freedom for granted. Under his "moral microscope" he saw "a sort of dry and flat Sahara . . . cities, crowded with petty grotesques, malformations, phantoms, playing meaningless antics . . . everywhere, in shop, street, church, theatre, bar-room, official chair, are pervading flippancy and vulgarity, low cunning, infidelity . . . everywhere an abnormal libidinousness, unhealthy forms, male, female, painted, padded, dyed, chignon'd, muddy complexions, bad blood."[31] It was a jeremiad that Hitler and Goebbels would have loved to quote to support their abhorrence of a cultureless America.

And yet, much more than the jubilant *Leaves of Grass*, it is this text—with its disdain for the depravity of the American business elite, with its fear of the future decline of a country that is still waiting for sustained progress in all matters cultural and social, and with its anger at a nation that is endowed with a vast body but has been left with little soul—that most convincingly argues for the crucial role of literature in a democracy. In a well-established and functioning democracy, culture was not much more than an ornament, the coda to a symphony. In a struggling democracy, however, a heavy burden was put on the poet who wanted to contribute to the betterment of the polity: "I demand races of orbic bards, with unconditional uncompromising sway. Come forth, sweet democratic despots of the west!"[32] Choosing *Democratic Vistas* as his main point of reference, Thomas Mann was well aware of the precarious future that lay ahead for the young and frail German Republic.

Emerson's Sponsors: Beethoven & Bettina

Walt Whitman had already made clear the precariousness of the situation in the United States in a letter to Ralph Waldo Emerson in August 1856, when he sent him the second enlarged edition of *Leaves of Grass*. The churches were a vast lie, the "heads of the public tables" and judges were pitiful, a rascal and thief had stolen the presidency. And yet America, "grandest of lands in the theory of its politics," was about to acquire a national character and an identity its citizens could be proud of. Literature would contribute to this process in an important way, not by pretending to be a substitute for politics, but by enriching it: "Strangle the singers who will not sing you loud and strong. Open the doors of The West. Call for new great masters to comprehend new arts, new perfections, new wants. Submit to the most robust bard till he remedy your barrenness. Then you will not need to adopt the heirs of others; you will have true heirs, begotten of yourself, blooded with your own blood."[33]

Founding an American literature of its own, "electric, fresh, lusty," one that did not develop out of traditions inherited from, if not imposed by, the English language, was not easy. The States had the mightiest printing presses, great bookshops, large libraries, and a vast array of newspapers—but they had still to develop a literature that walked out of the trodden paths of writing and reading as American politics had walked out of the trodden paths of European politics. Whitman was convinced, however, that this process would take place before long and that American poets and writers would follow the example of American politics in preventing any foreign tradition from shaping the United States: "The time is at hand when inherent literature will be a main part of These States, as general and real as steam-power, iron, corn, beef, fish."[34] The democratic ease with which literature was seen, not in tension with, but as a natural part of the polity must have attracted Thomas Mann. "Democratic ease"—these were the words Walt Whitman used to describe the atmosphere he had encountered when he visited Ralph Waldo Emerson for the first time.[35] Emerson and the transcendentalist movement were the background and the inspiration for Whitman's romantic hymn to the States and to the ideals of democracy.

In Emerson's 1837 Harvard Phi Beta Kappa address "The American Scholar"—the intellectual declaration of independence of the American people, as Oliver Wendell Holmes called it—he prophesied: "Our day of dependence, our long apprenticeship to the learning of other lands, draws to a close. . . . We will walk on our own feet; we will work with our own hands; we will speak our own minds."[36] He was thinking of the need to reduce the European influence in America and of the necessity for American authors to write themselves away from the English tradition, to "cut ourselves loose from the lead strings of our British grandmama," as William Carlos Williams described Edgar Allan Poe's aim.[37] To a certain degree this became the program of the transcendentalist movement, as expressed in an 1851 entry in Henry David Thoreau's *Journal*. Thoreau could not think of any existing poetry that adequately expressed the Americans' "yearning for the wild": "English literature from the days of the minstrels to the Lake Poets Chaucer & Spencer & Shakspeare & Milton included breathes not quite fresh & in this sense wild strain. It is an essentially tame & civilized literature reflecting Greece and Rome. Her wilderness is a greenwood her wildman a Robinhood. There is plenty of genial love of nature in her poets, but . . . Her chronicles inform us when her wild animals, but not when the wild man in her became extinct. There was need of America."[38] But America, too, needed help. As long as a genuine American tradition had not yet been established, distancing America from English traditions in thinking and writing required a large-scale orientation toward other national philosophical and poetic discourses. The void that a distanced yet never fully abandoned English heritage would leave was filled to a large extent by German traditions. On February 23, 1837, George Ripley, then minister of Purchase Street Church in Boston, asked James Marsh to contribute to a series of translations of some French and a dozen German authors called *Specimens of Foreign Standard Literature*. "With the exercise of the true German spirit," Ripley said, he hoped that American scholars would be able to do for their literature what "our elder sister, Britain, has failed to effect."[39]

Yet the book that had the greatest influence on the transcendentalist movement arguably was James Marsh's edition of Samuel Taylor Coleridge's *Aids to Reflection* (1829). But many transcendentalists would have agreed with the theologian and social reformer Theodore Parker's judgment that the mantle of the English genius had fallen, in modern times, on the Germans and not on the English. Shelley was the author of the sweeping dictum that "poets are the unacknowledged legislators of the world"—but only the Germans had taken it seriously.[40] Works by English writers like Coleridge and Carlyle and also Madame de Staël's *De l'Allemagne*—an American edition of which had been published in 1814 in New York and eagerly read by Emerson eight years later—promoted the German influence on American thought. At times this influence went so deep that an idolized Germany emerged that would hardly have been recognized by the Germans themselves. This is Emerson's outcry: "In that old rotten country of Germany it seems as if spontaneous character,—fresh outbursts of dear nature,—were less rare than in this country, called new & free. We are the most timid crippled old Uncles and Aunts that ever hobbled along the highway without daring to quit the sidewalk. I have no better Sponsors however at this moment in mind than Beethoven & Bettina."[41] The "New England Renaissance" sprang from German roots, and it was not least German influence that made transcendentalism appear, in James Elliot Cabot's definition, to be the "remarkable outburst of romanticism on Puritan ground."[42] Critics, however, spoke of German insanity that had come over New England like the plague, causing "a faction of discontented men and maidens . . . to love everything Teutonic, from Dutch skates to German infidelity," as Theodore Parker put it in the hilarious description of anti-German sentiment he used as a starting point to write one of the most emotional tributes ever paid to the German mind.[43]

For Emerson, traveling abroad was unnecessary after the German mind had made its imprint on American culture: "We imagine that in Germany is the aliment which the mind seeks or in this reading or in that. But go to Germany & you shall not find it. They have sent it to America. It is not without but within: it is not in geography but in the soul."[44] Despite a plea for American self-reliance that was reiterated in one of Emerson's famous essays, the German influence on the transcendentalist movement could hardly be overestimated—for better or for worse. When H. L. Mencken spoke of the "utter collapse of Whitman" and stated that American literature, "despite several false starts that promised much, is chiefly remarkable, now as always, for its respectable mediocrity," he saw one reason for this in the aping of German traditions. He belittled Emerson's effort as merely giving "a sonorous *Waldhorn* tone to what had been dreamed and said before."[45]

The German influence on the transcendentalists could easily be misunderstood. The transcendentalists saw society around them as seriously deficient. Walt Whitman admired their "democratic ease," but the transcendentalists might have said, anticipating the words of Ralph

Ellison, that "Deep down, the American condition is a state of un-ease."[46] Emerson spoke of America as a democracy in which no true democratic elements could as yet be seen. Thoreau claimed that health could be found not in society, but only in nature, and that writing was the work of art closest to life itself. Both men sounded like German authors who had turned away from society in celebration of inwardness. To follow the rhetorical attitudes of German romanticism, as Emerson and his New England friends did from the 1830s on, meant that they wanted to explore new ways of political action and civic engagement in which personal emotions and feelings were allowed to express themselves. Looking for an alternative way in American politics, they were influenced by German romanticism and its view of the creative individ-ual, to whom an important political role was ascribed. "The greatest action may easily be one of the most private circumstance," Emerson wrote in his essay on Goethe, where he also proclaimed that society has no greater interest than the well-being of the literary class. Emerson praised Goethe, the head and body of the German nation, for having "clothed our modern existence with poetry." For Emerson, Shakespeare was the greatest poet, but Goethe was the greatest writer in the world.

German romanticism exerted a huge influence on the transcenden-talists' program to change American democracy. At the same time, ro-manticism also changed. After its reception in the United States, it was much easier than before to detect the political core of a movement that had often been characterized, in German history, by its apolitical na-ture. Nowhere did this become more visible than in Thomas Mann's early speech in praise of the German Republic, this remarkable outburst of republicanism on romantic ground.

In the transfer of German philosophical thought and romanticism to the United States, James Marsh played a fundamental role. He trans-lated Herder's *Spirit of Hebrew Poetry* and wrote an essay, "Ancient and Modern Poetry," that turned the aesthetic credo of the German roman-tics into an American idiom. First at Dartmouth College and then as president of the University of Vermont (1826–1833), Marsh had a last-ing influence on American higher education, preferring the romantic view of an organic interaction between nature and man to Locke's proc-lamation of a passive mind. Among his students was Henry Jarvis Ray-mond, who would help to found the *New York Times* in 1851. The influence of Marsh's lectures on psychology was still discernible at Vermont when John Dewey studied there as an undergraduate in the late 1870s. When Dewey tried to establish a link between German philosophy and Nazi politics, he was lashing out at a tradition and a worldview that his teacher James Marsh had helped to bring to the United States. Dewey attacked a German system of thought that had deeply influenced the American mind.

German Culture Abroad: Victorious in Defeat

The Closing of the American Mind

On the occasion of the twentieth anniversary of the National Endowment for Democracy on November 6, 2003, George W. Bush reminded his audience of a speech by President Ronald Reagan. In June of 1982, Reagan had spoken to the British Parliament at Westminster Palace, predicting that a turning point was about to arrive in history: "President Reagan said that the day of Soviet tyranny was passing, that freedom had a momentum that would not be halted." Somewhat mischievously, George W. Bush added: "A number of critics were dismissive of that speech by the president, according to one editorial at the time. It seems hard to be a sophisticated European and also an admirer of Ronald Reagan." In the transcript of the Bush speech posted on the Web, an insertion was added at the end of this sentence: "(Laughter.)"

In his 1987 best-seller *The Closing of the American Mind*, Allan Bloom quoted President Reagan, who had recently called the Soviet Union the "evil empire." "Right-thinking persons joined in an angry chorus of protest against such provocative rhetoric," Bloom observes. The protestors did not object, however, when Reagan spoke of the different values that separated the United States from the Soviet Union. What the president's critics did not understand, Bloom argued, was that on both occasions he had said one and the same thing. Their misunderstanding pointed to a dramatic change in Americans' view of morality and politics that could only be compared to the substitution of Christianity for Greek and Roman paganism in antiquity: "There is now an entirely new language of good and evil, originating in an attempt to get 'beyond good and evil' and preventing us from talking with any conviction about good and evil anymore. Even those who deplore our current moral condition do so in the very language that exemplifies that condition." Reagan's critics found his use of the word "evil" arrogant—they were appalled by the American president's seeming certainty regarding what was good and what was bad. To replace words like "good" and "evil" with the neutral term "value" implied "the radical subjectivity of all belief about good and evil [and served] the easygoing quest for comfortable self-preservation."

These sentences appeared at the beginning of a chapter in Bloom's book in which he identified the main culprit for the deplorable change of the American state of mind: "The German Connection." Critics of President Reagan's speech, Bloom maintained, merely gave expression to German philosophical thought in its most advanced form.[1] For Bloom, the social and political problems of the United States in the second half of the twentieth century had their origin in a spiritual crisis. The time- and leisure-consuming use of high technology, the sexual revolution, and multiculturalism reflected a shift toward relativism and value neutrality that had also been caused by the influence of German thought.

The Closing of the American Mind should not be read as an empirically valid description of the influence of German thinkers in the United States, either before or during or after the Second World War. Bloom's book is a telling symptom, not a fitting diagnosis: a polemic, not a truthful account. His polemic, however, must be taken seriously, not least because it belongs to a specific tradition of attacks against the German mind. Bloom does not quote Julien Benda, but his book has its precursor in Benda's tract *The Treason of the Intellectuals*, first published in 1927, in which the mundane worship of relativism is ascribed to German thinkers, while the metaphysical cult of the universal is seen as the gift of Greece to humankind: "Here again, and moreover in its profoundest part, the teaching of the modern 'clerks' shows the triumph of Germanic values and the bankruptcy of Hellenism."[2]

It is important to see Allan Bloom in a tradition, unacknowledged by himself, together with Julien Benda in order not to misread his book or to overrate its impact. Its distortions and lacunae resemble those of Benda in his condemnation of German romanticism. Benda and Bloom join in an attempt at restoring the "tyranny of Greece over Germany."[3] Out of a Germany that had been so deeply influenced by Greek thought in the heyday of Weimar developed a tradition of historicist and relative thinking that, by rejecting the heritage of the Greeks, became a betrayal of classical German thought itself. Bloom, whose book could easily be read as an anti-German tract, tried to play off one strand of German thought against the other.

Nietzsche is a central figure in Bloom's attack on the German legacy in American thought. Bloom was as fascinated by Nietzsche as he was appalled by Nietzsche's American successors and imitators, whom Bloom saw as having transformed a tragic worldview into a cheap intellectual lifestyle. The Americanization of the German worldview inevitably led to its trivialization. Bloom hated Continental despair. What he hated even more was gloominess without a consequence, "nihilism with a happy ending," despair without the abyss. Yet "nihilism lite" has always been a part of American culture—playing with, yet finally refusing to indulge in, European-style existential sadness. In 1906 Edith Wharton invited the novelist and critic William Dean Howells to attend the New York premiere of "The House of Mirth," Clyde Fitch's dramatization of her novel. Wharton foresaw that the play was doomed to fail because she had refused to let her heroine survive. When Howells left the theater, he turned to Wharton and put the reason for the play's failure in a single sentence: "What the American public always wants is a tragedy with a happy ending."[4]

Inadvertently, perhaps, Bloom argued like an ardent follower of Nietzsche: he was fascinated by the power that culture could command in political defeat. While the Allies fought Nazi Germany, German thought conquered the West, not least the United States: "The self-understanding of hippies, yippies, yuppies, panthers, prelates and presidents has unconsciously been formed by German thought of a half-century earlier; Herbert Marcuse's accent has been turned into a Middle Western twang; the *echt Deutsch* label has been replaced by a *Made in America* label; and the new American life-style has become a Disney-land version of the Weimar Republic for the whole family."[5] While American troops, suffering terrible losses, went ashore at the beaches of Normandy, the United States underwent a fatal D-Day at home. The invasion of German culture led to a dramatic change in postwar

American philosophical thought. This outcome of the Second World War was even more unfortunate, from Bloom's perspective, since the war had not only been fought on the battlefield. It had been a culture war as well: "When we Americans speak seriously about politics, we mean that our principles of freedom and equality and the rights based on them are rational and everywhere applicable. World War II was really an educational project undertaken to force those who did not accept these principles to do so."[6]

To the dismay of Bloom, not only the defeated Germans but also the victorious Americans underwent a reeducation program after the Second World War. Americans became deeply influenced by German habits of thought and even adopted a new language they felt compelled to speak in talking about their own culture. Cabdrivers all of a sudden used words like "Gestalt," and Max Weber's complicated sociological terminology invaded everyday life, for instance at the "Charisma Cleaners," which Bloom, to his horror, found in Chicago. Even the movies, this most American of all arts, were now colored by German ideas. The scripts of Woody Allen, a "doctrinaire" in Bloom's view, were interspersed with thought bites of German philosophical fare and made it a household ingredient of the American entertainment market: without Max Weber, Heidegger, and Adorno, a movie like Woody Allen's "Zelig," featuring the other-directed man, would never have been created in the United States.

In the nineteenth century, when authors like John Stuart Mill and Matthew Arnold tried to soften utilitarian thought by propagating what they called the "culture of the feelings," they turned to German philosophy and poetry—as did the French whenever they tired of their Cartesian creed. Unwittingly, the same happened, Bloom argued, in the United States. Nietzsche's rejection of rationalism, Freud's discovery of the unconscious and the dark regions of the soul, Max Weber's attempt at disenchanting the world, Heidegger's Hellenism, Thomas Mann's mysteries and sufferings as described in *Death in Venice*—they all changed the rational project of American culture. Americans became utterly dependent on German missionaries for their knowledge of Greece and Rome, Judaism, and Christianity. Admiringly, Bloom tells the story of Alexandre Koyré, who was excited when, in 1940 in Chicago, one of his students, unaware that the ancient Greek philosopher was not his contemporary, always spoke in his paper of "Mr. Aristotle." Bloom's American dream was to send Professor Weber back to Heidelberg and Dr. Freud back to Vienna, while not only Messrs. Aristotle and Plato but also Mr. Locke and even Monsieur Rousseau—serious criticism of their works notwithstanding—would be granted permanent residency in the United States.

The German invasion of the United States affected classicists and theologians, political as well as moral thought, philosophy and psychology—but perhaps to the greatest degree sociology. An influential and seemingly so American author as David Riesman was in truth nothing but a Max Weber in disguise, Bloom maintained. The fashionable categories of tradition-, other-, and inner-directed behavior, for instance, developed in *The Lonely Crowd*, were a direct translation of the German master's three ideal types of legitimacy. Yet the German invasion could be successful only because it was the result of a misunderstanding, claimed Bloom. In truth, German culture was a system of thought and belief that did not travel. To imitate German thought only proved that the Americans knew nothing about its essence. American intellectuals sang a song they did not understand.

How could authors like Marx, Freud, Nietzsche, Weber, and Heidegger, all of them critics of rationalist thought, exert such an influence in a nation that had always been proud of its Enlightenment universalism? On the one hand, Bloom was convinced that nothing could have been more unwelcome to Nietzsche and Heidegger than the American embrace. On the other hand, Americans did not so much embrace these German authors as their indigenous fakes. The neo-Freudians turned the psychoanalytic adventure into a daily routine; Freud became a kind of family doctor. In the social sciences, Talcott Parsons trivialized Max Weber and was a living example of the routinization of charisma. Bloom despised the influence of German thought—and blamed American authors for not having been taken over by the German tradition to its fullest extent. Routinization and trivialization took the bite out of German thought. German nihilism was a matter of life and death; American nihilism was a mood that could be left behind over the weekend.

Bloom's invectives sometimes turned into parody. But he was right in his assessment of the influence the German *Geisteswissenschaften* (humanities) exerted on the American mind. There is no other national tradition of scholarship—with the exception of the British—that has played a similar role in the United States. If one concentrates on scholarly works that had to be translated or to be read in a foreign language in order to be taken into account at all, the impact of German books has been unparalleled—at least before French strands of thought like existentialism, structuralism, and deconstruction became popular in the United States. Durkheim and Pareto were never as influential as Max Weber; Bergson did not have the impact Heidegger still has today, and it would simply be unfair to compare anyone else with Marx and Freud.

In criticizing Bloom's view of German culture and the *Geisteswissenschaften* in particular, one would have to point to a specific selection, a peculiar distortion, and a far-reaching narrowing of German intellectual content in his book. In carefully selecting the authors he was talking about, Bloom could maintain that German culture, since Nietzsche and especially with Heidegger, took an incorrigible antirational turn. There were no alternatives. Authors who might be classified as forming, before and after Nietzsche, part of an enlightened and liberal tradition of German thought were either not mentioned or most inadequately discussed. Moreover, it was a distortion to speak of Nietzsche, Freud, Max Weber, Heidegger, and to a certain degree also Thomas Mann as authors who unanimously suggested that reason had to be abandoned and the exploration of the darker side of the human existence had to begin. Bloom forgot to mention that in the work of these authors a rational project can also be found, a serious and sometimes almost tragic attempt to secure the survival of Enlightenment thought in times of darkness. But there is no dialectic of Enlightenment for Bloom.

As an example of Bloom's narrowing of German traditions, the case of Thomas Mann is particularly instructive. In *The Closing of the American Mind*, Mann is discussed as the author of just two stories, *Death in Venice* and *Tonio Kröger*. The rest of his work does not exist. In Bloom's view, Mann seduced American students to follow the "mysteries and sufferings of sophisticated Europeans." Himself a sophisticated European par excellence, Thomas Mann, as expressed in the characters of his fiction that Bloom has chosen, longed to live out the hidden and primal drives of human existence that civilized behavior must tame. Civilized behavior was only a secondary satisfaction for him and not worth choosing if primary satisfaction was available. In fairness, it must be said that Bloom grants Thomas Mann the intention to depict the crisis of a civilization, the decline of the West. Allegedly, this was not understood by Mann's American audience, however, who read *Death in Venice* mainly as an early manifesto of sexual liberation. At the same time Bloom, who was teaching his students how to read Plato, called the interpretation of Plato's *Phaedrus* by Aschenbach, the hero of *Death in Venice*, appalling and attributed it to Mann himself: "There is no indication that Mann thought one could learn much directly from Plato about eros. One could learn something by applying Freud's insights to Plato and seeing how desire finds rationalizations for itself. Plato was [a] vile body for scientific dissection. Mann was too caught up by the novelty of the Freudian teaching to doubt whether sublimation can really account for the psychic phenomena it claims to explain. He was doctrinaire, or he was sure we know better than did older thinkers. They are mythologists."[7]

For Bloom, Thomas Mann was a foreigner whose work helped to fashion habits of thought and lifestyles that were then exploited by homemade American "doctrinaires." The Thomas Mann who had struggled to become a republican and a democrat did not exist for Allan Bloom—nor did Thomas Mann the European get any attention. Bloom missed the interesting blurring of European and American traditions in an author for whom Joseph could mature under the Californian sky and whose sexual fantasies were nurtured not just by the Viennese Sigmund Freud but also by the thunderer from Manhattan, Walt Whitman, whose "anatomical love-song" Mann had characterized as "Hellas—born anew out of the spirit of American democracy."[8] That Mann could exert such an influence on the American reader, as Bloom proclaimed, was not so much due to the reader's misunderstanding of European traditions that Mann represented. It had more to do with the fact that Mann himself had been influenced not only by American thought but also, and certainly in the case of Whitman, by an American "lifestyle" not in the shallow but in the deep sense of the term, before his feet had even touched American soil. It was not by chance that Ralph Ellison could speak of "many of us" who read "our first Hemingway, Fitzgerald, Mann in barbershops," naming these three authors together as the most natural thing in the literary world of the United States.[9]

Allan Bloom thus ascribed the closing of the American mind to the influence of German writers who had for a long time crossed the borders of their homeland. Yet it should have been impossible for Bloom to regard Freud and Marx, Nietzsche and Max Weber as primarily "German" authors. Even where standard editions or translations of their work did not exist, their thought had already long been incorporated into the humanities at large. This was not always a blessing, to be sure: Freudian thought, on its way from Vienna and London via Paris to New York and California, underwent curious changes and superficial adaptations indeed. And whenever someone who knows German reads Max Weber in an English translation and comes across a heading like "Some basic concepts," he cannot but regret that the neo-Kantian flavor of the German "Einige grundlegende Kategorien" has been completely lost. Yet most of Bloom's "German" authors were already classics, whose work had transcended its national context of origin and had become meaningful in other habitats as well.

Thinking of "influence" as a one-directional movement only, Bloom gave too narrow a view of one of the great sea-changes in the history of the humanities that was caused by the expulsion of German, notably Jewish, scholars from Germany. Emigration to other countries was considerable as well—but nowhere was its intellectual impact as far-reaching as in America. When Abraham Flexner, the founder of Princeton's Institute for Advanced Study, was asked who had been the greatest benefactor of the institute, he replied: "Adolf Hitler." In comparison, in France the deeply ingrained xenophobia of the country's institutions of higher learning made any substantial change in their basic intellectual orientation through the émigrés rather difficult. French intellectual resistance made a deep impression on Bloom. For him, every Frenchman was born either a Pascalian or a Cartesian and would not easily change his identity. With glowing admiration, Bloom relates that on a recent trip to France he overheard a waiter in a restaurant call one of his colleagues a "Cartesian."

After their migration to the United States, however, representatives of the German *Geisteswissenschaften* not only changed the American mind-set. Their ideas were not just stored in the United States, but were transformed considerably and later often returned to Germany in disguise. One does not have to go as far as Georg Simmel, who called pragmatism nothing else but what the Americans got out of Nietzsche. Phenomenological thought, for instance, which had played an important part in German philosophy, was later received as an American specialty in postwar Germany; Max Weber only became a classic through the integration of his ideas and categories into Talcott Parsons's *Structure of Social Action* of 1937—the best example perhaps of an American system of thought blending different European intellectual currents that had had almost no contact with one another in Europe itself. When the American sociologist Paul Lazarsfeld, who had been born in Vienna, traveled to Europe after 1945 to teach empirical social research, his visit was seen as part of an American invasion and, especially in West Germany, as an attempt at reeducation. But it also meant the return of a distinctly Viennese tradition of social science and sociologically oriented social-democratic policy to Europe. Gestalt psychology, a field whose proponents were all forced to emigrate, became transformed in the United States and eventually sounded so American, not only to Allan Bloom's cabdriver but to a broad swath of readers, that Thomas Kuhn, in his *Structure of Scientific Revolutions*, could use the term "Gestalt switch" as one of his key words.

The United States, in Bloom's words, had long been "a backwater and a consumer," dependent upon European intellectual traditions to establish its own identity. It was high time to realize that this dependency was no longer necessary. Europe was no longer the place where Americans went to learn and to train themselves. Bloom spoke of Europe, but what he was precisely aiming at was Germany. Locke, Hobbes, and Rousseau, not to mention Socrates, Plato, and "Mr. Aristotle," were still, as Bloom wrote, the acknowledged "Columbuses of the mind" to whom America could look for spiritual guidance, while the decline that the tradition of rational thought had suffered since Locke and Adam Smith was a result of the attack German irrationalism had mounted against it. Allegedly, the times were over when Emerson could write in his journal: "As the vegetable eye makes leaf, pericarp, root or bark or apple or thorn, as the need is, so and as the primal animal cell makes a stomach or a mouth or an eye or a nail according to the want; so, the world throws its life into a hero or a shepherd; so it puts it where it is wanted; Dante & Columbus are Italians then; they would be Americans & (Prussians) Germans today."[10]

Bloom spoke, as if anticipating today's neoconservative rhetoric, of the "American moment in world history" that required the United States to distance itself from its European origins and especially to reject its German heritage. Traditions had been blurred too much, though, to make such a severance possible. Bloom had forgotten that in the nineteenth century a British author named Charles Dickens wanted to "outamerica America" and that Thomas Mann had declared "I am an American" in an NBC broadcast as early as May 1940, four years before becoming an American citizen.[11]

The German Mind in Jeopardy

The Closing of the American Mind was translated into German as *Der Niedergang des amerikanischen Geistes* (The decline of the American mind). An equally if not more appropriate title could have been *Amerikanischer Geist in Gefahr* (The American mind in jeopardy). One year before the Nazis came to power, Ernst Robert Curtius, a well-known professor of Romance languages, published his book *Deutscher Geist in Gefahr*, a best-seller of sorts, too, for after just a few months it had to be reprinted. It is a learned and challenging, but also a cowardly, ambivalent book. In 1932 Curtius did not take sides—as Thomas Mann, for instance, did in his speech "Appeal to Reason" in 1930—but kept his options open. The book can be read as a sympathetic anticipation of the Nazi revolution—or as an early dissociation from it. There are traces of anti-Semitism in it, but these are so shrouded in ambiguous prose that at the same time they can be read as both an accusation against the Jews and an apologetic for them.

Curtius's publisher praised the book as a wake-up call. For Curtius, the German mind—which meant, above all, the German *Geisteswissenschaften*—was in danger because two important intellectual currents threatened its foundations: academic historicism drifting into value neutrality, on the one hand, and a forceful irrationalist movement on the other, culminating in a spiritual barbarism for which Nietzsche was mainly responsible. "Democratization" had been a key concept in the cultural policy of Carl Heinrich Becker, the Prussian minister for education and cultural affairs at the time of the short-lived Weimar Republic. He came under heavy attack from Curtius, who believed that the democratization and liberalization of the German universities had resulted in the weakening of traditional educational values and in a widespread contempt for culture (*Kulturhass*). What Germany now needed was a strong discipline of thinking and learning, a renewed reverence for reason, and a return to traditional values. Even more than the Western nations, France, England and the United States, Germany was in need of metaphysics, for which sociology, the fashionable new discipline, could not possibly be a substitute. Philosophy had to reign again as queen of the disciplines. Intellectuals had to return to the sources of ancient philosophy to acquire a new self-assurance. They had to remember that, in Europe, poetry came into being with Homer, sagacity with Plato, science with Aristotle, and mysticism with Plotinus.

The similarities between *The Closing of the American Mind* and *Deutscher Geist in Gefahr* are striking. The differences are equally interesting. Allan Bloom was writing his book at the "American moment in world history." Curtius was convinced that "the Anglo-Saxon day in world history is dawning."[12] It is an amazing parallel, but the two statements led to almost opposite conclusions. Bloom justifies the need to purify the American mind by liberating it from the influence of German thought. Curtius rejects any protectionism in the sphere of higher learning and education; he vigorously opposes attempts at cleansing the German mind by severing it from Western civilization. In the end, Curtius argued, the German humanistic tradition would suffer most if one tried to prevent it from mingling with the Western mind. Curtius knew what he was talking about when he derided the *Westfeindschaft*, the enmity toward the West that had shaped the intellectual currents of post- and prewar Germany. He had been thrown out of the inner circle around the seer-poet Stefan George because he had not been willing to distance himself from French and Anglo-American influences. Curtius was too much of a European and cosmopolitan to be acceptable to his nationalist colleagues.

Deutscher Geist in Gefahr sounds like a conservative manifesto, and it is a conservative text indeed. Yet at the same time it is rather antinationalist in tone, and its author prefers universalism to the provincialism of large parts of the German humanities. Writing shortly before the

Nazis came to power, Curtius promoted the universalism not of the Enlightenment but of medieval thought. In the same mood in which Bloom urged his American students to go back to the sources, that is, the philosophers of Greek and Roman antiquity, Curtius warned his readers that German culture could only survive if the bearers of culture renewed their ties with medieval humanism. This humanism, however, had been weakened not just in Germany but all over Europe. It was of great significance for Curtius, therefore, that the Mediaeval Academy of America had been founded in 1925 and began to publish, one year later, the journal *Speculum*. Curtius quoted the editors as wishing "to recognize satire, humor, and the joy of life as part of our aim. Art and beauty and poetry are a portion of our mediaeval heritage." The true humanist spirit was to be found in these words.[13] Hoping that what in Berlin and Weimar was threatened with destruction might survive in American universities like Harvard, Curtius followed the footsteps of Goethe, who, with a handwritten dedication, had sent his collected works to Harvard University in 1819, the same year in which the seventy-year-old told the chancellor, Friedrich von Müller, that he would sail to America if only he were twenty years younger.[14]

Allan Bloom wanted to reconnect the American mind with the immortal thought of the philosophers of Greek and Roman antiquity. He warned the Americans against continuing to walk on the German path, which had proved to be a dead end for any serious thinking about good and evil. What is so puzzling about Bloom's book, whose foreword Saul Bellow had written, and its huge success in the United States is the combination of an unmitigated trust in America's spiritual leadership—calling the United States one of the highest and most extreme achievements of the rational quest for the good life according to nature—with a sort of intellectual Monroe doctrine. Bloom made a plea not only for the de-Germanization but also for the de-Europeanization of American intellectual life. Bloom liked the role of the loner that inevitably gave to his writings a certain high tone and to his arguments a flavor of tragic futility. In retrospect, the high tone sounds considerably weaker after the publication of Saul Bellow's roman à clef *Ravelstein* in 2000, in which the tragic outlook of the hero became inextricably linked to his lust for the high life.

A Calm Good-Bye to Europe

In distancing himself from European strands of thought, Bloom was following a tradition that had been part of America's quest for identity from the moment when the first pilgrims landed on the shores of Massachusetts. Even as late as 1841, however, Theodore Parker thought "we are, perhaps, yet too young and raw to carry out the great American idea, either in literature or society."[15] One hundred years later, Lionel Trilling wrote that the European influence, "as a large, definitive, conscious experience of the American intellectual," had come to an end and that this was all to the good.[16] A shallow cosmopolitanism had reigned over American letters. Nowhere did the American intellectuals look more provincial than in their imitation of European mores. Whereas Bloom bade Europe a dramatic farewell, Trilling calmly said good-bye. His serene dissociation from European influence came in an essay entitled "The Situation of the American Intellectual at the Present Time" (1952–53). Though consisting not only of intellectuals in the narrow sense of the term, an intellectual class, Trilling observed, was for the first time playing a role in the political and social life of the United States. Adlai Stevenson, who publicly admitted to being an intellectual, lost the presidential race against Eisenhower in 1956 but had won the Democratic nomination and received a large popular vote. It was still difficult to imagine that in a country as big as the United States an elite could exert a decisive political influence. Yet "art and thought [were] more generally and happily received and recognized—if still not wholly loved—than they [had] ever been in America."[17] The nation enjoyed an increased power of the mind. An author like Trilling must have been especially pleased with this diagnosis, for he had once proclaimed that it should no longer be possible to think of politics except as the politics of culture. Now culture could rightly be defined as the meeting of literature with social action.[18] Trilling dismissed European influence at exactly the moment when he rejoiced at the happy union between culture and politics in the United States.

At the same time that Trilling published his observations on the present situation of the American intellectual, in another essay he glanced backward at one of the great American intellectuals of the twentieth century. Edmund Wilson was the only person, Trilling said, whom he was sure that he would want to read his upcoming book on Matthew Arnold. Trilling valued Wilson's readership because Wilson was an exemplary author who was not only deeply convinced that the literary life mattered, but who had been able to make it attractive to others as well. One might have expected Trilling's essay on Wilson to be an example that confirmed what he had said about the American intellectual and literary life in general. Yet this was not the case. Taken together, the two essays, written more or less in the same year, read like the script for a *Rashomon*-like movie. Looking back at Edmund Wilson and remembering the role he had once played, Trilling went so far as to judge that American literary life, though "quite indispensable to civilization," did not play a major role in American politics anymore.

When Edmund Wilson was writing for the *New Republic*, the magazine became the perfect context in which American culture was seen as an important part of the nation's moral destiny. But times had changed, Trilling observed: "We have nothing in our intellectual life today like *The New Republic* of that time, no periodical, generally accepted by the intellectual class, serving both politics and literature on the assumption that politics and literature naturally live in a lively interconnection."[19] It was an interconnection that had, of course, existed long before Wilson began to write. It had accompanied American literature's attempts to free itself from European influence. That the image of the man of letters in a community with his peers no longer pleased or commanded public attention, as Trilling said, made one nostalgically think of a period in which Emerson could claim that "society has really no graver interest than the well-being of the literary class."[20]

When Newland Archer, the hero of Edith Wharton's novel *The Age of Innocence*, asked himself whether the humanities were as meanly housed in other cities as they were in New York, he had forgotten, though he was an occasional traveler to Boston and a regular visitor at Newport, that New England had already answered this question with a resounding "no." One should be careful, however, not to mistake a New England phenomenon for an American reality. At the same time that Emerson praised the literary class, the good society of Old New York was proud to be a small world that had no need of letters at all. Reading a book was seen as an "inherent oddity," and "people who wrote" lived far down West Twenty-Third Street, together with dressmakers and bird-stuffers, "scattered fragments of humanity [which] had never shown any desire to be amalgamated with the social structure." Wharton thus described her own experience as an author whose writings New York's society only regarded as "a drawback and an embarrassment" while the "literary men foregathered at the Century Club, and continued to turn a contemptuous shoulder on society."[21] In New England, however, the writings of Emerson and Thoreau gave the impression that literature naturally dealt with man in society. This was a view that Stanley Cavell would underline when pointing out that Thoreau's *Walden* was written at a moment when philosophy, literature, and theology could not yet be separated from each other. This had also been the German romantics' view.

Trilling had put his two essays in radically different settings, which explain why they read so differently. The essay on the American intellectual culminated in saluting his liberation from European influence, a liberation that had permitted the intellectual class to assume a pivotal role in American public life. In the essay on Edmund Wilson, however, Trilling argued that the American intellectual had played an even bigger role in the past. Compared with the status of a towering figure like Edmund Wilson, the present situation of the American intellectual looked less exciting. Both essays are similar in the rather subdued tone in which they were written. Literary life was commented upon with much common sense and a lack of either anger or excitement. Deploring the decay of American culture, Trilling, rather than being outraged, just sighed: "We are all a little sour on the idea of the literary life these days." Allan Bloom must have been appalled when Trilling, using one of the terms with which Max Weber had changed the American vocabulary, wrote that it was not a propitious sign that the reading public had become "disenchanted" with literary life.

When Trilling published his essays at the beginning of the fifties, the fact that the American intellectual allegedly had cut his ties with Europe had no political repercussions. Only a few years earlier, NATO had been founded. There were disagreements between the United States and Europe, notably with France, but during the cold war the West stood firmly together against the Soviet bloc. In this context, internal cultural disagreements played only a minor role. When Bloom published *The Closing of the American Mind* in 1987, the situation was different. President Reagan ventured to predict the coming fall of communism. The Europeans rejected the Manichaean language of American politics. The clash was an anticipation of the derailment of American-European relations, both in politics and in culture, that would ensue as a consequence of the end of the cold war.

It is easy to overrate the impact of a book that became a best-seller. That *The Closing of the American Mind* was displayed on the coffee tables of hundreds of thousands of American homes does not yet prove that Allan Bloom changed the worldview of his readers or was able to influence the course of American politics. Bloom's symptomatic book was an anticipation of America's resolve to leave its self-doubts behind and become proud and strong again. Two years after *The Closing of the American Mind*, with its praise of Ronald Reagan, had been published, Mikhail Gorbachev did what President Reagan, in a speech given in front of the Berlin Wall, had asked him to do: he opened the Wall. The neoconservatives became a force in the Republican Party and the "Contract with America," drafted by Newt Gingrich in 1994, paved the way for the defeat of the Democrats and the first presidency of George W. Bush. Stronger than ever before, ideology became a crucial element of American politics at home and abroad. And more explicitly than ever before, one man was hailed as the inspiration for the neoconservative movement: Leo Strauss. Strauss, a Jewish-German émigré, came to the United States in 1937, taught at the University of Chicago, and died in 1973. That he could exert such an influence on American politics was a puzzle: "How could an obscure German-Jewish biblical scholar, historian of ideas, admirer of Plato, Alfarabi, and Maimonides become the leading intellectual inspiration of America's Republican party?"[22] The question itself is part of what Mark Lilla has called a "wild speculation about Straussian influence in American government," including "even the suggestion that Strauss's 'esoteric' method of reading texts might lie behind a duplicitous foreign policy, especially in the recent Iraq war." It was indeed highly speculative to see in Strauss, whose separation of "the life of philosophy" from "the life of the city" was reminiscent of Julien Benda's admonishment to the intellectual not to mingle with politics, the mastermind behind the partisan politics of neoconservative Republicans. Still, the irony remains that American

politicians who engaged in a cultural war against "Old Europe" saw fit
to claim the legacy of a scholar whose work was the epitome of classical
European thought.[23]

Allan Bloom had studied with Leo Strauss. One could argue that
The Closing of the American Mind is a popularization of Straussian ideas,
an updated sequel to *Natural Right and History*, the Walgreen Lectures
that Leo Strauss gave in 1949, the year two separate German states
were founded. The book was published in 1953. More radical than any
American-born author, a German émigré deplored the influence of a
certain strand of German thought in America. Leo Strauss asked
whether the American nation still believed in its original faith, that is,
the self-evidence of the natural and divine foundations of the rights of
man. Strauss came to the conclusion that there was no longer any difference between the abandonment of the idea of natural right and adherence to it. The difference between German thought, on the one hand,
and that of Western Europe and the United States, on the other, had
completely vanished. Washington threatened to become Weimar. Leo
Strauss concluded: "It would not be the first time that a nation, defeated
on the battlefield and, as it were, annihilated as a political being, has
deprived its conquerors of the most sublime fruit of victory by imposing
on them the yoke of its own thought."[24] Victorious in defeat, German
culture had proved its fundamental assumption: not only could it compensate, but it could even take its revenge on politics.

The publication of Bloom's book coincided with the beginning of
American revenge. Soon the neoconservatives spread the belief that the
"principles of freedom and equality and the rights based on them are
rational and everywhere applicable" and that it was justifiable "to force
those who did not accept these principles to do so."[25] America had liberated itself from the pernicious German—and European—influence.

5

French-German Culture Wars

Two Revolutions

It may well be argued that the "culture wars" characteristic of the English departments of American universities in the 1980s and 1990s were more the result of a "Gallic invasion" than of the intrusion of German irrationalism.[1] Yet it would be difficult to separate French and German influences from each other. The selective and distorted view of the German humanities, of which Allan Bloom's polemic against the "German connection" is but one example, was exacerbated by the fact that, after the Second World War, German traditions survived in the United States not least through their French mediators. With the possible exception of Claude Lévi-Strauss, French authors who influenced American thought were indebted to German thinkers: Jean-Paul Sartre to Husserl and Heidegger, Raymond Aron to Max Weber, Michel Foucault to Nietzsche, and Jacques Derrida to Nietzsche and Heidegger. Since the rise of romanticism in the late eighteenth and early nineteenth centuries—"the privilege and curse of the German mind"[2]—Germany had always served as a reservoir for French authors who referred to German irrationalism and speculative thought. They sought thereby either to strengthen their own Cartesian views or, on the contrary, to claim more vehemently than the Germans themselves that the borders between reason and unreason were fluid and that madness could be found in almost any method. The appropriation of German thought served those French intellectuals—*universitaires* as well as *hommes de lettres*—who wanted to sharpen their public profile by distancing themselves from the reigning ideas and the gate-keeping institutions in Paris. Sartre, Foucault, and Derrida were virtuosi of this strategy that paid off at home and perhaps to an even greater degree abroad, notably in the

United States. German irrationalism crossed the Atlantic via Paris. Americans bought it second-hand.

When Theodor Adorno returned to Germany after the war, he witnessed, much to his astonishment, the resurrection of German culture. He felt as if a time machine had propelled him back into an era where a "dull philosophical book" like Fichte's *Theory of Knowledge* influenced public opinion more than any political action.[3] Unwittingly, perhaps, Adorno's remark was proof of how much anything that happens to German culture must be understood in relation to France—and vice versa. Adorno was alluding to a famous statement by a romantic author, Friedrich Schlegel, who, in 1789, had known how to offend a neighbor by calling the French Revolution, Fichte's *Theory of Knowledge*, and Goethe's *Wilhelm Meister*—not necessarily in that order—the highest achievements of the modern epoch, thus daring to set a German philosophical tract and a German novel equal to the revolution in France.[4] German readers must have been surprised and French readers—at least the republicans among them—must have been dismayed.

Schlegel offered an explanation. Whoever rejected a revolution that was not "noisy and material," that is, one that was not a political revolution in the narrow sense of the term, was not yet able to look at human history from an elevated point of view. Schlegel's present was a time when a small book that was neglected by the multitude could have a greater influence on the course of history than any action this multitude would ever be capable of. There were two ways to look at the French Revolution. On the one hand, one could see it as the most important phenomenon in the history of nations, a global event, the prototype of all revolutions, and a gift to humankind. On the other hand, one could see in the French Revolution nothing but the expression of the French national character, in which all its paradoxical elements were tied together and came to the fore: a grotesque play of history, the most complete assembly of all known prejudices, a tremendous tragicomedy of the human race.[5] The German romantics did not altogether reject either of these opposing views. They reserved, however, the right for the German observer to decide for herself how universal a French claim to universalism really was. For Schlegel, France was a "chemical nation" and the French Revolution took its inevitable course like an experiment in chemistry. After the "chemical epoch" an "organic epoch" would follow that one might also call a German epoch. When one looked back from this later German standpoint, the French Revolution would appear as nothing more than a youthful exercise of humankind.

Goethe had always decided for himself whether to accept a French claim to universality. On August 2, 1830, the news of the French July Revolution reached Weimar. Three days of upheaval, the so-called *trois glorieuses*—July 27, 28, and 29—had finished the Bourbons. King Charles X had gone into exile. Frédéric Jean Soret, a liberal republican from Geneva and a mineralogist whom Goethe held in high esteem, came to visit the poet in the afternoon. Goethe was excited: "What do you think of this great event? The volcano has come to an eruption; everything is in flames, and we have no longer a transaction with closed doors!" "A frightful story," replied Soret. "But what could be expected under such notoriously bad circumstances, and with such a ministry, otherwise than that the whole would end in the expulsion of the royal family?" Perplexed, Goethe responded: "We do not appear to understand each other, my good friend. I am not speaking of those people, but of something quite different. I am speaking of the contest, so important for science, between Cuvier and Geoffrey Saint-Hilaire, which has come to an open rupture in the academy." This reply came so unexpectedly that Soret, in his own words, "did not know what to say, and for some minutes felt [his] thoughts perfectly at a standstill."[6]

Bad harvests had led to enormous price increases and had caused famines in many parts of France. The number of unemployed grew steadily, and more and more people were forced to live in poverty. The domestic and social policies of the Bourbons had failed. In many provincial towns the inhabitants were up in arms and the tricolor flag could be seen—a sign that in the middle of the Restoration period the revolutionary spirit was still alive. The name of Napoleon, who had remained for many a symbol of social justice and equality, was often invoked. And yet, in a heated atmosphere of resistance and revolt, the largest room in the Academy of Sciences in Paris was filled to capacity on July 19, 1830. What would be the outcome of the verbal duel between Georges Cuvier and Etienne Geoffroy Saint-Hilaire, who had once been friends? Who would shape the sciences of man in the years to come, the system builder or the evolutionist? It was a question that interested not only the scientific community but the whole educated world. Writers and poets could not escape its spell. Some of them had difficulties deciding whom to support. Balzac, for instance, referred to Geoffroy Saint-Hilaire at the opening of the Comédie Humaine and dedicated one of its novels, *Le père Goriot*, to him. In an earlier novel, *La peau de chagrin*, however, he had praised Cuvier as the greatest poet of the century, an immortal scientific genius who was able to re-create new worlds out of the dry bones of animals that had been dead for thousands, if not millions, of years.

In Goethe's view, Cuvier was far too systematic. The poet's favorite was Geoffroy Saint-Hilaire, who must, in his view, win the duel against Cuvier. It meant the victory of the idea of evolution that Goethe himself had pursued vigorously without finding many allies, at least not at the beginning of his own career as a scientist: "And now Geoffrey Saint-Hilaire is decidedly on our side, and with him all his important scholars and adherents in France. This occurrence is of incredible value to me; and I justly rejoice that I have at last witnessed the universal victory of a subject to which I have devoted my life, and which, moreover, is my own *par excellence*."[7] Goethe praised French scientists for engaging in a controversy over problems of natural history in times of political turmoil. Yet it would be wrong to assume that he was not interested at all in the political developments in France, as the anarchist Gustav Landauer claimed in an essay on Goethe's politics written immediately before the German "revolution" of 1918.[8] In his conversation with Soret, Goethe simply left no doubt that he would decide for himself what to regard as an event of universal interest and to what he was willing to attribute only local importance. The July Revolution was a political episode and, public opinion notwithstanding, a local French affair, whereas the breakthrough of the idea of evolution was a cultural event, a universal victory for humankind.

This famous misunderstanding between Goethe and Soret has often been retold. It is incomplete, though, without a follow-up conversation between Eckermann and Goethe that was to take place a year later, on Sunday, the 20th of June 1831. Eckermann and Goethe talked, as they often did, about problems in natural science. On this day, they addressed the imperfection and insufficiency of the language that scientists have at their disposal to describe the procedures and results of their

research. Eckermann delighted Goethe when he gave the highest marks
to the German language and contrasted it with the French, an idiom
that is "at once material and vulgar" and altogether unfit for proper
scientific use. Thereupon Goethe attacked his former hero, Etienne
Geoffroy Saint-Hilaire, "a man who has certainly a great insight into
the spiritual workings of nature; but his French language, so far as he
is constrained to use traditional expressions, leaves him quite in the
lurch." Besides the term *Materialien*, the use of one word especially
roused Goethe's ire, the word *Komposition*.

Eckermann, as so often his master's voice, echoed Goethe's damna-
tion of the terrible word, whereupon the poet almost exploded in his
fiery rejection of it: "It is a thoroughly contemptible word for which we
have to thank the French, and of which we should endeavour to rid
ourselves as soon as possible. How can one say, Mozart has *composed*
(*componiit*) Don Juan!—Composition! As if it were a piece of cake or
biscuit, which had been stirred together out of eggs, flour, and sugar! It
is a spiritual creation, in which the details, as well as the whole, are
pervaded by *one* spirit, and by the breath of *one* life."[9] The twentieth of
June 1831 clearly did not count among his "French days," as Goethe
used to call those times when words came easily and everything seemed
to be going smoothly. There was nothing playful in his attack on the
French language.

Why had French become the universal European language? This had
been the prize question in a contest the Berlin Academy of Sciences
organized in 1784. Did the French language deserve this prerogative?
Was it likely to last in the years to come? Antoine de Rivarol was one
of the two prizewinners, arguing that a natural bond existed between
the use of French and clarity of thought and expression. If something
was not clear, it could not be French. This view did not remain uncon-
tested. Under the spell of Louis XIV's political supremacy, French culture had invaded Germany, and French had become the language of the
German courts after 1648. By the mid-eighteenth century, however,
poets and philosophers tried to restore German pride by writing in German and by distancing themselves from French culture. Goethe, while
he was attacking Geoffroy Saint-Hilaire, took aim at the French language for what he saw as its lack of precision and its inaptitude for

grasping the essence of scientific understanding. The German poet thereby dealt the most terrible blow the enemy could possibly expect in the French-German culture wars.[10]

Goethe in Exile

But the French took their revenge. On April 30, 1932, one hundred years after Goethe's death, Paul Valéry gave an address in honor of the German poet in the Grand Amphithéâtre of the Sorbonne. Valéry had great difficulties in preparing his speech, as he wrote in a letter to André Gide. He knew no German and not much of Goethe, having read few of his works, among them *Faust* in French translation and some biological stuff on the intermaxillary bone and the metamorphosis of plants, *crâne et plante*, which he called, somewhat condescendingly, "not bad at all." It had taken him five whole days to type the speech on his old Remington and when it was written he no longer wanted to read it. There was something in Goethe that bothered him: *Il y a quelque chose qui me gêne chez Goethe.* And yet there is perhaps no greater tribute to Goethe, "the most complex figure in the world," than this speech. Valéry used the opportunity to dwell on a theme that had been the basic idea of many of his own works: how might the world, and especially Europe, have developed if political and intellectual power "had been able to join forces, or at least if the relations between them had been less precarious?"[11] Valéry never stopped hoping for what he called a *politique de l'esprit*, but knew that he was only dreaming: "The two forms of power may well be incommensurable quantities; and it is no doubt necessary that they should be so."

Among the handful of men in whom Valéry's dream had come true were Napoleon and Goethe, "one of them no doubt . . . the wisest, the other perhaps the maddest of mortals . . . , both of them . . . the most exciting characters in the world."[12] Valéry seemed to repeat the juxtaposition of Napoleon and Goethe that had been a centerpiece in Emerson's portrait: "I described Bonaparte as a representative of the popular external life and aims of the nineteenth century. Its other half, its poet, is Goethe, a man quite domesticated in the century, breathing its air, enjoying its fruits, impossible at any earlier time, and taking away, by his colossal parts, the reproach of weakness, which, but for him, would lie on the intellectual works of the period." Together, the writer and the emperor represented their epoch in its entirety: "You and I, Monsieur Goethe, possess the strange virtue of completeness," Napoleon had said. Valéry goes on to say that this is why the year 1808, when Goethe and Napoleon met in Erfurt, was such a priceless moment in world history: "Coquetry was essential at such a meeting. Each wanted to appear at his ease, and carefully arranged his smile. They were two Magicians attempting to charm one another. Napoleon assumed the role of emperor of the mind and even of literature. Goethe appeared as the embodiment of mind itself." Napoleon knew that the fate of the world "was certainly in his beautiful hands; but [that] the fate of his Name was in the hands that hold the pen." Goethe thought what an ideal figure Bonaparte would make for a third part of *Faust*.[13]

Valéry's description of the Erfurt meeting is extraordinary, a drama in itself, full of a tension that has lost nothing of its vibrant power after more than seventy years. Valéry seems to follow André Gide, who had called Goethe "the most un-German of all Germans" because he did not retreat into inwardness and distance himself from politics. For Valéry, Goethe is a "courtier, confidant, minister, a diligent official, a poet, collector, and naturalist" at the same time; the great, in Germany perhaps the greatest, "apologist of the world of Appearances. . . . In the evening of his days, in the heart of Europe, himself the center of attraction and admiration of all intelligent people," Goethe probably thought of Napoleon, "perhaps his greatest memory, whose look still lingered in his eyes."[14] How could a French intellectual not admire a German writer who admired a French genius?

And yet, at the end of his speech, Valéry's eulogy for Goethe sounds as if he wanted to take revenge for the German poet's criticism not so much of France as, worse, of the French language: "What a noble sunset! What a view of the plenitude and glory of life when, in extreme old age, he contemplated, nay *composed* his own twilight, from the splendor of the immense spiritual riches his labor had assembled, and the immense spiritual riches his genius had scattered abroad."[15] In his criticism of Geoffroy Saint-Hilaire, Goethe had once taken the verb *composer* as an example of the French language's inability to describe natural phenomena and do justice to human achievements. And now

Valéry, who had almost certainly not read this passage, not only used the verb *composer* but put it in italics to describe the German genius.[16]

Goethe had always been admired as a world genius who lived, as Emerson wrote, "in a small town, in a petty state, in a defeated state, and in a time when Germany played no such leading part in the world's affairs as to swell the bosom of her sons with any metropolitan pride, such as might have cheered a French, or English, or once, a Roman or Attic genius. Yet there is no trace of provincial limitation in his muse."[17] Valéry admired Goethe no less. But into his admiration, brought to the fore in the intellectual center of Paris, the Sorbonne, the French writer stirred a pinch of disturbing and in the end devastating critique. It is a critique not so much of Goethe as of the German understanding of him: "Wolfgang von Goethe was to die a little more than ten years after the death of the Emperor, in that little Weimar which was a sort of delicious St. Helena for him."[18] Weimar, *une sorte de Sainte-Hélène délicieuse*—this analogy meant that the happy coexistence of political and intellectual power had been nothing but an episode in German history, a remote island, an exile from which no Goethe would return. In Germany, there had once been a political promise in culture that had not been fulfilled.

"Culture Wars" and Their Origin

Samuel Huntington did not invent the idea of a "clash of civilizations"; the term "war of cultures" is to be found in one of the most severe scoldings of intellectuals ever written, in Julien Benda's 1927 pamphlet *The Treason of the Intellectuals*. From the beginning of the nineteenth century on, Benda argued, political passions no longer served national interests alone, but had to be pursued in the name of universal ideas. Nations pretended to follow moral principles in foreign affairs; political hatred now needed an intellectual organization. Cultures fought cultures, patriotism became belligerent and had to be based on cultural ideals. Benda agreed with, of all authors, Heinrich von Treitschke, the most nationalistic among German historians, who had claimed that wars would never disappear from the earth once they had turned into

culture wars. More than in any other nation, culture in Germany became a shield with universal mottoes behind which particular interests
were pursued. The Prussian war of liberation against Napoleon was, in
Benda's view, the first "war of cultures" (*guerre des cultures*).[19]

Although one might doubt Benda's claim that culture wars were "entirely an invention of modern times," one can hardly deny that culture
wars were always at the center of French-German conflicts. Whenever
one country was defeated on the battlefield, cultural policy served the
need for revenge until renewed spiritual strength made retaliation in a
"real" war possible. This holds true for Germany after the defeat at Jena
and Auerstedt in 1806, when the Prussian king's cry that the state must
now replace by spiritual forces what it had lost in material strength
eventually led to the founding of Humboldt's university. It holds true
for France after the lost war of 1870–71, when the desire to regain
Alsace-Lorraine could best be fulfilled, in the eyes of French politicians,
by learning from the enemy and sending the best of the young French
scholars to the universities in Leipzig and in Berlin. It holds true for
Germany during the First World War, when its intellectuals compared
the mobilization of the German army reserve, jubilantly cheered by the
whole population, to the *levée en masse* of the French Revolution. At
last, the "Ideas of 1789" were superseded by the "Ideas of 1914." And
how could one not laugh at a civilization where country inns were
named *A l'idée du monde* and even fishing trawlers were called *Pensée* or
Honneur et dévouement moderne, as Thomas Mann pointed out in 1918?
French universalism had become a joke. How could a soft civilization
that raised its youth in the illusions of democracy survive the attack of
the armored German cultural state?

French-German reactions were not only characterized by culture
wars. There was also mutual attraction, if not admiration, between the
two countries. Frederick the Great preferred speaking French and
would have loved to have Voltaire preside over cultural life in Prussia.
Arguably, no one did more to spread the high regard for German culture
than Madame de Staël with her book *De l'Allemagne*. For her, France
and Germany were connected by the same moral chain. They were the
twin nations upon whom the future of Europe depended. On the eve
of the First World War, Romain Rolland echoed Madame de Staël's

view in his novel *Jean-Christophe*. He called France and Germany "the two wings of the west—whoever breaks one of them, impedes the flight of the other." The Germans were no less emotional. In 1928 Annette Kolb, *femme de lettres*, daughter of a French mother and a German father, traveled to Paris to meet Aristide Briand, then the French minister of foreign affairs and the partner of Gustav Stresemann, who had served as chancellor in 1923 and was now Germany's foreign minister. In retrospect, she mused: "What did 'politics' mean to me? For me, it meant above all that Germans and French should unite. Our planet turned around the novel of these *Promessi Sposi*; it must be brought to a good end, nothing else counted much. The other countries were only supernumeraries, England played the role of a relative. Did the East, the Balkans, the Russian Empire, the states on the Danube exist at all? They were all not important, their turn would come later. First, the empire that already existed under Charlemagne, that could exist indeed, had to be restored. Then, the world would be redeemed."[20] These pleas for a French-German alliance were even more impressive because they entailed a coalition of opposites: the French saw the typical German as a romantic dreamer, the Germans saw the typical Frenchman as a notary public.

Political attempts to reconcile the enemies had been numerous. In 1868 François Guizot, the former French minister of foreign affairs, published an article in the *Revue des deux mondes* reminding France and Prussia of their specific responsibility for the peace in Europe.[21] Sainte-Beuve, the great French critic, later got to know this article. Whereas Guizot confined himself to an appeal directed at diplomats and generals, Sainte-Beuve was convinced that a genuine cultural rapprochement was needed to achieve a lasting French-German peace. While he had been working one day—in the fall of 1867—on his weekly literary column in his home on the Rue du Montparnasse in Paris, detonations and the sound of military maneuvers could all of a sudden be heard in the direction of the southwestern suburb of Meudon. Sainte-Beuve interrupted the dictation of his article and talked to his secretary about the necessity of French-German reconciliation: "I don't know what they are planning. . . . France and Prussia are at the pinnacle of European civilization. Instead of setting these great powers like dogs against each other it would be much better to bring them close together. . . . Because of its military strength and its scientific genius, an alliance with Prussia seems logical for us, since we are strong and a progressive country. . . . It would be better, instead of a confrontation between our two towering nations, to set up two schools, one in Berlin and the other in Paris. Their youth would come to us to moderate and smooth themselves: they would not thereby lose any of their strength and would take on some of our courtesy of spirit; we, in turn, would send the elite of our colleges to their laboratories, which are much better equipped than ours, so that they would strengthen themselves in contact with this rough people, which, if you will, is as barbaric as the Macedonians. . . . Oh yes, they are the modern Macedonians and all the more to be feared."[22] Sainte-Beuve hated what he called "transcendental chauvinism" and regarded Alfred de Musset's patriotic song "Le Rhin Allemand" as the worst of all French poems. He admired Goethe for his refusal to endorse German nationalism. In October 1869 Sainte-Beuve died. Less than one year later, the Franco-Prussian War broke out. It did not last long and France suffered a terrible defeat.[23]

After the lost war, nothing could console the French more than the ominous warning of a simple Prussian soldier and medic named Friedrich Nietzsche: "At the very moment when Germany emerges as a great power," Nietzsche wrote, "France achieves new importance as a *cultural power*. A lot of new seriousness, a lot of new spiritual *passion* has already emigrated to Paris. The question of pessimism, for example, the question of Wagner, virtually all psychological and artistic questions are considered there in an incomparably more refined and profound way than in Germany—the Germans are simply *incapable* of this kind of seriousness.—In the history of European culture, the rise of the '*Reich*' means one thing above all: a *shift of the center of gravity*. It's already known everywhere that in what really counts—and what really counts is still culture—the Germans are no longer worth considering. . . . There is no end of amazement at the fact that there is not a single German philosopher anymore."[24]

The relations between France and Germany were not a zero-sum game in which military power was exchanged for cultural supremacy. The realization of the German dream of the Reich became a nightmare for France. Modern Macedonians ruled Germany. A nation of poets and thinkers turned into the blood-stained military regime of Bismarck's Prussia. The German chancellor's successful attempt to transform the German *Kulturvolk* into a powerful *Kulturstaat* resembled the moment in antiquity when ancient Greece became united under a Macedonian military monarchy.[25] French intellectuals, who, in the tradition established by Madame de Staël, admired German philosophy and German literature and did not want to give up on them, now faced a dilemma. Loving German culture and disliking Prussian politics made it necessary for them to distinguish between two Germanys, a good and a bad one.[26] There was no consensus, however, among French intellectuals on whether Prussia's military might was irreconcilable with German philosophy. Some of them argued that in the works of a Prussian philosopher, Immanuel Kant, the universal norms could be found that Bismarck had violated. Others, like Charles Maurras, the nationalist writer and founder of the right-wing Action Française, held the contrary view: the exact formula not just for German but for any barbarism had originated in Kant's mathematical head.[27] For Maurras, it was no coincidence that so many scientists, philosophers, historians, and jurists served as officers in the Prussian army. France fought a military power that consisted of "educated Attilas." And these "educated Attilas" refused any attempt to separate the two Germanys. As the ninety-three signatories of the manifesto "To the Civilized World" had insisted, Prussian militarism and German culture were not just compatible with one another, they were two sides of the same coin. Without the military, these proponents claimed, culture would not have survived in the country of Kant and Bismarck.

Disappointed love and mutual hatred were the prevailing, yet not the only, attitudes in the French-German culture wars. In the nineteenth century, the historian Edgar Quinet claimed that the French loved German culture because they did not know it. The same might have been said about the French contempt for German culture—"haters without knowledge," as Theodore Parker had once called the foes of German culture in the United States, could also be found in France.[28] Sometimes, neither love nor hatred but a conspicuous lack of awareness was characteristic of French-German intellectual relations. The history of the social sciences offers more than one example of this.

A Puzzle in the History of Sociology

In 1885 Emile Durkheim, who was born in Alsace, was sent to Germany, one of those bright young scholars whom the French Ministry of Public Education wanted to study the enemy. In the same year, a reserve officer in the German army underwent his first drill in Strasbourg. He once remarked that there was no rational choice between French and German cultural values; their relationship resembled an eternal struggle between different gods that would last forever. The officer's name was Max Weber.

The nonrelationship between Durkheim and Weber remains a puzzle in the history of French and German sociology.[29] The two greatest sociologists at the turn of the twentieth century pretended to be ignorant of each other to such a degree that only willful neglect can have been the reason for it. There is not a single reference to Weber in Durkheim's writings and there is not a single one to Durkheim in Max Weber's published works and letters. The moment came, though, when the French colleague's neglect must have appeared rather benevolent to Max Weber. It was the day when his wife, Marianne, showed him the review in which Durkheim had torn apart her book on the legal status of wife and mother in history (*Ehefrau und Mutter in der Rechtsentwicklung*, 1907).

To secure a safe spot in the French system of higher education, sociology—an embattled discipline if there ever was one—had to prove its distinct national profile and separate itself from German social science. The German mind, as Durkheim readily acknowledged, was characterized by a shrewd awareness of the complexities of social life; but the Germans were, as a rule, thought to be only mediocre analysts and gave up early when something became too difficult—social facts showed a tendency to appear so complex to them that they seemed no longer intelligible. Durkheim was therefore convinced that sociology would remain a pseudoscience for the Germans, who had given up the search for social laws in the strict sense of the term. They were content to point out regularities, approximations, and all sorts of exceptions in social life. The French, however, dyed-in-the-wool Cartesians, had not stopped believing that the universe was indeed intelligible as a whole and could be completely translated into a scientific system. Only French sociology could confidently embark on a journey to universalism: Durkheim began to form a doctrine and a school that was first called the School of Bordeaux, then the sociology of the New Sorbonne, then the French School of sociology, and, finally, sociology pure and simple.

In the wake of the First World War and as a belated consequence of the eternal Dreyfus Affair, Durkheim's journey to Germany almost dealt a deadly blow to sociology's aspirations in France. The French attacks against him, the son of a rabbi, were tainted by overt anti-Semitism. Critics fumed that the term "French school of sociology" was nothing but camouflage. In truth, a philosophical system *made in Germany* was hidden behind it that served as a fifth column and was about to take over the Sorbonne. Durkheim responded by writing two books against Germany and its bellicose politics, by supporting the French propaganda effort, and by publicly expressing his contempt for those German colleagues who once belonged to the same moral community as the French. Now they had turned into savage creatures, aggressive and unconscionable, "whom we hold up to public indignation." It was telling enough that an outspoken antisociologist, the historian Heinrich von Treitschke, had contributed, through his aggressive nationalist views, to the outbreak of social pathology that came to be called the First World War. Never before in his life, Durkheim claimed, had he worked as hard as he did for the French propaganda effort. But his enemies continued to misinterpret his pilgrimage to Leipzig and Berlin; as late as 1916, a Parisian newspaper called Durkheim a German spy. In the same year, his only son, André, whom he had seen as his intellectual heir, was killed in action. In 1917 Durkheim died.

Ten years later, Durkheim's nephew Marcel Mauss contrasted the fragmentation of the social sciences in both the United States and Germany with the unity sociology had achieved in France—thanks to Durkheim. After criticizing various German sociological schools, Mauss came to the conclusion that "the late Max Weber, although he never quoted Durkheim and the work that was done under his direction, came much closer to our own point of view [than other German sociologists]. Compared with him, there seems to be only regress [in German sociology today]."[30] That there must have been a certain affinity between the Durkheimians and Weber had already become obvious to Mauss when, several years earlier, he had visited Heidelberg. There, on a shelf in the late Max Weber's library, were the complete volumes of Durkheim's journal, the *Année sociologique*. And not a single sentence by Durkheim on Max Weber could be found in them.

A Mediator: Maurice Halbwachs

Not a sentence by Durkheim himself—but it would have been impossible not to mention Max Weber's name at all. The *Anneé sociologique* informed its readers about Weber's better-known publications. As a rule, one or two short sentences were devoted to them—if any comment was given at all that exceeded bibliographical information. The second part of Weber's seminal essay *The Protestant Ethic and the Spirit of Capitalism* received the following comment: "A very interesting paper, the consequences of which have yet to be seen." In all likelihood, the anonymous author of these one-liners was Maurice Halbwachs, who became an influential Durkheimian of the second generation. Born in 1877 as the son of a German teacher from Sélestat in Alsace, he was one of the first French intellectuals to publish in a German scholarly journal again after the First World War. Halbwachs was well informed about the developments in Germany. He had studied German philosophy and had written his first book on Leibniz, had been a lecturer at the University of Göttingen in the academic year 1902–1903, and had later done research in Berlin. In 1921 he assumed a teaching post at the Center for German Studies at Mayence in the Rhineland, which was occupied at the time by French troops.

In the 1920s Maurice Halbwachs turned his one-liners, step by step, into full studies of Max Weber's life and work. In 1925 he chose, appropriately enough, the journal of the faculty of Protestant theology at the University of Strasbourg to publish a long essay on Weber's *Protestant Ethic*, which would not be translated into French until 1964. In 1929 Halbwachs published a portrait of Max Weber in which he closely followed Marianne Weber's biography. Halbwachs opened his paper with the remark that Weber was a truly German author indeed—*Max Weber était allemand, très allemand*—but that he was of French origin as well, since his maternal grandmother, Emilie Souchay, came from an Orléans-based Huguenot family that had migrated to Germany in the seventeenth century. What is so striking about Max Weber, Halbwachs said, is that he never ceased revising his ideas; each time he finished a project, it seems that he found a new impetus to proceed even further. One could easily compare him to the captains of industry of the heroic era, so well described by him, who felt naturally obligated to reinvest everything they had earned in new enterprises. Halbwachs, who was not uncritical toward the achievements of German sociology in general, concluded with the remark that everyone who worked on similar problems should in all confidence take the direction that Weber's work indicated.

In 1919 Halbwachs had first been appointed professor of sociology and education at the University of Strasbourg. Later his chair became the first one in France devoted to sociology and nothing but sociology, and it was to remain the only one of its kind for a long time. In 1935 Halbwachs was appointed to the Sorbonne in Paris, and he became a professor at the Collège de France in 1944. From 1872 until 1918, Strasbourg, called Straßburg, had been the home of the German Kaiser-Wilhelms-Universität. Here, in the least anti-Semitic of all German universities—Friedrich Meinecke, an anti-Semite in his youth, even called it *judenfreundlich*, or friendly toward Jews—Georg Simmel, a Jew, finally was appointed full professor of sociology. After the First World War, the University of Strasbourg received generous support from the French government—in order to accelerate the reintegration of Alsace-Lorraine, to prove French superiority, and to extend French cultural influence in Europe. Both the French and the German government used the university as a wedge in their culture wars. Still, the motto that the German professors had given their university could remain in use after 1918, since it was written in Latin and displayed a kind of neutral patriotism only: *Litteris et Patriae*, dedicated to letters and the fatherland. Among both the French and the German faculties, a scholarly ethos survived that simply refused to succumb to nationalistic day-by-day politics. Simmel could not be talked into propagating the ideals of pan-Germanism, and Halbwachs's stubborn resistance to engaging in cultural propaganda let his enemies talk of his unacceptable stance *pro Germania*.

The sociology chair to which Halbwachs was appointed in Strasbourg had been established because such a chair had already existed when Straßburg was German. It was in the French University of Strasbourg, the capital of French-German cultural competition, that Weber's growing influence in France became most conspicuous, notably in the *Annales d'histoire économique et sociale* that Marc Bloch and Lucien Febvre founded in 1929. Halbwachs was a member of the editorial board of the *Annales*, its only sociologist. There were no scientific solutions to human problems, an early editorial said, and many sociologists had therefore misunderstood human reality. The time had come to turn to a skeptic like Max Weber, whose views were broader and more productive and whose writings had opened up new perspectives for the social sciences that had been overlooked in France.

The lasting French neglect of Max Weber eventually led to repercussions that transcended the rivalry of the two national schools of social science. French sociologists' belated reading of Weber made them aware of their lack of political perspicacity. Three years after the Nazis had come to power in Germany, Marcel Mauss went so far—too far, perhaps—as to admit the Durkheimians' blindness to the core conflicts of modern civilization. The French School of sociology had always been proud of its universalistic approach. But in fact, Mauss complained, it had remained rather provincial. It had not foreseen the degree to which the totalitarian movements of the twentieth century would be able to throw modern societies back into barbarism. When one of his students despaired of ever understanding the caste system, Durkheim replied: "Dear friend—from an objective point of view there is absolutely no reason for despair. The social facts cannot escape us. We shall be able to discipline them all before long." Now Mauss called it a tragedy that French sociology had not given due attention to the social facts that had led to the rise of modern totalitarianism. Raymond Aron, who had studied in Cologne and had acquired an intimate knowledge of not only German sociology but also German society, repeated Mauss's words. Whenever he read Max Weber, Aron heard "the rumors, the creaking of our civilization, the voice of the Jewish prophets and, as a sardonic echo, the ravings of the Führer."[31] Aron was indebted to Max Weber for a worldview that he called "active pessimism." Compared with

Weber's lucid analyses that always paid tribute to political reality, Durkheim's sociology floated above the real world.

Mauss expressed his self-criticism in 1936.[32] In the same year, the French philosopher and mathematician Jean Cavaillès visited Germany. After having read Hitler's *Mein Kampf,* Cavaillès dryly remarked that this was the typical book of a German politician: before coming to power, he had to write six hundred pages of pseudophilosophy. When Cavaillès, who had met with opponents to the Nazi regime in Hamburg-Altona, returned to France, he spoke of the "demons" he had seen in Germany. In the writings of French social scientists, for whom Max Weber had become more and more important, we find a kind of precognition, still chilling today, of the fate that Nazi Germany would prepare for philosophers like Jean Cavaillès, historians like Marc Bloch, and sociologists like Maurice Halbwachs.

An Expulsion from Berlin

In 1909 Maurice Halbwachs went to Berlin to study German municipal institutions. In December 1910 he was expelled from Prussia as a "bothersome foreigner." The authorities in Berlin claimed that, as a special correspondent for the socialist Parisian newspaper *L'Humanité,* Halbwachs had reported unfairly about the Prussian police's violent dispersal of a meeting of striking workers, the so-called Wedding riots. Allegedly, the German chancellor Theobald von Bethmann Hollweg felt personally attacked by an article in which Halbwachs accused the police of having used *agents provocateurs* in their clash with the workers. The expulsion of Halbwachs, whom police agents had spied upon for quite a while, was criticized on the front pages of the Berlin newspapers. In the Christmas issue of *L'Humanité,* an editorial commented upon Halbwachs's expulsion. The article bore the title "Police Politics" (*Politique policière*), and its author sought to limit the damage that Halbwachs's eviction might do to French-German relations: "As everyone knows, we are not among those who want to exacerbate the differences and misunderstandings between France and Germany. We don't for a minute seek to hold the German people responsible for a shabby and impolite act—as little as we blame the republican-thinking French people for the missteps of the French police. Indeed, the European reaction is awkward and brutal everywhere, and without inflating the incident [involving Maurice Halbwachs], it will still be permitted to say that such reactions invite the proletarians and democrats of all countries to grow even closer together from day to day and to close their ranks—so that their common action will one day bring about governments in Europe that rely less upon the police, thus being more popular, and a civilization that is at once more rational and more refined."

The editorial was written by Jean Jaurès, the leader of the French socialists. Halbwachs, himself a member of the Socialist Party since 1906 who admired Jaurès, must have been as pleased with the article as with the fact that, during the Prussian parliament's debate on the budget, a delegate condemned Halbwachs's expulsion from Berlin in the sharpest terms. The delegate was the socialist leader and journalist Karl Liebknecht. Nine years later Liebknecht would be murdered, together with Rosa Luxemburg, by soldiers of a right-wing Free Corps, the "Nazis of the future," as Halbwachs called them. We know today that Traugott Achatz von Jagow, the Berlin police commissioner, had acted very much on his own initiative when he gave orders to expel Halbwachs. Troubled by the negative reactions at home and the scandal the expulsion of Halbwachs had provoked in Paris, Jagow had to report to Johann von Dallwitz, the Prussian minister of the interior, two weeks later. Von Bethmann-Hollweg himself had inquired whether the expulsion of Halbwachs could be revoked. A kind of "Lex Halbwachs" was created: in the future, the police commissioner would not be allowed to order an expulsion that was based on political grounds.

On the one hand, Jaurès published his editorial at a moment when the possibility of a great European war was already looming. On the other hand, the European nations had not yet lost the chance in 1910 to come to an understanding that would maintain the peace. For Jean Jaurès, Maurice Halbwachs's expulsion was a European incident that pointed to the ruthless politics of the Continent's reactionary forces. In contrast to Jaurès, Halbwachs did not see his expulsion as an incident that could have occurred in almost any European country. For him it was essentially an affair of present-day Germany, an anomaly that pointed to a drastic change in German political attitudes. Thirty years later, Halbwachs remembered his time in Berlin with almost nostalgic feelings. Long after the First and in the midst of the Second World War, he found it hard to imagine that his expulsion had been seen not only in France but also in Germany as a thoughtless and unfriendly act toward a European neighbor. An incident like this had been the exception, not the rule; and Halbwachs added that, to the best of his knowledge, not a single other French citizen had been expelled from Germany for political reasons between 1871 and 1914.

The Murder of Maurice Halbwachs

In 1944 Halbwachs amused himself—these are his own words—by putting old papers in order. Among these papers were documents from his stay in Berlin that he commented upon in a six-and-a-half-page, handwritten note, called "Une expulsion," in which he described the circumstances of his eviction from Berlin in December 1910, including the article by Jean Jaurès.[33] *Tout cela est bien loin derrière moi*, Halbwachs wrote, "All this is way behind me"—but nothing could have been further from the truth. Forcing himself to adopt a cheerful tone, Halbwachs sounds as if he wants to banish a coming catastrophe back into the past. At the same time he sounds as if he were anticipating the terror that lay ahead for him.

On December 19, 1910, Maurice Halbwachs had been summoned to the headquarters of the Berlin police. To get there, he had to cross a giant square, the Alexanderplatz. "I will long remember this impression," he wrote at the time. "Suddenly I noticed a colossal building made of red bricks; in the middle, at the entrance, were two enormous rotundas that resembled helmets. This was the headquarters of the police." To reach the office to which he had been summoned, he had to walk through what seemed like miles of dark corridors and climb countless steps. Finally he entered a hall: it was full of civil servants, all of them standing and hardly distinguishable from one another; they resembled noncommissioned officers, and they stared at Halbwachs through the smoke of their cigars. "I feel their cold, terrible glances, which seem to photograph me and which stick to me like flies." Finally he was let through to an official, who explained to him the reasons for his expulsion. Halbwachs, whom the police had mistaken for a political correspondent, kept his composure. It was not altogether bad that he had to leave Berlin: "I think that, after Berlin, I will like Vienna a lot."

Disbelieving, the Prussian police officer noted that Halbwachs had not listed any religious denomination in his personal papers. "But you just told me you are a high school teacher and a civil servant!" Halbwachs, who was born into a Catholic family but would in all likelihood have called himself an agnostic, explained that information on one's religion was not required in France—and tangible in his words was pride in the Third Republic and its separation of church and state. It was the republic that arose in France as a consequence of its defeat in the Franco-Prussian War and that, since its founding, had been preparing vengeance on Germany—not only on the battlefield but also in the fields of culture and of scholarship. Thirty years later, Halbwachs proudly recalled that he had been able to follow his police interrogation in Berlin in minute detail: *J'étais assez maître de mon allemand*—"I was quite sure in my mastery of German."

In his characteristically neat script, Halbwachs gave his note the character of both a personal document and a social legacy. An experience of bureaucratic fright is captured in these handwritten pages, but Halbwachs's premonitions are nowhere clearer than in his reaction, more as a calligrapher than as a graphologist, to the signature of the Prussian commissioner of police, Traugott Achatz von Jagow. "Should you fail to comply with this directive, you will be confronted with forcible corrective measures." Halbwachs: "This is followed by a heraldic signature: Jagow, in black lines, like the wings of a raven, the *J* a thick, straight, vertical and rising beam, the flourish at the end—*le paraphe final*—thin, but still rising, even higher, like an arrow." *Paraphe* can mean not only flourish but also—according to the dictionary of the time, the 1893 edition of the Sachs-Villate French-German dictionary—a slap to the face. The raven is traditionally regarded as the harbinger of doom and death. Halbwachs must have written his note a few weeks before he was deported to Buchenwald.

Both of Maurice Halbwachs's sons, Francis (b. 1914) and Pierre (b. 1916), had joined the French Resistance. Halbwachs was thus threatened with penal liability. On July 23, 1944, the Gestapo arrested him while he tried to help his Jewish wife escape from their apartment in Paris. In August 1944, Halbwachs was deported to the Buchenwald concentration camp. He died there on March 16, 1945. Pierre, who had been deported to Buchenwald with his father, survived the camp—and later committed suicide, as so many former inmates of the camps did. To the volume *Visages de la Résistance*, published in 1987, Pierre Bourdieu contributed the chapter "L'assassinat de Maurice Halbwachs"—"The Murder of Maurice Halbwachs."[34] But Maurice Halbwachs was not murdered. He underwent even worse: he was compelled to die slowly while his body fell apart. At the end he was ashamed to die the way he did. The writer Jorge Semprun, who had attended Halbwachs's classes at the Sorbonne and who became his fellow inmate at Buchenwald, has described how his former teacher died: "Maurice Halbwachs . . . was obviously past all desire, even the desire to die. He had clearly gone beyond all that, into the pestilential eternity of his decomposing body. I took him in my arms; I drew my face close to his; I was enveloped in the fetid, fecal smell of death, which was growing in him like a carnivorous plant with a poisonous flower, rotting splendidly away."[35]

The exactness of Semprun's description has been challenged.[36] Yet there can be little doubt that Maurice Halbwachs was forced to die under conditions that are reminiscent of the headline he gave to his note describing his expulsion from Berlin in 1910: "Une expulsion." In the Sachs-Villate French-German dictionary, the French word "expulsion" has two meanings. It denotes an eviction and at the same time it represents a medical phenomenon: the voiding of the body by the action of the body itself. When his life came to an end, Maurice Halbwachs was no longer the master of himself and of his body—as if his murderers wanted to take revenge for the proud and ironic sentence with which, thirty-five years earlier, Halbwachs had reacted to his expulsion: "I was quite sure in my mastery of German."

Strange Defeat

While Maurice Halbwachs was looking back on his 1910 expulsion from Berlin, France suffered a swift yet terrible defeat by the German army. As in 1918, the armistice between Germany and France was signed in Compiègne on June 22, 1940. This time the roles of conquerors and conquered were reversed. On Sunday, July 14, 1940, the anniversary of the outbreak of the French Revolution, the *Völkischer Beobachter*, the aggressive mouthpiece of the National Socialist movement, carried on its front page news of German victories and British war cruelties. The editorial was written by Alfred Rosenberg, the leading Nazi ideologist. Its title was "The End of the French Revolution."[37] Rosenberg proclaimed that, after the military defeat of France, the era of the French Revolution was over. French governments had used its legacy to promote anti-German cultural policies at home and cultural propaganda abroad. Germany, on behalf of a Europe that had grown tired of democratic politics, not only had defeated France militarily but had thereby also put an end to French claims to cultural supremacy once and for all. Now, a so-called positive revolution, orchestrated by the Nazi movement, was about to shape Europe's future, in which Germanic culture would play the leading role. Founded after the defeat of France, the "Office Rosenberg" promoted the dominance of Germanic culture by plundering European museums and private art collections and abducting their masterpieces.

In 1870 Flaubert had written to George Sand that the Franco-Prussian War would destroy the legacy of the French Revolution. As it turned out, his prediction was premature. Only seventy years later, the Nazis seemed able to carry out what the Prussians had only attempted to do.[38] Hitler was convinced that the French Jacobins had failed because they trusted human virtue too much; the Nazi regime would be victorious because it took human vice into account. The French fascists, however, to justify their sympathy with the Nazis were obliged to see in the German revolution the survival of their own Jacobin traditions. It was not sufficient to admit that the Roman idea of empire had been restored to vigor in the Third Reich. Therefore they detected forerunners of the *soviets* and *fasci* in the militant groups found in villages all over France in 1792.[39] In his hatred for the "so-called French Revolution," Charles Maurras went as far as to call any *fait révolutionnaire* a *fait boche*: "1789, this is Luther, Kant, Rousseau."[40] This sounded a bit odd, yet even Marc Bloch, who was perhaps the intellectually most courageous, outspokenly self-critical member of the French Resistance, and who was later tortured and shot by the Nazis, reluctantly confessed in his book *Strange Defeat*, written in 1940, that it made sense to establish a link between the National Socialist movement and the French Revolution: "I detest Nazism, but, like the French Revolution, with which one should blush to compare it, it did put at the head, both of its armed forces and of its Government, men who, because their brains were fresh and had not been formed in the routine of the schools, were capable of understanding 'the surprising and the new'. All we had to set against them was a set of bald-pates and youngish dotards."[41] France's "strange defeat" was made even worse by the fact that Germany's triumph was not only a military but also an intellectual victory.

It seemed as if the prophecy of a German writer exiled in Paris, Heinrich Heine, had come true. In 1833, a few years after the July Revolution, he had given the most graphic description of the French-German revolutionary contest and where it might eventually lead: "It seems to me that a methodical people, such as we are, must begin with the reformation, must then occupy itself with systems of philosophy, and that only after their completion could it pass to the political revolution. I find this sequence quite rational. . . . Give yourselves no anxiety however, ye German Republicans; the German revolution will not prove any milder or gentler because it was preceded by the 'Critique' of Kant, by the 'Transcendental idealism' of Fichte, or even by the Philosophy of Nature. These doctrines served to develop revolutionary forces that only await their time to break forth and to fill the world with terror and with admiration. . . . The thought precedes the deed as the lightning the thunder. German thunder is of true German character: it is not very nimble, but rumbles along somewhat slowly. But come it will, and when ye hear a crashing such as never before has been heard in the world's history, then know at last the German thunderbolt has fallen. At this commotion the eagles will drop dead from the skies and the lions in the farthest wastes of Africa will bite their tails and creep into their royal lairs. There will be played in Germany a drama compared to which the French Revolution will seem but an innocent idyl."[42]

Intellectual Resistance

Theodore Parker sounded as if he knew about Heine's prophecy when he spoke, in 1841, of the revolutions that were to be found in Kant's thoughts: "His books are battles."[43] John Dewey quoted Heine's prophetic words in 1915 and again in 1942 when he described what he saw as the dismal affinity between German philosophy and German politics. Alfred Rosenberg might as well have used Heine's words in his sarcastic farewell to the French Revolution—if the Nazi propaganda minister had only been able to be ironic and allow himself to agree with a nineteenth-century Jewish émigré.

In his attempt to come to terms, in 1940, with the "phony war," Marc Bloch realized that the French had first of all lost a culture war. They had become lazy and did not want to learn anymore; they lacked the intellectual techniques that were indispensable for survival in the modern world. He blamed the leaders of France's chemical industry for having preserved the mentality of premodern alchemists. He complained about French municipal libraries that were less well stocked than the field libraries the German army had carried with it in the First World War. He accused the French bourgeoisie of not having read enough and of not having understood the little it had read: "We read, when we do read, with the object of acquiring culture. I have nothing against that. But it never seems to occur to us that culture can, and should, be a great help to us in our daily lives."[44] In contrast to the Germans, the French had forgotten since the First World War how to use culture as a means of intellectual survival and as a preparation for political warfare. This amnesia was partly the sociologists' fault. Bloch shared the anger of Marcel Mauss when he described the wall of ignorance with which the French elites had surrounded themselves. Who, if not the French School of sociology, could be held responsible for the inability of the French elites to analyze the social realities of their own country? It had perhaps been impossible to anticipate the Nazis coming to power. An aggressive German revival, however, had seemed unavoidable to careful observers, John Maynard Keynes first among them, after the Treaty of Versailles.

For Maurice Halbwachs, the collective memory of the French after 1945 would have offered a vast field for research. He could have taken issue as much with a resistance that clouded itself in heroic myth as with a downplaying to insignificance of French collaboration with the Germans. During the First World War, Paul Valéry underscored the importance of what he called a *politique de l'esprit*, a politics of the mind. In the same vein, one could talk of a resistance of the mind. In the French *Résistance des intellectuels*, two elements were of special importance. The first was the willingness of these intellectuals to act in groups and their ability to "get ahead collectively." The second was their conviction that individual political actions had to be seen as the consequence of a belief in universal values.

Getting Ahead Collectively is the title of a book by the economist Albert Hirschman, a German émigré from Berlin who became an American citizen.[45] I am using the title of his book, though written in another context, to describe the rule of conduct of many French intellectuals who joined the Resistance. One cannot but recognize the parallels between the French *Résistance des intellectuels* and Albert Hirschman's clandestine, group-oriented engagement in the *Centre Américain de Secours* of Varian Fry, who, in Marseille in 1940–41, was so courageous in helping refugees from all over Europe escape from Nazi persecution.

Loners by definition, intellectuals in France were always, to an astonishing degree, forming groups and engaging in collective action. For this, their colleagues abroad despised and envied them. German intellectuals watched incredulously when, in 1920, not only was a union of intellectual workers (Confédération des Travailleurs Intellectuels) founded in France but also an additional union, the Compagnons de l'Intelligence, for those intellectuals who were publicly known not to want to unionize, the so-called *esprits réputés ingroupables*.[46] Reading about the circles and networks of the Resistance, one is reminded of Emile Durkheim's wish that the early sociologists should assemble in small groups, *cercles de sciences sociales*, that, ideally with the support of local politicians, would spread the sociological message. Mauss described this strategy when he later revealed the extent to which he had been educated by the collectivism of the Durkheimians: "I cannot divorce myself from the work of a School," he wrote. "If there is any individuality, it is immersed in voluntary anonymity. Perhaps what characterizes my scientific career, today even more than before, is the feeling of working together as a team—, and the conviction that collaborating with others is a drive against isolation and the pretentious search for originality." "Immersed in voluntary anonymity"—a better expression could hardly be found to describe the spiritual core that held together Resistance groups like the Réseau du Musée de l'Homme, the Libération-Sud, or the Réseau Cohors, which was founded by Jean Cavaillès. Halbwachs, with Marc Bloch and Lucien Febvre, belonged to an antifascist group, the Comité de Vigilance des Intellectuels Antifascistes, which had been founded in 1936. Later he joined a resistance group that named itself for the fight at Thermophylae.

The central chapter in Marc Bloch's book *Strange Defeat* is titled "A Frenchman Examines His Conscience." In this chapter Bloch wrote, "We had tongues and brains in our heads and pens in our hands. But we were all of us either specialists in the social sciences or workers in scientific laboratories, and maybe the very disciplines of those employments kept us, by a sort of fatalism, from embarking on individual action."[47] Bloch was as overcritical as Marcel Mauss. His life and death would become a refutation of his own self-critical statement.

The second important element in the resistance of the intellectuals was the close connection between scholarly convictions and political commitment, in which the claim of universalism played a crucial role. Georges Canguilhem, to take one example, was an eminent French scholar who had been a hero of the Resistance. Close to the second-generation Durkheimians, Canguilhem would later become one of the great historians of science in the twentieth century and, precisely because he preferred to remain in the background of academic fights and fashions, perhaps the most important teacher of French intellectuals—their *maître à lire*—after the Second World War. Canguilhem had been a student of the philosopher Alain, and—together with Maurice Halbwachs's sister Jeanne—had thus become an adherent of what Alain and his students called their "militant pacifism." When asked how he could have changed from a militant pacifist to an active Resistance fighter, Canguilhem said only, "When the Germans attacked France, I knew that the time for pacifism was over." Yet he never talked about himself and his admirable role in the Resistance; he only talked about the courage of colleagues and friends. At the same time, Canguilhem made sure to distance himself from those French intellectuals who saw themselves above all as individual heroes. They were, as a rule, associated with existentialism and spoke so much about themselves, as he ironically remarked, because only they were in a position to speak about their resistance, it had been so discreet.

For Canguilhem, his comrades' dedication to the Resistance and their calm and unflinching courage could be understood only on the basis of their fundamental belief in universal values. National Socialism was an ideology of race that contradicted any claim of universalism. Since the Nazi ideology was intellectually unacceptable, political resistance against it was unavoidable. Scholars became political resisters out of intellectual necessity. They were willing to fight for their country and for the life of the mind, as Jean Cavaillès did, a professor of mathematics and logic who got used to carrying hand grenades in his briefcase and knew how to handle dynamite. He acted—as Georges Canguilhem put it—without political ambition, but with a highly developed political consciousness.[48] Political consciousness without political ambition is a description that fits many members of the resistance of the mind. They came from an intellectual milieu in which experimental rationalism and intellectual courage were paired.[49] They were convinced that the political activity of intellectuals need not be dreamlike or utopian: "Before it can become the sister of the dream, action must be the sister of rigor."[50] Normally, Canguilhem said, a philosopher who wrote a textbook on ethics was prepared to die at home and in his bed; but in the years when Cavaillès was in danger of being arrested, tortured, and killed by the Nazis, he wrote a textbook on logic.

Shortly after the Nazis came to power, Marcel Mauss deplored the Durkheim School's inability to come to terms with the inner conflicts of modern civilization and the dangers of totalitarianism. Halbwachs shared this criticism. At the same time, his disenchantment with German sociologists grew. It seemed to him that they turned away from Max Weber and the task of analyzing their country's obvious difficulty in becoming a modern nation; they lost themselves in fruitless debates about lofty notions like *Geist* and *Kultur*. They had not really emancipated themselves from metaphysical speculations, and they displayed an increasingly open contempt for the rationalist and universalistic approach of French sociology. Others nourished the illusion of belonging to a "socially unattached intelligentsia" and pretended to practice pure scholarship uncontaminated by political interests and goals. All this contributed to create a collective consciousness in Germany that helped to foster the most abhorrent kind of nationalism and racism. Halbwachs, however, was a militant of universalism, as Pierre Bourdieu would later call him, and therefore refused "to divide [his] existence into two parts, one part devoted to the strict requirements of science and another that abandon[ed] itself to the political passions."[51]

That this separation, painful though it was, could not be overcome, had been the view of Max Weber, the German sociologist Maurice Halbwachs had introduced to France and the only one he exempted from his criticism when he denounced the inability of his German colleagues to deal with their country's difficult journey into modernity. In two speeches on politics and on science as a vocation, Max Weber maintained both that the scholar cannot give answers which only a prophet or a savior is able to provide and that man must live with the distressing insight that something can be sacred and not beautiful, or beautiful and not good. Weber gave his two speeches in 1917 and 1919. In 1918, Thomas Mann published his *Reflections of a Nonpolitical Man*. Mann sounded like Weber when he reminded his German readers of a simple truth—that intellect and action are, as he put it, "quite different and poorly compatible things."[52] But whereas Weber resigned himself to the insolubility of a timeless problem and faced its tragic consequences, Thomas Mann sought a specifically German solution to a problem that had basically been created, he said, by the French. In his view the French Revolution had been responsible for the illusion that intellect and action are indeed compatible—with disastrous consequences that had led Europe into a series of deadly conflicts culminating in the First World War.

For Thomas Mann, the rallying cry "The intellectual must act!" was a highly literary slogan, a fashionable doctrine, and nothing but sensational food for the newspapers: "The intellectual who becomes convinced he must act is immediately at the point of political *murder*—or, if not this, then the morality of his action is always such that political murder would be the consequence of his way of acting. The slogan, 'The intellectual must act!', as far as it is meant in the sense of pure intellect, is a rather questionable slogan, for all experience definitely teaches that the intellectual who is carried by his passion into reality enters an element that is wrong for him, in which he behaves badly, dilettantishly, and wretchedly, suffers human damage and must immediately cover himself in the melancholy martyrdom of moral self-sacrifice in order to stand up at all before himself and the world."[53]

Intellectuals like Maurice Halbwachs acted from their convictions—not so much to measure up before the world as to keep the world worth living in. Even if it were true, as T. S. Eliot maintained, that good prose cannot be written without convictions—and it probably isn't true—the melancholy insight remains that the convictions that good prose serves can be bad as well as good.[54] Maurice Halbwachs believed in an undivided reason that not only shapes our knowledge but also guides our actions. He fought for French universalism against the murderous particularism of Nazi ideology.

Limits of the German Revolution

In the twenties, French and German politicians, scholars, and intellectuals tried hard to create an enduring entente between their two countries. And yet conspicuous lack of awareness also remained an intellectual option, an attitude on both sides of the Rhine. This was true not least for attempts to create a sociology of the intellectual and of intellectual life, which were abundant in both France and Germany. Two of the most important contributions to the sociology of the intellectual were published during that period, Julien Benda's *The Treason of the Intellectuals* (1927) and Karl Mannheim's *Ideology and Utopia* (1929). Benda and Mannheim had presented the main arguments of their books in earlier publications that were easily available. That they did not take notice of each other—Julien Benda did not mention Mannheim in a new edition of his own book published in 1946—was even more astonishing since a curious intellectual crossover characterized both books. The Hungarian Karl Mannheim's major aim was to professionalize German sociology and to provide it with a secure institutional frame. Yet perhaps no German sociologist was as indebted to the spirit of the French Enlightenment as Mannheim in his essays on the sociology of knowledge or—as he sometimes called it—the sociology of the mind. When Mannheim spoke of intellectuals as "sentinels of an otherwise pitch-black night," he sounded as if he were quoting a paragraph from the entry on the *philosophe* in the French *Encyclopédie*. On the other hand, Julien Benda sounded as if he were quoting Mannheim's description of the "socially unattached intelligentsia" when he called it "one of the gravest responsibilities of the modern State . . . that it has not maintained (but could it do so?) a class of men exempt from civic duties, men whose sole function is to maintain non-practical values."[55]

In truth, however, Benda's book had to be read as a pamphlet directed against the sociology of knowledge and against the "German connection" that had influenced the French mind to such a large degree since the times of romanticism.[56] For Benda, the social context did not matter at all in the realm of ideas. Whereas Mannheim's intellectual was bound to use his social detachment to influence what was going on in the city and to teach politics to the citizen, Benda's intellectual, a hero of the universal, could not have been more different from the modern sociologist. For Benda, the intellectual is a solitary figure who, even as a hermit, remains a rationalist. He is a Cartesian who refuses to join the Enlightenment project. Attacks against Germany and the German mind play a central role in Benda's pamphlet. In the Prussian wars of liberation against Napoleonic France, poets and thinkers developed the intellectual patriotism and the "philosophy of national morality" that eventually led to the treason of the intellectuals and their giving up on universalism. It was even more deplorable, therefore, that with the philosophy of Henri Bergson, whom Benda fought throughout his life, German irrationalism was invading the French educational system. Germany had lost the First World War, but was about to conquer the French spirit. Benda anticipated the complaints of Leo Strauss and Allan Bloom after the Second World War when he declared that the intellectuals were denouncing adherence to universal ideas and praising attachment to the particular: "In the world of spiritual things the victory of Germany is now complete."[57]

For Mannheim, giving the irrational its due would have been the end of sociological thinking, its unconditional surrender. One had to argue on the assumption of a prevailing rationality in men's words and deeds as long as possible. Benda, "the eternal rationalist, a clever and naïve descendant of the nineteenth century,"[58] looked at rationalism in two different ways—depending on whether he was engaged in domestic or in foreign intellectual policy. In the context of French culture, rationalism for him was a pre-Enlightenment, Cartesian affair. It was the attitude of the individual, disinterested thinker who did not want to become engaged in the mundane problems of the city and only cared for the universal and the eternal. In this context, Benda preferred, deviating from an established French tradition, the aloofness of the scholar, the *universitaire*, over the worldly interests of the *homme de lettres*, the man of letters. In foreign cultural policy, however, rationalism for him changed into a national trait of which the Latin countries could be proud. For Benda, any attempt to reconcile German romanticism with the skeptical project of Latin rationalism was doomed to fail.[59] Like Leo Strauss and Bloom after him, Benda attacked German irrationalism with the rational weapons the Greek and Roman civilizations had developed. Europe—that was France, Italy, and Greece. Benda's love of Latin cultures led him, who allegedly hated all kinds of nationalism, to demand that in the future French would have to become, once again, the language of a united Europe. His *Discours à la nation européenne*, in which he made this request, was published in 1933, the year when the Nazis came to power in Germany. At this date, Benda felt compelled to remind his European readers that since the early nineteenth century, German authors had tried to lead the irrational to triumph over the rational and to stress the dark and strange elements of the human soul. Opting for a renewed hegemony of the French language and of France, the "reasoning nation" (*la nation qui raisonne*) was an attempt to preserve the survival of the rational mind.

Whoever tried to promote German intellectual traditions in France after 1933 ran the danger of being regarded as unpatriotic by his fellow countrymen. It required courage and intellectual stubbornness not to follow the mainstream of French reasoning and at the same time to avoid the danger of becoming a mental *collaborateur*. This delicate balance was achieved by Raymond Aron, who defended his thesis on the German tradition in the philosophy of history at the Sorbonne in 1938—two weeks after Hitler's troops had forced Austria to join the Third Reich. Aron knew Germany well. He had been assistant to the Austrian-born literary theorist Leo Spitzer in Cologne, where he read Marx's *Capital* for the first time. In Berlin he had given French lessons to the famous theater director Max Reinhardt, he had witnessed Hitler's coming to power and watched incredulously, together with Thomas Mann's son Golo, the Nazis' book-burning on the square before the Berlin opera on May 10, 1933—a deliberate reference to the year 1817, when the fraternities assembled at the Wartburg castle had burned books that threatened the cultural fabric of the German people. As early as 1935, Aron published a book on the history of German sociology.

The shrewdness and open sympathy with which Aron defended German traditions of thought in 1938 impressed the members of his doctoral committee. They were puzzled, though, by the style of his reasoning, which did not follow the established French model at all. They felt repelled by Aron's muddled style of writing that might perhaps have made sense for a German reader but sounded like an offense to the French language and its nature-given clarity. Aron seemed to prefer a German concept like *Verstehen* to the French *explication*; his pessimistic outlook befitted a milieu in which Mephistopheles played a leading role in the national drama—but not the nation of Voltaire and Condorcet. Aron, though, was too intelligent to fail an exam: he passed with honors. Bidding him farewell, the members of his committee expressed their wish that the young French intellectuals would not follow his example. Some committee members were old Durkheimians, including Maurice Halbwachs.

Aron must have thought of his exam when he gave his inaugural lecture at the Collège de France in 1970. He had set as his main task to explain why, throughout his whole intellectual life, he had preferred Max Weber to Emile Durkheim. His own political experience in Nazi Germany had been primarily responsible for this intellectual preference. Whoever tried to understand the mechanism of a totalitarian state, Aron argued, could not learn much from Emile Durkheim, but had to follow the insights of Max Weber—the "Machiavelli from Heidelberg." That Max Weber did become a classic of German sociology again was due in great part to two foreign social scientists, the American Talcott Parsons and the Frenchman Raymond Aron.

When Aron published his *Memoirs* in 1983, he described how much German culture had enchanted him in his youth. For a whole year he did nothing but read Kant and become acquainted with the richness of German philosophical thought. In France, only literature could command a similar attention from him. In the end, no niche was left for Durkheim's sociology between German philosophy and French literature, between Kant and Proust. Compared with Kant's intelligible character and Proust's Albertine, neither Durkheim's *Division of Labor* nor his *Suicide* touched a nerve in Aron. Formed by German culture, he became able to understand modern societies much more fully than if he had been a disciple of Durkheim. Whereas many Germans saw culture as a refuge from politics, culture opened the vast and difficult field of politics for Aron, who would later become *le premier sociologue de France*, France's first and foremost sociologist.

On November 4, 1989, a huge demonstration in East Berlin organized by artists and writers anticipated the fall of the communist regime. German intellectuals suddenly felt they were *philosophes* who had worked all their lives for the revolution. The French Enlightenment thinkers' dream of a *politique de l'esprit* seemed in the offing in a renewed socialist Germany. When the masses in East Germany took to the streets that autumn and finally made the Berlin Wall collapse, they evoked the image of the Bastille, whose storming had started the French Revolution. French observers tried, in vain, to remind the jubilant Germans that the French Revolution had had no territorial limits. Robespierre was convinced that the Revolution was nothing less than an anthropological mutation and that the French, a new species, were forging ahead on a path all of mankind would take. The French Revolution had not been a French episode or a European affair. It had been a universal event.

Nineteen eighty-nine was not only the year when the Berlin Wall finally came down. It was the year of European revolutions that marked the end of communism. Intellectuals from Central and Eastern Europe sparked a debate over whether the events of 1989 did not designate the end of an era that had begun with the French Revolution of 1789 and that had found its culmination in the Russian Revolution of 1917. François Mitterrand had wanted to rejuvenate the remembrance of the French Revolution with huge ceremonies in 1989—yet the events at the end of this year would show that he had only organized its funeral. German exceptionalism took a new turn. The nonviolent character of the German revolution was used as a cultural and political asset. German politicians and intellectuals could not hide the triumphant feeling that the belated nation had not only finally caught up with France's revolutionary head start, but had surpassed it. After two hundred years, differently than Heine foresaw and much differently than Hitler wanted, a revolution without *terreur*, and therefore morally far superior to the French Revolution, had succeeded in East Germany.

The triumph did not last long. After having realized the failure of the denazification program, Hannah Arendt had written in 1950: "The only conceivable alternative to the denazification program would have been a revolution—the outbreak of the German people's spontaneous wrath against all those they knew to be prominent members of the Nazi regime. Uncontrolled and bloody as such an uprising might have been, it certainly would have followed better standards of justice than a paper procedure."[60] Given the enormous legal difficulties the German courts had after 1989 in sentencing those who were responsible for the crimes of the East German dictatorship, one is reminded of Weber's remark that the tragedy of German history was that, unlike the Stuarts or the Bourbons, a Hohenzollern had never lost his head. It was difficult for a German citizen, however, to entertain the somewhat cynical view that a bit of *terreur* would not have been a bad thing after all for the German revolution of 1989.

A foreigner could be blunt. When the two German states were reunited, the playwright Arthur Miller, who had close connections to German culture and German politics, asked, "Does the Federal Republic of Germany arouse lofty democratic feelings in its citizens' minds, or is it a system that is simply a matter of historical convenience invented by foreigners?" To ask this question was to negate it: Arthur Miller came to the conclusion that the Republic did not imbue the Germans with "sublime sensations." There was something insubstantial and artificial in the idea of democracy for them. As a German friend said to Miller, one could not trust the Germans' civic instinct when they were confronted with the task of building a free society. At the moment of reunification, Miller doubted the stability of German democracy because the Federal Republic was born "without a drop of blood being shed in its birth. . . . What Germans lack now is the consecration by blood of their democratic state."[61] In the eyes of an American observer, Germany was still lacking a "real" revolution like the French Revolution of 1789.

German Culture at Home: A Moral Failure Turned to Intellectual Advantage

The German Catastrophe

In 1949 Leo Strauss complained that German thinking had become indistinguishable from Western thought in general. In retrospect, one must see this complaint of a German émigré as the prophecy of one of the great political success stories of the twentieth century. After the end of the Third Reich, first the Federal Republic and then a reunited Germany became part of the West. Germany's special path eventually flowed into the mainstream of parliamentary democracy, the market, and the rule of law. Playing off culture against civilization no longer made sense. It also no longer made much sense to think of culture as a substitute for politics. Immediately after the war, however, things had looked different.

On August 17, 1946, Hannah Arendt apologized to her teacher, the philosopher Karl Jaspers, for not responding to his last letter for over a month. She could not yet write back because she had immersed herself in reading his book *Die Schuldfrage* (The question of German guilt), which had been published in the same year. She was troubled by the book, because Jaspers was speaking of Nazi crimes as if they could be dealt with in court: "Your definition of Nazi policy as a crime ('criminal guilt') strikes me as questionable. The Nazi crimes, it seems to me, explode the limits of the law; and that is precisely what constitutes their monstrousness. For these crimes, no punishment is severe enough. It may well be essential to hang Göring, but it is totally inadequate. That is, this guilt, in contrast to all criminal guilt, oversteps and shatters any and all legal systems. That is the reason why the Nazis in Nuremberg are so smug."[1] When Hannah Arendt wrote her letter, verdicts in the Nuremberg trials had not yet been reached. Göring committed suicide by poisoning himself on October 15, 1946, two hours before his scheduled hanging.

Hannah Arendt's objections to Jaspers's book were raised in a firm but friendly way. Heinrich Blücher, her husband, had been much more appalled by it. Rather than brood about their metaphysical guilt, the Germans should be ashamed of what they had done and try to act accordingly, he wrote to his wife. It was preposterous to invite the world, once again, to ponder the specifics of the German national character. The task of the time was not to find out what was typically "German" in the Nazi crimes, but what was right and what was wrong in the behavior of the German people. Karl Jaspers was a scholar without the slightest talent for political insight, Blücher fumed. The philosopher's lofty ethical speculations were of no practical value or political consequence whatsoever.[2] Given this harsh rejection of Jaspers's book, it must have come as a surprise to Hannah Arendt and Heinrich Blücher that his reply was not lofty at all. It was rather pragmatic and a sensible refutation of what Jaspers regarded as Arendt's poetic view of the Nazi crimes.

Jaspers too did not react immediately to his former student's letter, which was written in August. He waited for two months, until October 19. Then, after thanking Hannah Arendt for regularly sending food packages that allowed him and his wife to live in almost grand style, as if the war had never happened, he rejected Arendt's critique. In return, he now took issue with her own view of how the Nazis should be treated: "You say that what the Nazis did cannot be comprehended as 'crime'—I'm not altogether comfortable with your view, because a guilt that goes beyond all criminal guilt inevitably takes on a streak of 'greatness'—of satanic greatness—which is, for me, as inappropriate for the Nazis as all the talk about the 'demonic' element in Hitler and so forth. It seems to me that we have to see these things in their total banality, in their prosaic triviality, because that's what truly characterizes them." Years later, Hannah Arendt would use the phrase "banality of evil" as the subtitle of her book *Eichmann in Jerusalem*. Jaspers liked the title and called it brilliant. He had been told that Heinrich Blücher blamed himself for suggesting the phrase and thereby causing so much trouble for his wife. I find it hard to believe, though, that Jaspers's early letter from 1946 was not the point of departure for Arendt from which her own thinking developed toward the idea of the banality of evil.[3]

In his letter, Jaspers goes on to defend his view of how the Nazi leaders should be judged. He reproaches Arendt for trying to substitute drama for criminal justice: "I regard any hint of myth and legend with horror, and everything unspecific is just such a hint. My more sober outlook is hardly widespread in Germany. Many people make a great thing of it that Göring managed to escape the gallows, when nothing but the sheer incompetence of the prison staff was responsible. Your view is appealing . . . [but by] the way you do express it, you've almost taken the path of poetry. And a Shakespeare would never be able to give adequate form to this material—his instinctive aesthetic sense would lead to falsification of it—and that's why he couldn't attempt it."[4] The Nazi crimes had to be dealt with by disciplines like psychology, psychopathology, sociology, and above all jurisprudence. The path of poetry did not, in Jaspers's view, lead to an understanding of why the German people had followed Adolf Hitler. One had to refrain from thinking in aesthetic terms altogether when dealing with the Nazis. There was nothing grand buried deep within their cheapness and vulgarity.

Hannah Arendt took her teacher's advice seriously. Nevertheless, she must have been pleased when her friend Mary McCarthy, in a theater review written in June 1962, spoke of the "return of the irrational in the Fascist nightmare" that brought one to see the most modern of all Shakespeare's characters in bloodstained Macbeth. McCarthy called Macbeth a murderous Babbitt, a "commonplace man who talks in commonplaces, a golfer, one might guess, on the Scottish fairways." To compare a politician to a Shakespearean character did not necessarily turn him into a heroic figure, McCarthy seemed to say. It was almost the opposite: Shakespeare's greatness consists in his ability to show us the commonplace, the trivial, in human evil.[5] *Eichmann in Jerusalem* triggered a fierce debate, notably among New York intellectuals, that must have reminded Hannah Arendt of Jaspers's early warnings. Whereas Norman Podhoretz wrote that Arendt "with . . . surprising boldness, rids her story of melodrama altogether and heavily underlines every trace of moral ambiguity she can wring out of it,"[6] Lionel

Abel, in an article in *Partisan Review* entitled "The Aesthetics of Evil: Hannah Arendt on Eichmann and the Jews," charged that in writing *Eichmann in Jerusalem*, Arendt had made Eichmann aesthetically palatable and the Jews aesthetically repulsive. He also called Shakespeare to witness that a man can be a clown and a monster at the same time, whereas Hannah Arendt allegedly had claimed that Eichmann should not be regarded as a monster because he was nothing but a clown, and mediocre.[7]

In 1946, the year in which Jaspers's *Question of German Guilt* appeared, Friedrich Meinecke, the eighty-four-year-old, half-blind doyen of German historians, published a volume of reflections and recollections with the title *Die deutsche Katastrophe* (The German catastrophe). Meinecke had been, if somewhat reluctantly, a defender of the Weimar Republic. During the Third Reich, he had basically been a bystander. He was no racist and no longer an anti-Semite;[8] in his professional actions he remained untainted by the Nazi ideology and he courageously tried to help Jewish colleagues. Yet he admitted feelings of pride and happiness over the success of the German armies in Poland and in France. It is doubtful whether Meinecke would have written a book with the title *The German Catastrophe* had the Nazis won the Second World War. After the war had been lost, Meinecke declared Nazism to be a phenomenon that had been imposed upon the Germans from the outside. *The German Catastrophe* was a book that had a tragic element in it; it was a catastrophe itself.

The lesson that Max Weber tried to teach German intellectuals after the First World War had been completely forgotten. In contrast to received wisdom, Weber had argued that the political problems of the present could not be solved by looking back to intellectual achievements of the past. No eternal German spirit existed from which recipes for successful political actions could be distilled. To read the Weimar classics was useful because, after Versailles, they reminded the Germans of the fact that a country could be a cultural leader in times of political defeat and foreign domination. Beyond this, however, they should be read only for pleasure and for the formal training of the mind—not for political advice. The political and economic ideas of the German classics were molded by their descent from a deeply apolitical epoch: "The modern problems of parliamentary government and democracy, and the essential nature of our modern state in general, are entirely beyond the horizon of the German classics." Max Weber admiringly quoted Alexander Herzen, who proclaimed that his native Russia should be the land not of its fathers, but of its children. Weber wished that the same could one day be said of the German fatherland.[9]

Nothing could be further from the core of Meinecke's book than Max Weber's warning not to look back to the classics for political advice. *The German Catastrophe* must have been widely read; it went through four printings in the first three years after its publication. Had the German mind survived the disaster the Nazis inflicted upon Germany? There were, Meinecke gladly observed, signs of life: "One hears of culture leagues and culture communities in the cities. One hears of theatrical productions in which the treasures of German drama are again rising into the light. Young men and old crowd to concerts in which the great old German music is played."[10] What was needed now, Meinecke wrote, was an intensified development of the Germans' inner existence. More than ever before, they had to rely on religion, culture, and learning to regain credit in the world. Meinecke imagined a specific organization where the spiritual rebirth of the nation would be undertaken. What he longed to see in the future, in addition to the formation of small religious groups, were communities of like-minded friends of high culture that he called "Goethe communities." To these communities "would fall the task of conveying into the heart of the listeners through sound the most vital evidences of the great German spirit, always offering the noblest music and poetry together." The "regular music and poetry festal hours" would have much in common with a religious service. Meinecke wanted to schedule these hours for a weekly late Sunday afternoon, if at all possible in a church. On these occasions the Germans would "detect something indestructible—a German *character indelebilis*—in the midst of all the destruction and misfortune of our Fatherland."[11]

One was reminded of the Fichte Society that had been created in 1914 and had found two years later, in the midst of the First World War, nothing more important to do than to engage in the reorganization of the German theater. The therapy Meinecke prescribed to the Germans in 1946 was the same he had administered to himself in 1918. At the outbreak of the First World War, he declared that the time had come to bridge the distance between culture and politics and that culture must be a weapon in the hand of the state. When Germany was defeated, Meinecke brooded over the impossibility of reconciling power and culture; he found consolation in reading Goethe's poems.

Meinecke's suggestion to found Goethe communities all over Germany has been widely cited. Yet the specific historical context into which Meinecke himself put his idea has not often been mentioned. This context is important, because Meinecke had insisted, even before 1933, that some of the ideas the Nazis propagated were not their intellectual property but belonged to the heritage of a better German past. In 1948, Meinecke was speaking about favorable experiences from which the Germans could profit in the attempt to reconstruct their culture after the country had been defeated militarily: "Some . . . come even from the Third Reich. The sly Goebbels knew very precisely, for example, how one could snare harmless souls by putting a couple of good articles worth their price in the show window of the Nazi party. Every Sunday morning at church time when he wanted to keep people from attending service he offered them on the radio a little 'Treasure Chest' that gave the most beautiful German music and choice poetical pieces to those who listened in."[12] An important strategy of Nazi propaganda had been the deliberate production or performance of "apolitical" works of art, in which movies played a crucial role. This led Leni Riefenstahl, for instance, to later pretend that she had distanced herself from the Nazi regime because the movie she produced during the war, *Tiefland*, was a romantic film, "the opposite of politics and war."[13]

Meinecke's recollections make it obvious why he did not want the repair of German cultural life to become a part of the Allied denazification process. Cultural repair was the Germans' business alone. It could not be done by foreigners and it could not be attempted in the sphere of politics. The harmless soul of the historian fell prey to the "sly Goebbels" when he declared that "spiritual life and the striving for spiritual values are their own justification and work most deeply where their movements can be most free from political tendencies." Meinecke wanted the Nazi megalomania, with its uncultured spirit, to disappear after 1945. Yet when he warned that it should not be replaced by "pale, empty, abstract cosmopolitanism," he sounded as if he were alluding to Goebbels' militant utopia of a German cultural state that fought any

Western influence.[14] It is thus difficult to understand how H. Stuart Hughes could interpret *The German Catastrophe* as proof that Meinecke had "gone back to the late eighteenth century, when Germany had not yet diverged from the Western European norm . . . he had gone back to the last and greatest products of the Enlightenment."[15]

In 1935 the Nazis had forced Meinecke to resign as editor of the most important history journal in Germany, the *Historische Zeitschrift*. After 1945 Meinecke belonged, with Gerhard Ritter and Hans Roth-fels, to the group of distinguished German historians who were in desperate search of a spiritual remedy for the defeated nation. When the war was over, they tried to tell a countertale in which the good Germany had prevailed and Goethe had triumphed over Bismarck.[16] Meinecke wanted above all to keep the remembrance of the other, good Germany alive. In *The German Catastrophe*, he took great pains to point to the sacral elements of German culture. He thereby contributed to the survival of the aesthetic legacy of the Nazi regime that had attracted the German masses and many members of the cultural elite, not least through its sacral rituals. In the end, Meinecke's book became a symbol of the German catastrophe it claimed to analyze.

The Resurrection of Culture

After 1945, émigrés who returned to Germany witnessed a miracle. Apparently high culture had survived the war and the atrocities of the Nazi regime unharmed. What Theodor Adorno had expected was dullness, apathy, and cynical mistrust. Yet all things spiritual now seemed to evoke an even greater interest in young Germans than in the years before the Nazis came to power. Adorno felt as if a time machine had propelled him back into the days of early romanticism, when a book like Fichte's *Theory of Knowledge* exerted more influence on public opinion than a political action did. Only then, he wrote in his essay "The Resurrection of Culture" (1949), had the Germans immersed themselves in problems of the mind to the same degree as in the present. The country resembled Prussia at the dawn of the wars of liberation, fought against Napoleonic France, when the Germans thought, prematurely as it turned out, that they had found their national identity. The renewed enthusiasm for culture overwhelmed Adorno not least because in America he had been "liberated from a certain naïve belief in culture and [had] attained the capacity to see culture from the outside."[17]

On December 28, 1949, Adorno wrote a long letter to Thomas Mann. Enthusiastically, he told him about a seminar he was giving in Frankfurt. He was overwhelmed by the passion and the seriousness of his students. Hard though it is to believe, the philosopher had great difficulties making himself heard in his own class. The reader gets the impression that the "kids," as he calls his students, skip their break because there is a point in Kant's transcendental dialectics they have not yet quite understood, or that they insist the seminar must continue into the vacation period. How could they relax without having finished Hegel's *Phenomenology of the Spirit*?[18] Three years before, Jaspers had told Hannah Arendt about a similar experience in his philosophy class: "We recently heard a superb report on the 'idea' in Plato and Hegel, totally abstract, followed by a discussion that was as alive and intense as if we were dealing with the most current of problems."[19] At first sight, Adorno and Jaspers write as if in sympathy with the cultural utopia Friedrich Meinecke had dreamed of in *The German Catastrophe*. Yet both Adorno and Jaspers draw conclusions from their experience of a resurrected German culture that could not be more different from those of Meinecke.

Without sacrificing the rigor of reasoning, Karl Jaspers regarded himself as a political philosopher with a moral obligation to address the political issues of the time. In the winter of 1946–47, he gave a lecture course on "The German Present and Philosophy"—a title that pointed to his future engagement both as a professional philosopher and as a concerned citizen. Jaspers was therefore disappointed with his students' lack of interest in politics. In his letter to Arendt in September 1946, Jaspers continued: "These few excellent young people have no interest at all in politics, only scorn and mistrust," whereupon Arendt was reminded of her own youthful attitude—the traditional aloofness from politics that had been so characteristic for large segments of the German cultural elite. In her response to Jaspers, Arendt told him how much she was troubled by his seminar: "What frightens me about your gratifying seminar students is that they, like us in our time—of unblessed memory—are not interested in politics."[20] Three years later, Arendt wrote that nothing had changed: "Sometimes I wonder which is more difficult: to instill an awareness of politics in the Germans or to convey to Americans even the slightest inkling of what philosophy is all about."[21] These words came from an author whom another émigré called a gifted philosopher with no talent for politics.[22]

In her "Report from Germany," published in 1950, Hannah Arendt ventured into the field of political prophecy. What she saw in Germany was an escape from reality that was also an escape from responsibility. The Germans treated facts as though they were mere opinions and believed "this nihilistic relativity about facts to be the essence of democracy." One could not but admire the fanatic devotion of young Germans to their studies, but their future was uncertain. German universities, Arendt was convinced, would produce "a whole class of frustrated and starving intellectuals." Their country did not need them, because it had no political future. "Neither a regenerated nor an unregenerated Germany" would play a role in a unified Europe: "And this knowledge of the ultimate futility of any political initiative on their part in the present struggle is not the least potent factor in the Germans' reluctance to face the reality of their destroyed country."[23]

After the Second World War, all visitors to Germany observed a cultural enthusiasm that went hand in hand with an almost visceral abstinence from politics. This avoidance was understandable enough, given the previous experience with life under a totalitarian regime, the uncertainty about how to behave under occupation, and the necessity to move forward into the hitherto unknown territory of democracy. For Adorno, both cultural enthusiasm and political abstention were the result of collective self-deception. The Germans had not yet realized that culture, in the traditional sense of the word, had perished. Illusions of a quick political recovery ran even deeper. Abstaining from politics was seen by some as only a temporary act; the first priority was to get back to a normal private life. A climate of provincialism prevailed among the German population, in which it felt quite at ease. "Wait and see" was the motto. But it was no longer up to the Germans to decide whether and how to act politically.

In his letters to Thomas Mann, Adorno continues comparing the apolitical atmosphere he encounters in postwar Germany to the situation in which Prussia found itself at the dawn of the wars of liberation.

In the universities, the postwar German youth talked again about logical and metaphysical problems as if they were talking about politics. The young Germans had no other choice, Adorno wrote in an almost triumphant tone, because politics in the traditional sense did not exist anymore in their fatherland. Germany was no longer a political subject. In the future, the country would not be able to exert any influence whatsoever on world politics. Consequently the Germans would have to resign themselves to survive in the shadow of the great powers. They would become poor in deeds and full of thoughts again, as their forefathers had been around 1800. Now, however, no great war of liberation was looming on the horizon. It had already been fought—not by the Germans but against them. Karl Jaspers went even further when he spoke about Germany's future between the United States and the Soviet Union, "a battleground for both of them, a garbage heap where all those people are tossed whom nobody wants anywhere else."[24]

What Friedrich Meinecke regarded as promise, Jaspers saw as an irritation and Adorno as an illusion. The three observers could not have differed more in their judgment of what was happening in German culture and politics after the war. In his Californian exile, Adorno had been flattered when Thomas Mann asked for his help while writing the musical passages of *Doctor Faustus*. After his return to Germany, Adorno tried to please the much-admired Mann by taking his distance from Jaspers. In Adorno's view, Mann, an American citizen by now, was a public moralist—the only one who had been able to confront the Germans with their guilt and their shame in an adequate way. When the Protestant pastor Martin Niemöller—whom the Nazis had interned in a concentration camp—and Karl Jaspers talked about the question of German guilt, their writings only displayed, in Adorno's verdict, a mixture of helplessness and vanity.[25]

This was an unfair remark of which the sociologist Adorno could not be proud. His allegation did not take into account the different social and historical contexts in which Mann, Niemöller, and Jaspers had written about German crimes and German guilt. Adorno's remark was not only unfair; it was also superfluous and repulsive. Against its author's intentions, it played into the hands of the German conservatives and supported the restorative tendencies in Adenauer's Republic. The spirit in which it was pronounced prevented the early formation of a "moral coalition" (*Gesinnungsgemeinschaft*) that could have acted much more forcefully against those tendencies.[26] Unwilling to strive for a compromise, Adorno argued like an apolitical man in a situation in which Germany needed nothing more than the will to a democratic politics.

At the same time, Adorno's criticism of Niemöller and Jaspers revealed a rift among German intellectuals that, for a long time to come, would shape the cultural and political debates in Germany. Adorno had spoken with the authoritative voice of the émigré. The émigré's authority to give his verdict on German culture, however, would soon be challenged. In 1950, the critic Max Rychner, a close friend of Carl Jacob Burckhardt, took issue with Adorno's essay on the resurrection of German culture in an article for the Swiss magazine *Die Tat*. It was not without malice that he introduced Adorno to the Swiss reader as the author who had achieved a certain degree of notoriety mainly through his contribution to the musical passages in Thomas Mann's novel *Doctor Faustus*.

Inner Emigration and Its Discontents

When the Nazis came to power, the émigrés coined the phrase that would remain their token of consolation: "The German mind has emigrated." The phrase, Rychner said, sounded right abroad and could also be easily memorized—but it was wrong. Adorno believed in the phrase—and thus fell prey to emigration propaganda. When he returned to Germany and found, contrary to his expectations, that culture was alive and well, his astonishment only revealed how little he had known about what was really going on in Nazi Germany. Still, in Rychner's opinion Adorno had to be praised for the sincerity with which he admitted his wrong expectations and later corrected his views. When Germany left the League of Nations in October 1933, Max Rychner had written a moving article in which he mourned Germany's solitude. After 1945, he insisted that Germany, isolated under Nazi rule, had remained a breeding ground for works of art that could not be used by the Nazis for purposes of cultural propaganda. The only observers who could now speak of a solitary and sterile Germany were those who did not know what had happened inside the country during the twelve years of the Nazi regime. Views from within were badly needed to do justice to the recent cultural developments in Germany and thereby make a realistic prediction about the country's political future.[27]

Rychner's 1950 criticism of Adorno was a reminiscence of the "great controversy" that had erupted immediately after the Second World War.[28] Walter von Molo, head of the literary section in the Prussian Academy of Arts (1928–1930), had written an emotional letter to Thomas Mann in which he begged him to return to Germany and help restore his destroyed home country. Mann did not answer immediately. While the German public was waiting for Mann's reply, the novelist Frank Thiess mounted a vicious attack against him. Thiess, a mediocre author, must later have been especially annoyed by Thomas Mann's *Doctor Faustus*, his novel about recent German history. In 1946 Thiess published an article with the title "Return to Goethe," arguing that Goethe's spirit alone had prevented the total self-destruction of the German nation. Not only émigrés but also the "internal exiles" could claim his legacy. They even enjoyed a moral superiority over the émigrés who had left their homeland: never and nowhere had Goethe been read more intensely than in Germany in the twelve years under Nazi dictatorship.

In a self-congratulatory article entitled "The Inner Emigration", published in August 1945 in the Münchner Zeitung, Thiess claimed—unjustifiably as it turned out—to have coined the term in 1933. He attacked Thomas Mann for his charge that only the émigrés had lived and written in distance to the Nazi regime and had suffered from it. Whoever had remained in Germany had by his sheer presence contributed to legitimate the Nazi regime, Mann said. Books written during the Third Reich were stained with blood and shame. Thiess not only countered that a large number of German artists and writers had lived miserably under the Nazi regime. He pretended that, by hiding in an intellectual cave during the Third Reich, the "internal exiles" had contributed, more than the émigrés, to the survival of the German spirit. They had prevented the worst possible catastrophe—the demise of German culture. Deliberately refraining from any political commitment had been an act of great courage and resistance. Meanwhile, émigrés like Thomas Mann had lived a comfortable life and had given cheap advice to those who did not need it. Mann and his coterie could not know what had really happened in Germany in the past twelve years. Not only Thomas Mann but all émigrés should return, correct their views, and help rebuild the country.

It was a strange coincidence that German writers, complaining how much they had suffered in internal exile, attacked Thomas Mann for his alienation from Germany at exactly the moment when Mann thought, certainly not of resuming his German citizenship, but of becoming a "German" writer again. He had paid for his adherence to republican ideals, democratic values, and a cosmopolitan worldview with the loss of his nationality. The American citizen felt entitled to come to the defense of German inwardness again, to distance himself from Western values, and to criticize, if necessary, the policy of the Western allies.

Goethe had once suggested that the Germans should not be allowed to use the word *Gemüt* (soul) for thirty years.[29] In 1941 Thomas Mann added *Tiefe* (depth) to the index of prohibited words. What the Germans needed instead, he wrote, was *Anständigkeit* (decency). Only "decent" German poets and writers would have the right again to defend German inwardness and "depth" against Western rationalism: "That is what I have done earlier, and I must say how impatient I feel to do it again."[30] In the speech he gave at the Library of Congress on May 29, 1945, with the title "Germany and the Germans," it became obvious how eager Thomas Mann was to reintroduce the word "depth" into the German language. Talking about Faust, who was filled with arrogance because he surpassed the world in "depth," Mann gave an answer full of sympathy to the question of what constituted this attitude that was so alien to non-Germans: depth was "simply the musicality of the German soul, that which we call its inwardness, its subjectivity, the divorce of the speculative from the socio-political element of human energy, and the complete predominance of the former over the latter."[31] Could an echo of the *Reflections of a Nonpolitical Man* be heard in these words? *Doctor Faustus*, a novel about a German composer, was written by a German writer who thought, once again, of his Germanness.

Thomas Mann was therefore even more furious when the "internal exiles" attacked him. Thiess and others sounded as if the Third Reich had been another Augustan age for the arts. In an open letter with the title "Why I will not return," Mann reiterated what he had said before, notably in *Listen, Germany!*, his "messages to the German people" that had been aired by the German Service of the BBC. He responded less as an émigré than as an American citizen. When he addressed Walter von Molo directly, he did not preclude the possibility that he might return to Germany—but only as a visitor, he almost forced himself to say, not as a German-born writer who was coming home.

Mann was also accused of a lack of forgiveness: in 1944 he had refused to become chairman of the Council for German Democracy that had been founded in the same year that the communist National Committee for a Free Germany was created in Moscow. Intellectuals like Paul Tillich, Reinhold Niebuhr, Heinrich Mann, Bertolt Brecht, Ernst Bloch, Max Reinhardt, and others drafted a declaration in which they tried to convince President Roosevelt that Germany must be defeated, but that it must receive a just peace, rather than being destroyed or dismembered, and that as soon as possible it should find an adequate place in the European system of states again. Thomas Mann did not sign this declaration—nor did Theodor Adorno or Max Horkheimer. Thomas Mann resented what he called the émigré patriotism of German left-wing intellectuals.

Bitterness among émigrés and internal exiles ensued. In Germany, one reason for such enmity was the similarity of the opponents' attitudes—substantial differences of their political positions notwithstanding. Neither Thomas Mann nor his attackers attempted a political explanation for why and how the Nazis could have come to power in the first place. Both sides mystified culture. The "internal exiles" reiterated their belief in the sanctity of the cultural realm that had prevented them from becoming tainted with the crimes of the Nazi regime. Thomas Mann saw the reason for Germany's political aberrations in the field of culture as well: inwardness, originating with and fortified through the Protestant tradition, and irrationalism, justified and even indispensable in the arts, had determined the course of German politics.

In Princeton, Thomas Mann had interrupted his work on the Joseph novels to write *The Beloved Returns* (*Lotte in Weimar*)—a tribute to German culture if there ever was one. The Weimar novel was deliberately written as a cultural, and not a political, rejoinder to the recent developments in Germany. *Doctor Faustus* was planned as the political rejoinder in the form of a novel. In a letter to Tillich written in 1944, Mann said that his new novel was "the most consciously, emphatically and deliberately Germanic" he had ever undertaken, "a mixture of theology, music and genius = pathology, that continuously suggested the term 'German' with the words 'tragic' and 'demonic.'" Adrian Lever-kühn, the novel's hero, was born in Thuringia, the German province Luther had come from. Mann described Leverkühn's life as a symbol of German history in the first half of the twentieth century, during which it eventually "plunged into the abyss of fascism, feverish with inwardness." Pointing to the tragic and demonic aspects of German culture, however, was not enough to understand German politics. To speak of a pact with the devil that had caused the German catastrophe was not an explanation but an obfuscation of the Nazi period. The tale of German inwardness and the tragic transformation of inwardness into crime became a strangely apolitical masterpiece.

Doctor Faustus did not turn out to be the novel in which the Germans could recognize themselves and their recent history as in a mirror. The *praeceptor Germaniae* must have felt especially hurt when younger German critics declared that they found the Middle Ages depicted in *Doctor Faustus* as strange and unconvincing as the painting of the Nazi period. Thomas Mann's remark that Zeitblom, the novel's narrator, was a parody of himself, was quoted with a vengeance. The author of *Buddenbrooks* and *The Magic Mountain* had become too alienated from the country's reality for German youth to accept him as a teacher any-more: "Thomas Mann has never been a stranger for us; he belonged to the many who represented a better than the existing Germany. A communal feeling began to form between us. Now we are even more disappointed. There is a Germany that Thomas Mann loved, and there is a Thomas Mann whom we loved and still love. But this is not the author of 'Doctor Faustus.'"[32] In only one way did Thomas Mann de-velop a truly political vision for Germany that was more far-reaching than anything his opponents had to offer: out of the experience of exile, the vision of a transnational world was born. A unified Europe was dreamed up in which Germany would be welcome as a member and find its legitimate place.

In the end, the "great controversy" between internal exiles and émi-grés led to a blurring of moral responsibilities. Both sides took it for granted that their way of looking at the interplay of culture and politics had been adequate and far-sighted. In truth, both had given undue weight to cultural aspirations and achievements—at the expense of political analysis. The dividing lines that really mattered had to be sought elsewhere, as Henry Pachter, an émigré, convincingly argued: "The experience of the Third Reich has made me more tolerant—or better: more than tolerant. The great discovery of the 'thirties' was that the dividing line is not between Left and Right but between decent people and political gangsters, between tolerant people and totalitarians. Not between those who stayed in Germany (and perhaps had to be involved in the daily life of the Third Reich) and those who emigrated for whatever reason, but between those who enjoyed the atmosphere of the Third Reich and profited from it, and those who lived as aliens either in their own country or in another."[33] This lesson, however, was one that the Germans did not learn, at least not for a long time.

Among the few writers of rank who remained in Germany after 1933 was Gottfried Benn, whose poems and prose had tested the limits of the German language to the extreme. In the summer of 1948 he wrote a letter from Berlin to the editors of *Merkur*, the magazine that was to become a leading intellectual publication in postwar Germany. Benn had been blacklisted by the Allies for his alleged adherence to the Nazi regime. In his letter, he offered a sweeping explanation for the past and future catastrophes of his times: "In my view, the West is doomed not at all by the totalitarian systems or the crimes of the SS, not even by its material impoverishment or the Gottwalds and Molotovs, but by the abject surrender of its intelligentsia to political concepts. The *zoon politicon*, that Greek blunder, that Balkan notion—*that* is the germ of our impending doom."[34] Distancing himself from the real world outside had always been a prerequisite for Benn's own poetic production: "In war and peace, at the front and behind it, as an officer and as a doctor, among generals and profiteers, before rubber and jail cells, over beds and coffins, in triumph and decay, I never lost the trance-like feeling that this reality did not exist."[35] For the poet, social life and politics were nothing but part of a virtual reality.

Benn, a master of surprising prose, turned the traditional problem of Germany's intelligentsia upside down. He did not deplore the distance of German artists and intellectuals from the public realm that had made them easy prey for the Nazis—he pretended that intellectuals had failed to remain apolitical and thereby contributed to a political catastrophe. Benn was a great admirer of Plato's *Republic*, which he called the most impressive vision of mankind ever conceived. In the *Republic*, Socrates explains why poetry must be exiled from the city.[36] Benn too wanted to separate poetry from politics. But whereas Plato had banned poetry from the city because it was concerned with neither truth nor virtue, Benn turned things around and took Plato's proscription as a warrant for cultural escapism. When Benn learned that Martin Heidegger, after having been allowed to teach again, had begun his first class by reading five of his, Benn's, poems, he felt that his own poetical existence was now redeemed. Though much indebted to cynicism and irony, he acted like a seer who claims a privileged point of view—thus sounding a strange echo of the ambitions that a free-floating intelligentsia had hatched during the Weimar Republic.

Benn closed his letter, written during the Berlin airlift by Western powers to supply vital necessities to West Berlin in response to the Soviet Union's land and water blockade, in bitter irony: "And so farewell, and greetings from this blockaded city without electric power, from the very part of the city which, in consequence of that Greek blunder and the resulting historical world, is on the brink of famine. Written in a room of many shadows, where there is light for two hours out of twenty-four; for a dark, rainy summer, incidentally, robs the city of its last chance of brief happiness, and the spring lays autumn over these ruins. But it is the city whose brilliance I loved, whose misery I now endure as that of the place where I belong, the city in which I lived to see the Second, the Third, and now the Fourth Reich, and from which nothing will ever make me emigrate. Indeed, one might prophesy a future for it now: tensions are developing in its matter-of-factness, changes of pace and interferences are developing in its lucidity, something ambiguous is starting up, an ambivalence such as centaurs or amphibia are born from. Finally, let us thank General Clay, whose Skymasters will, I hope, convey this letter to you."

Written in his nervous and original prose, Benn's letter displays the German mind-set immediately after the end of the Second World War: the lack of any feeling of responsibility or regret; boundless self-pity;

and unwillingness to learn from past experience. If one had to explain why reeducation in Germany was bound to fail in the years immediately after the war, this letter could provide the key. Yet neither the open disdain for democracy nor the tacit acceptance of the Nazi regime as a legitimate period in German history is the most important passage in this disturbing document. Speaking of the "Second, the Third, and now the Fourth Reich, and from which nothing will ever make me emigrate" made it obvious that the poet could not emigrate—because he perceived himself as already living in exile. Berlin, the blockaded city, is the metaphor for an existence in exile; and Benn—who had been expelled from the National Chamber of Writers (*Reichsschrifttumskammer*) in 1937, who had been no anti-Semite and had never even thought of joining the Nazi Party—believed himself to have lived in exile for most of his life, artistically as well as politically.

German and Jewish Diaspora

When the war ended, emigration and exile had become, in Germany, blurred genres of existence.[37] For much of the German intelligentsia—scientists, artists, and writers alike—blurring past moral options became the prerequisite for mastering the present and planning for the future. It was accompanied by an attempt to obliterate the boundaries between the public and the private spheres. Undeniable individual suffering was enlisted to shed collective responsibility. "I mention my family," Benn wrote after the war. "Three of my brothers died in battle; a fourth was wounded twice; the remainder, totally bombed out, lost everything. A first cousin died at the Somme, his only son in the recent war; of that branch of the family nothing is left. I myself went to war as a doctor, 1914–1918 and 1939–1944. My wife died in 1945 in direct consequence of military operations. This brief summary should be about average for a fairly large German family's lot in the first half of the twentieth century."[38] In this tale, sad and true, one's own suffering alone counted. There was neither a quest for a cause nor a search for responsibility. The parallel to Meinecke's *German Catastrophe* is obvious. It is indeed, as Lionel Gossman writes, "hard to avoid the impression that

... there would have been no *Katastrophe* had Germany been victorious." Benn, like Meinecke and many others, remained "disappointingly silent on the persecution of the Jews and the Holocaust."[39]

Not 1945, the year in which the Second World War ended, but 1948, the year of the monetary reform, must be seen as the turning point in the history of postwar Germany. Not bad conscience but a new currency propelled the change that brought with it a new society. Neither the year 1945 nor the year 1933 marked a break—at least not for large segments of the intelligentsia and the cultural elite. When intellectual temperaments, similar in their antidemocratic resentment and yet as different from one another as the philosopher Martin Heidegger, the jurist Carl Schmitt, the poet Gottfried Benn, and the writing officer and anarchist Ernst Jünger, expressed their sympathy for the Nazis' seizure of power, one must see this not as a conversion but as a sign of continuity. If 1933 could be regarded as a turning point in German history, it meant the return to a Germany that had not lost its self-respect after Versailles. In this perspective, the year 1933 was not a break; it marked the fulfillment of German history. As Gottfried Benn put it, the new state of the Nazis had to be commended because it promised to give culture its due: the separation between politics and culture that Prussia had already tried to overcome was finally about to end. In the state of the Nazis, the cultural nation would be reborn under the umbrella of an "expressionist politics."

In West Germany, culture did not merely survive the war. It fared well after defeat and capitulation. Politics seemed to be discredited forever; a remilitarization of the country was unthinkable, only culture—not least because of the "internal exile" in which so many intellectuals had taken refuge—was left with a legitimate past and hopes for the future. At the same time, culture in Germany was shaped by experiences of emigration, exile, and reimmigration. It became difficult to identify purely German traditions of thought and scholarship; as a rule, a mixture of domestic and foreign, especially Anglo-American, traditions prevailed. The Federal Republic's political and military loyalty to the West was thus enhanced by its cultural Westernization. In 1964, when German sociologists recalled that an economist named Max Weber had written some interesting stuff around the turn of the century, the scholars they invited to talk about him were an émigré philosopher, Herbert

Marcuse, who was then teaching in California; a French political scientist who had studied in Berlin, Raymond Aron; and an American sociologist who had studied in Heidelberg, Talcott Parsons. It is almost beyond belief that in France an author like Emile Durkheim could have become a French classic only after a detour abroad. Ideas and ideologies of German origin, methods, and men were not simply stored in exile; they survived in another cultural milieu by actively adapting to it before they returned to West Germany.

In West Germany, denazification foundered. The old elites were reactivated rather quickly. The confrontation between émigrés and fellow travelers, between opponents of the regime and its collaborators, between Jews who had been driven out of their fatherland and anti-Semites who had been responsible for their flight led to the production of works of art and scholarly books that were provocative and full of innovative energy. West German culture, both in the arts and in the sciences, blossomed because a moral failure turned into an intellectual advantage. To this day, German historiography is interesting not least because German historians are still caught in bitter feuds over their professional legacy, haunted by past masters who displayed both moral cowardice and intellectual bravado in the Third Reich. In philosophy, the intellectual tension created by a constellation of thinkers like Heidegger, Jaspers, Karl Löwith, and Arendt was awesome. In sociology, the confrontation of the Frankfurt School with the émigré Karl Popper, on the one hand, and scholars like Arnold Gehlen and Helmut Schelsky, both members of the Nazi Party, on the other, shaped the development of the discipline. It is amazing to see to what a large extent Theodor Adorno and Arnold Gehlen could agree in their views behind the veil of their private correspondence. Political differences melted away when matters of culture and philosophy were at stake.[40]

After his return to Frankfurt, Adorno was convinced that Germany would never again become a player on the stage of world politics. Germany would only survive as a double appendix to the great political powers in the East and the West. Whoever dreamed of Germany's political recovery was lost in illusion. Adorno made this remark in an essay in which he marveled at the resurrection of German culture, personified by his students, who, though suffering under dismal living conditions, insisted on devoting their time to problems that had no practical import at all. They were hungry, but their hunger for culture was even greater. Whether a theory was true or not did not matter. What was of greatest importance for them was their fight over divergent interpretations of a text.[41] Adorno compared his Frankfurt seminar to the atmosphere in a Talmudic school.

That statement was ambiguous, to say the least. On the one hand, it could be read as an ironic attempt to bridge the gap between two opposite intellectual environments; on the other, it could be understood as a reminder of German-Jewish affinities that, though often in a rather clandestine way, had been a topic of debate in the nineteenth century. Adorno's remarks contrasted with Victor Klemperer's reactions while visiting a Talmudic school thirty years earlier. Victor Klemperer was a German Jew who would later become famous for the diaries he was courageous enough to write under the Nazi regime. In 1918 Klemperer was working as a censor for the German military government in Vilna when he was invited to visit a Talmudic school. His reaction resembled Goethe's rather unpleasant description of the Frankfurt ghetto in his autobiography *Poetry and Truth*. Klemperer was repelled by what he saw: "I did not belong to them, even if my own father would have been a pupil here. I belonged to Europe, to Germany, I was nothing but a German and I thanked my creator to be a German. Not as a student in Geneva and Paris, not among my Zionist fellow students in Prague, not in Kovno, not even in the Vilna ghetto had I felt this as strongly as in this half hour in the Talmudic school."[42]

Adorno's observation belongs to a tradition of pointing out German-Jewish similarities of which Bogumil Goltz, the nineteenth-century ethnographer, was a prime example. Goltz had claimed that, not least in their love of knowledge, the Germans had "a Jewish-Talmudic inventiveness and skill at categorizing, Jewish toughness, indestructibility, a Jewish sense of envy and private quarrels."[43] Yet Adorno went even further. Speaking of the overzealous students in his Frankfurt seminar, it seemed to him, he wrote to Thomas Mann, as if the spirit of the murdered Jews had entered the German mind.[44] Adorno's remark must also be seen as part of a tradition that, by comparing Jews and Germans, had developed the idea of the Diaspora as a compensation for an unwarranted or adverse nationalism. For this view, Hermann Cohen's essay *Deutschtum und Judentum*, published during the First World War in

1915, is perhaps the most striking and far-reaching example. For Cohen, the "sorrow of the Diaspora" had entailed engagement with what George Steiner called a "universalistic humanism older and more tenacious than that of the Enlightenment. To this faith, nationalism was adverse. . . . Cohen felt it was the German idealist tradition and German pre-eminence in European learning and higher education which provided the chosen ground for the unfolding of Judaism within a Gentile and even nationalist matrix."[45] In a more secular way, Fritz Stern followed the same tradition when he described the importance given to cultural religion (*Kulturreligion*) as the main reason why Germany had been so attractive for Jewish intellectuals throughout German history. The fusion of the Jewish spirit and the German mind could only be endured because Germany would never become a political subject again, Adorno assured Thomas Mann—and himself. The Germans knew that access to the political stage was closed, and they resigned themselves to remaining a cultural nation. A divided Germany that had been stripped of its nationalist ambitions by force would finally join the Jews in their sorrow of the Diaspora.

Thomas Mann answered on January 9, 1950—in a rather trivial letter with long digressions on various medical problems he had had with his nose and his throat, the fact that he was still regarded as a fellow traveler, a complaint about the taxes he had just paid, and a sideswipe at Arnold Schoenberg, who could not stop being angry at Thomas Mann's use of his own musical ideas. Mann obviously had forgotten or, rather, suppressed the recollection of how close Adorno's postwar remarks on German-Jewish affinities resembled his own earlier views. In July 1934, Erika Mann came to visit her parents and her brother Golo in Küsnacht. The family speculated about the fate of the German people after the end of the Nazi regime. Thomas Mann asked himself how the defeated and humiliated Germans would be able to survive as a second-rate people: "Perhaps history has in fact intended for them the role of the Jews, one which even Goethe thought befitted them: to be one day scattered throughout the world and to view their existence with an intellectually proud self-irony."[46] In the same month, he repeated this view when bidding farewell to his old friend Ernst Bertram, who had welcomed the Third Reich. Thomas Mann told him that he implored the world spirit to liberate the German people from politics altogether. Anticipating the coming fate of Germany, Mann wished that the Germans should be dispersed throughout the world, "like the Jews with whom [they are] connected through quite similar tragedies."[47]

Neither during the reign of the Nazis nor immediately after the end of the Second World War did it come as a surprise that Thomas Mann wanted Germany stripped of its national ambitions. It was surprising, though, that he had already done the same in 1918, while still endearing himself to the German national conservatives. In the *Reflections of a Nonpolitical Man*, Mann indulged in a long if not the longest quotation of his book to pay tribute to "a strange man . . . Bogumil Goltz by name, humorist, philosopher and critic of the times, a writer who thought deeply and wrote much about Germany and the German character." Writing around 1860, at a time when Bismarck was already steering Germany toward becoming the Reich, Goltz maintained that "*the German nation can have no character the way other nations can*, because through literature and education in reason it has generalized and ennobled itself as a nation of the world that all humanity is beginning to recognize as its teacher and educator. Yes, we are, we were, we remain the schoolmasters, the philosophers, the theosophists, the religious teachers of Europe and of the whole world. This is our genius, our ideal national unity, honor and mission, *which we must not trade for the thing or phantom that the French or the English call nation*."[48] Being the first and foremost cultural state in the world, Germany had no need to aspire to political nationhood. It is difficult to say whether this was, in the case of Thomas Mann, a sour-grapes argument, given that it became more and more likely that a defeated Germany would have great difficulties in upholding its national stature. With a defeat of the German troops likely in the offing, Mann had to present his argument not in a tone of resignation but with aggressive pride. This may also explain why he did not mention that Bogumil Goltz had pointed to the similarities between the German and the Jewish character. In 1918 it was impossible to relate the German willful neglect of nationhood with the Jewish fateful orientation toward the Diaspora.

To point to this relation, however, became almost a common figure of speech for Thomas Mann the émigré during the Third Reich and at the end of the Second World War. There was nothing philo-Semitic in these remarks—quite to the contrary. Rather, Mann described with scathing irony the connection through a common fate that could please neither the Germans nor the Jews. In a diary entry from July 15, 1934, he wondered at a scandalous rapprochement between German Jews and Nazi Germany. Is it not a paradox indeed, he asked himself, that the Jews were stripped of their rights by a regime which some of them had helped to come to power—by supporting the cause of antiliberalism? It was not only members of the circle around the poet Stefan George like Karl Wolfskehl who would have gladly accepted life under Nazi rule if they had only been allowed to do so. Deep in their soul, Mann wrote, the Jews might perhaps even cherish their role as merely tolerated guests in Germany who paid their taxes but did not have to participate in its public affairs. Mann went so far as to ask why the Nazis had murdered an author like the "quite disgusting" Theodor Lessing, who called himself a socialist. In truth, Mann said, Lessing shared his way of thinking with that of his murderers.[49]

Since Thomas Mann knew Dorothy Thompson quite well, he may have known and later perhaps even approved of her statement that for the Nazi leaders "Germanism seemed to be a kind of Zionism. Hitler was born in the Austria of the Hapsburgs and loathed it. He looked wistfully across the borders into the German promised land. Hess was born in Cairo; Darré was born in the Argentine; Rosenberg was born in Estonia. Ernst Bohle, head of the 'Service for Foreign Germans' was born in England. I am sure that there is something significant in this. For to these men Germany is not a place, an existing organized society, but an idea."[50] In this respect, a critical view of the way Jewish nationhood was achieved in the state of Israel became almost inevitably linked to the German model. On October 31, 1948, Hannah Arendt wrote to Karl Jaspers: "Monsieur [Heinrich Blücher] says, in his despair: 'If the Jews insist on becoming a nation like every other nation, why for God's sake do they insist on becoming like the Germans?' There is, alas, some truth to that."[51] On September 7, 1952, Arendt quoted her friend Kurt Blumenfeld, who used to say that he was "a Zionist by the grace of Goethe" and that Zionism was "Germany's gift to the Jews."[52]

Goethe was the central reference in Mann's German-Jewish rapprochement. In 1936, paraphrasing Goethe, Mann went so far as to see one reason for the chronic German anti-Semitism in the fact that Germans and Jews resembled each other so deeply.[53] He repeated this argument almost verbatim eleven years later in the speech he gave before the Library of Congress on "Germany and the Germans." It was the year 1945; Nazi Germany had been defeated. Mann reminded his American audience, admitting his deep sympathy for this view, of Goethe's wish for a German Diaspora. " 'Like the Jews,' he [Goethe] said, 'the Germans must be transplanted and scattered over the world!' And he added: '. . . in order to develop the good that lies in them, fully and to the benefit of the nations.' " Goethe had made remarks of this kind to several people, including Wilhelm von Humboldt.[54] Goethe claimed that the Germans let themselves be suppressed everywhere, like the Jews, but that they were, again like the Jews, "indestructible" (*unvertilgbar*). The Germans kept close together only when they had no fatherland. Like the Jews, they would not perish, because they were individuals.[55]

In a famous epigram, Goethe and Schiller admonished their compatriots not to try the impossible: "To learn to form a nation, you hope, Germans, in vain / learn instead, you can do it, more freely to become human." To justify breaking up postwar Germany into several states after the Second World War, Henry Morgenthau quoted Goethe: "I have often felt a bitter pang at the thought of the German people, so estimable as individuals and so wretched in the whole."[56] Goethe anticipated that German culture, and with it the whole civilized world, would profit more from a German Diaspora than from a successful German nation-building that was only a remote possibility in his own time. After Germany had disappeared as a political subject immediately at the end of the Second World War, the Diaspora seemed to become a German option indeed, if only a forced one. As early as July 1934, Thomas Mann had asked himself whether the "depoliticization" of Germany that would be an inevitable result of the Nazi era could not be seen as a liberation of the German soul. At a sad and paradoxical moment, Germans and Jews, the murderers and their victims, resembled each other more than ever before.[57] They resembled each other not least because both—members of the cultural nation par excellence and the "people of the book"—used to take refuge in a religion-like reverence for culture.

German culture was reborn after the end of the Second World War. A Jewish émigré like Theodor Adorno could imagine only one price the Germans would have to pay for the resurrection of their culture: the loss of political sovereignty. Poems could be written again, for Adorno had been too severe in this respect. The political unity of the nation, however, seemed to be lost forever.

The Survival of the Typical
German: Faust versus Mephistopheles

Goethe in the Polls

In 1949, the year the Federal Republic was founded, the Allensbach Institute, the German equivalent of the Gallup Institute, asked a representative sample of Germans about their knowledge of and their relation to Goethe. Generously funded by a large public television station (ZDF), the Goethe poll was repeated in 1999, when the 250th anniversary of the poet's birth was celebrated with pomp and circumstance.[1] Mentioned abroad, these polls sound rather funny—at home they were and still are taken seriously indeed. In 1949, in another poll, Germans were asked whether, after 1945, they had had "a major spiritual experience." Only a disappointing 46 percent answered "Yes"—a result the pollsters judged so dismal that it had to be compensated by the answer of a publisher, who claimed he had a major spiritual experience each day. Somewhat mischievously, he added: "This is a stupid question indeed. I would go so far as to say that any German who had not had a major spiritual experience since 1945 had better hang himself."

The Goethe polls make it possible to contrast the answers Germans gave in 1949 with the answers fifty years later and to compare East and West almost ten years after unification. Asked in 1949 whether they considered Goethe the typical German, half of the West Germans answered "Yes." In 1999, however, only 31 percent of the West Germans regarded Goethe as the typical German, but 50 percent of the East Germans still did. In 1949, 40 percent of the West Germans could recite a poem by Goethe, compared with only 10 percent fifty years later. Once more, the East Germans did much better: 25 percent of them knew a Goethe poem by heart. Most striking was the East-West divide when the Germans were asked if they had read Goethe's *Faust*: 19 percent in the West were greatly outnumbered by 50 percent in the East. East Germans seemed to feel much closer to Goethe and his spiritual heritage than West Germans did. The German press found much food for thought in the fact that, in 1949, the majority of Germans considered Faust the most important character in Goethe's drama, whereas fifty years later Mephistopheles had sneaked into first place—if only in the West. In the East, Faust still played the leading role. The pollsters attributed this difference to the fact that Mephistopheles incorporated the unabashed longing for a life of luxury—a wish that appealed to the West Germans, who had produced an economic miracle and now pursued happiness and adopted hedonism as their preferred attitude. The pollsters were convinced, however, that this East-West divide would not last. After a few years, hedonism would take over the East as well and Mephistopheles would reign supreme in the whole of Germany.

A more trivial explanation for Mephistopheles' success in the West was conceivable. In 1957 Gustav Gründgens had directed *Faust I* at a theater in Hamburg, the Deutsches Schauspielhaus; three years later a movie of this theater production was made that became a huge popular success in the Federal Republic. On the stage and in the movie, Gründgens not only directed but also played Mephistopheles. He was much better than Faust, who was merely good and was played by Will Quadflieg. No wonder, then, that the generation of Germans who saw the play and/or the movie voted for the more impressive actor when they were asked to name their favorite character from Goethe's *Faust*. Still, this more mundane explanation was laden with political symbolism: Gründgens had had a remarkable career under the Nazis that continued uninterruptedly into the first decades of the Federal Republic. As early as 1936, Klaus Mann had published *Mephisto*, "the novel of a career," a barely disguised *roman à clef* about Gründgens, who had been married for a while to Erika Mann, Klaus Mann's sister. *Mephisto* was also an early attempt to refute the claims of fellow travelers, who had disguised themselves as "internal exiles," that they had preserved the better part of Germany during the time of the Third Reich. It was only appropriate therefore that Klaus Mann's father, Thomas Mann, the representative of German emigration, would call his German novel of 1947 *Doctor Faustus*.[2]

The most intriguing aspect of the Goethe polls lies not in the answers they yielded, but in the importance both the interviewers and the public attributed to these surveys. It is hardly imaginable that the BBC could have done the same with Shakespeare or that a Spanish television station would test, after the death of Franco, the acceptance of the country's new democratic structures by asking the people whether they preferred Sancho Panza to Don Quixote. In Germany, however, the people's image of Goethe was seen as a litmus test for the state of the nation. Two results were especially reassuring. First, Goethe's popularity had not dramatically diminished since 1949. Second, Goethe was even more popular in the East than in the West. These findings meant that the cultural nation was alive and well. They also meant that the unification of Germany, which had occurred in 1990, had turned out to be an asset, not a liability, in the attempt to preserve the best that Germany has to offer to itself and to the world: culture. The polls also showed some alarming results: why, for instance, do only 27 percent of those Germans who regard themselves as moderately leftist see in Goethe the typical German, whereas 48 percent of the political right do? This question has remained unanswered, because unasked.

The Goethe polls should not lead to the conclusion that German history in the 19th and 20th centuries was in general characterized by a Goethe cult. Goethe was not always worshipped and certainly not always by each and every German. At almost any point during this period, however, the public image of Goethe was used to adopt or to reject a specific political vision—in both East and West.[3] Goethe was so attractive because he had been, as Thomas Mann wrote admiringly, a citizen and a man of letters who was at ease in both the social and the intellectual sphere: "Goethe's conception of the German people, as an unpolitical, intellectual nation, centred upon human values, receiving from all and teaching all, will it not always have its profound justification, even in times of violent over-compensation and national self-correction?"[4] It was a rhetorical question. To ask it in 1932, one hundred years after Goethe's death, meant to answer it in the affirmative.

When the hundredth anniversary of Goethe's birth was celebrated in 1849, though, he might have seemed almost forgotten in Germany.

After the revolution of 1848 had failed, Schiller became more popular, as the festivities for his hundredth birthday in 1859 demonstrated; the occasion was celebrated throughout the German lands in a mood of patriotic fervor. Two years earlier, the Goethe-Schiller monument had been erected in Weimar; but only after the Prussian victory over France in the war of 1870–71 did it become a national place of worship. Germany's political topography now had two centers: Berlin and Weimar. They symbolized the attempt to reconcile politics and culture after the Reich had finally been founded proclaimed by Bismarck at Versailles in 1871. Goethe did not escape the nationalist and chauvinist turn of German politics that followed. A narrow patriotism was ascribed to him that was alien to the great cosmopolitan who had put forward the idea of a "world literature." Nietzsche could therefore rightly claim that the life of Goethe, "not only a good and great human being but a *culture*," was an episode without consequence in the history of the Germans. Schiller and, though to a lesser degree, even Lessing belonged to the world of German politics, but certainly not Goethe. Goethe, said Nietzsche, was no representative of a national literature: "He stands towards his *nation* in the relationship neither of the living nor of the novel nor of the antiquated. Only for a few was he alive and does he live still: for most he is nothing but a fanfare of vanity blown from time to time across the German frontier."[5]

This judgment did not prevent the continuation of a misunderstanding on both the right and the left side of the political spectrum. In imperial Germany, Goethe's skepticism toward the realm of politics in general was misused as an argument against party politics in particular—as if political parties, which so piqued the Kaiser, had already existed in Goethe's time. The mistrust of parliamentary democracy that would later contribute to the downfall of the Weimar Republic was also nourished by reference to a distorted picture of Goethe. Friedrich Ebert, on the other hand, who opened the constituent assembly of the Republic on February 6, 1919, in Weimar, could not possibly do so without reference to Goethe, the author of *Faust* and of *Wilhelm Meister's Years of Travel*. Ebert, a man of modest origins, was ridiculed by the Left as well as by the Right for his pathetic "discovery of Goethe," but the president of the Republic had no choice. He had to call upon Goethe when he urged the German people to switch from imperialism to idealism and to aspire to spiritual greatness instead of world power. The "Spirit of Weimar" was a lofty but useful device: it could legitimize anything.

When Thomas Mann traveled to Weimar to give his speech in honor of Goethe on the hundredth anniversary of his death in 1932, he was appalled at the mixture of Goethe worship and "Hitlerism" that he encountered all along the way. To show his anger was admirable, and his reaction was an accurate indicator of things to come—in contrast to Ernst Robert Curtius' foggy complaint in the same year that Germany was in jeopardy because the nation was living in a constellation far from Goethe. That prediction was risk-free, whereas Thomas Mann's open contempt toward "Hitlerism" in the name of Goethe required considerable courage, even though the Nazis had not yet seized power.

March 21, 1933, was the "Day of Potsdam." It marked the end of the Weimar Republic, staged by Goebbels on the date when after the proclamation of the new "Reich," the Reichstag had met for the first time in 1871. The handshake between Hitler and President Paul von Hindenburg at the opening ceremony of the new Reichstag was a clear sign that Hitler had won over the conservatives for the Nazis. Goethe had died on March 22, 1832. That the shrewd Goebbels had not chosen this date for the ceremony was a sign that reverence for Goethe would not become a topic of central importance for the Nazi leadership. The later claim of Frank Thiess, Thomas Mann's ferocious opponent in the debate over the legitimacy of "inner exile," that a widespread reading of Goethe's works during the Nazi era proved that the Germans, in their innermost breast, had withstood the temptations of a totalitarian regime, was shallow and did not prove anything.[6] In the same way that readers and followers of Stefan George became both executioners and victims in the Nazi death camps, Goethe was used by the Nazi leadership and by opponents of the regime alike. Rudolf Hess, for instance, proclaimed, in the name of Goethe, the rebirth of classicism in Germany. On the surface one might indeed detect a certain affinity between the cosmopolitan views of Goethe and those Nazi doctrines of cultural policy that preferred the legacy of Imperial Rome and classical Greece to Teutonic ideologies and Germanic mythology. Cosmopolitanism, however, was an idea intrinsically alien to the Nazi mind-set. At the

Nazi core was a racially motivated eagerness to dominate the world, rather than to appreciate and celebrate it.

The German classics also provided spiritual guidance to resistance groups, in which intellectual sympathy did not necessarily lead to idolatry, as had so often been the case in German history. Hans Scholl, for instance, together with his sister Sophie a founder of the resistance group "White Rose," whose members would be executed by the Nazis in February of 1943, was an outspoken Goethe skeptic. He had great difficulties accepting Goethe as a spiritual leader. In one of his leaflets, Hans Scholl had called upon the Germans to resist and had asked for the rebirth of a spiritual Europe. To envisage a new and democratic Europe in the midst of the Nazi dictatorship, however, came as close to the worldview of Goethe the cosmopolitan as one could imagine. At the same time, Goethe was a beacon of hope for many inmates of the Nazi camps, even if they were not Germans. Jorge Semprun engaged in imaginary conversations with Goethe while he was an inmate of Buchenwald, the concentration camp that had been built in the immediate vicinity of Weimar, and the Dutch communist Nico Rost described how literature helped him daily to survive in a book with the telling title *Goethe in Dachau*.[7] Martin Walser has used the term *Kulturvertrauen* (trust in culture) to explain, for instance, why a Jewish woman who would later be deported to a concentration camp and murdered there, could write: "It's up to *us* to save Goethe."[8]

Goethe after 1945

After 1945, the work of moral repair in East and West Germany could not be accomplished without reference to Goethe. Goethe became the eagerly sought moral handyman. In the West, Friedrich Meinecke urged his compatriots to form Goethe communities as a means of spiritual redemption. He also suggested to Theodor Heuss, the first president of the Federal Republic, to choose August 28, Goethe's birthday, as the date for the German national holiday. Heuss, with his characteristic Swabian banter, did not think much of this proposal: with the economic miracle well under way, most Germans would be on vacation at the end of August and nobody would be there to celebrate. In the

East, Goethe became nothing less than a godfather for the socialist state. Karl Jaspers and Richard Alewyn were among the few who criticized the renewed all-German Goethe cult. When Jaspers received the prestigious Goethe Prize in 1947, he gave a speech with the title "Our Future and Goethe," in which he finished off any attempt to use a quotation from the author of *Faust* to find a justification or excuse for what had happened in Germany. In 1949 Richard Alewyn condemned the misuse of Goethe as a moral and political alibi in German public debate. Richard Alewyn was a Jewish émigré who had been forced to flee from Germany in 1933—one year after he had been called to the University of Heidelberg as the successor of Friedrich Gundolf, the famous literary scholar who once had been a close ally of Stefan George. Alewyn was stunned by the nonchalance with which the Germans used Goethe to come to grips with their recent past. He insisted that one could not praise Goethe and at the same time forget Hitler. Humanism and bestiality existed together in Germany; the country's moral topography was forever characterized by the proximity of Weimar and Buchenwald.

Alewyn's ire must also have been directed against authors like Frank Thiess, who justified the "internal exile" by the extensive reading of Goethe under the Nazi dictatorship. Immediately after the end of the Second World War, the emphasis on Goethe was no less explicit in the East, whose premises often contradicted those in the West. Johannes R. Becher, a poet and the first minister of culture in East Germany, maintained that Hitler's barbarism would not have been possible if Goethe's legacy had remained alive after 1933. As early as 1934, in his Moscow exile, Becher had seen in Goethe the symbol of another, better Germany. Since after 1945 the East would become the better Germany, as Becher was convinced, Goethe necessarily had to play a crucial role there. In a speech delivered on August 28, 1949—Goethe's two hundredth birthday—Becher praised Goethe as the "liberator" of Germany, using vocabulary that was communist on the surface yet colored by explicit religious undertones. Goethe had to come to the rescue of the damned German soul. Forgotten were the words of Friedrich Engels, who had seen in Goethe above all a victim of Germany's miserable plight. The Hungarian writer and critic Georg Lukács was criticized by Becher and others because, at least in some of his writings, he had called Weimar classicism nothing but an intermezzo, a fatal reaction to the French Revolution that had propelled German poets' and thinkers' flight into inwardness and accelerated their turning away from politics. In 1952 Hanns Eisler's opera *Johann Faustus* and Bertolt Brecht's production, with the Berliner Ensemble, of Goethe's *Urfaust* provoked similarly harsh criticism from party officials. They disapproved of any attempt to create a Goethe for modern times who was not worshipped but acclaimed with playful distance and irony.

Two pictures from 1945 were an anticipation of the future cultural politics of the German Democratic Republic (GDR). In May, three soldiers of the Red Army staged the raising of the flag over the Reichstag in Berlin that had first happened on April 30. In July of the same year, pioneers of the Red Army were photographed while they removed the brickwork around the Goethe-Schiller monument in Weimar that had been erected there to prevent possible damage from the Allies' air raids. Twelve years after the Nazis had walled in the classics, Soviet soldiers liberated them and gave them back as a gift to the first socialist German state. In this state, the long-awaited union of Berlin and Weimar, that is, of politics and culture, would finally become a reality. A forced political optimism was accompanied by the firm belief that the formation of a new political consciousness could be achieved with the help of culture. Becher and others went so far as to admit that it would be much too difficult to start with reading Marx and Engels in order to reeducate the German people. They would have to read Goethe and Schiller first. Reading and learning from the classics were the first steps in a process at whose end a new man would be born in the GDR.

Culture was seen for a while as a common meeting ground for East and West. Until 1947–48, the Kulturbund zur demokratischen Erneuerung Deutschlands (Cultural Union for the Democratic Renewal of Germany) was a national institution through which intellectuals from East and West tried to keep the idea of the cultural nation alive. Then the Cultural Union was transformed into an instrument of propaganda. The official cultural policy of the GDR now regarded the liberation of the German classics as its own, specific moral point of departure. Goethe became the founding father of the eastern Republic—not of a reborn and peacefully reunited cultural nation. Unwittingly, however, the efforts to found Goethe circles and Goethe communities bespoke the similarities of cultural policies in East and West: Meinecke, after

all, had made the same proposal. Although the Goethe Society, which
had been founded in 1885 and had its seat in Weimar, officially remained an all-German organization, institutional unity could not hide
the political rifts behind the hermeneutical differences with which
Goethe's work was interpreted. When the Federal Republic regained
its political independence and joined the West, that act was condemned
by politicians in the East as an abandonment of culture for civilization,
a sacrifice of national pride for cosmopolitan pretension, and the giving
up of a warm and lively communal life for the formalities of parliamentary democracy. Goethe's legacy was now used as an arsenal providing
the weapons for an antimodernist attack against the West. Members of
the East German secret police infiltrated the Goethe Society in the
GDR. Although even in the East Goethe was called, from time to time,
a symbol of spiritual unity in a politically divided Germany, he was not
at all a common good that East and West were willing to share.

The East also put much greater emphasis on Goethe as its guide and
witness for cultural policy. In 1958 Walter Ulbricht, first secretary of
the Socialist Unity Party (SED), gave a simple answer to the question of
where the GDR was heading: it sufficed to read the *Communist Manifesto* and Goethe's *Faust* to anticipate the future development of the first
socialist state on German soil. The GDR would become a cultural state,
a pedagogical province as Goethe had foreseen in his novel *Wilhelm
Meister*. Even stronger was the affinity to *Faust*, notably its second part.
In *Faust II*, Goethe had described not a peaceful utopia, but a world to
fight for, not a ready-made land, but an earth that had to be created by
man's own hands and made fertile by the rhythm of regular work in
daily life. *Faust II* reflects the influence that the socialist ideas of Saint-
Simon exerted on Goethe in his later life, a time when he also wrote
many pages with the New World, America, in mind. Now the outer
and inner landscape of *Faust II* were seen as an anticipation not of the
USA but of the GDR—a somewhat paradoxical change of perspective,
considering the aggressive anti-Americanism that was part of the Socialist Unity Party's ideology.

Against the declared wishes of the Soviet government, Walter Ulbricht, who, after the end of the Second World War, had become first
chairman of the Communist Party and then of the Socialist Unity Party
in East Germany, insisted on including the term "German Nation" and

a reference to the political goal of German reunification in the newly written East German constitution of 1968. It was also Ulbricht who had prevented an early split of the Goethe Society, one of the few remaining all-German cultural institutions. In 1962 Ulbricht went so far as to see the GDR itself as a kind of Goethe play: it represented *Faust III*. The play that Goethe certainly would have written had he lived in Ulbricht's lifetime, the first secretary seemed to say, should now be written by an East German author. The order to write a socialist *Faust*, however, was not an innocent wish, as the novelist Anna Seghers realized. She must have remembered Georg Lukács's pathetic claim that the great October Revolution of 1917 had chased Mephisto and his magical powers from the political stage once and for all. Therefore Seghers asked the party chairman: "Fair enough, Comrade Ulbricht— but how will we deal with Mephisto?" Ulbricht, however, too convinced of the communist cause to be irritated by this question, replied: "Comrade Seghers, don't worry, we will also be able to solve the Mephistopheles problem!"[9]

Goethe was more widely read in East Germany than in West Germany. This fact was one not too surprising finding of the Goethe polls conducted by the Allensbach Institute. This result must be seen not so much as a consequence of communist cultural policy but, paradoxically enough, as proof of the thesis that the GDR was a country where people led a middle-class way of life in the absence of a bourgeoisie. After the Weimar Republic and the horrific interregnum of the Third Reich, a communist Weimar Monarchy had been established in the East. Only in this "monarchy" could a new classicism develop, of which the authors Heiner Müller and Peter Hacks were the best-known representatives. A preponderance of the state was necessary for such a classicism, which never came to life in West Germany. In one important aspect, the cultural policy of the GDR resembled the cultural policy during the Nazi period: it was characterized by a kind of polycratic chaos. Such chaos makes it difficult to speak of one and only one role that Goethe played in this policy.

There was less emphasis on Goethe in the West. The foreign cultural policy of the Federal Republic was basically carried out by the Goethe Institutes, but using his name did not imply a direct or even an indirect reference to his works and thought. As a consequence of the student

revolt of 1968, which was among other things an attempt to repoliticize
the German cultural scene, Weimar classicism was attacked because of
its alleged quietism and submission to existing political power. Goethe
the Weimar minister was despised as a reactionary. At the same time,
his animosity toward the political sphere was cited with as much contempt as was a letter from Schiller to Herder, in which Schiller had
written that it was necessary for the poetic genius to withdraw from
political reality into an ideal world. Weimar was no longer part of a
living cultural memory, but only a legend that had misled the Germans
and should be forgotten as quickly as possible.[10]

During a visit to Hamburg, Gustav Stresemann, who had become
German chancellor in 1923, paid a visit to the Warburg Library. Aby
Warburg received the chancellor and honored him with a private lecture
on one of his hobbies: aspects of political sovereignty as displayed on
postage stamps. Stresemann was shown current French and English
stamps, whose dignity and elegance adequately represented the cultural
aspirations and political ambitions of both nations. Then Warburg
showed Stresemann a current German stamp, with Goethe's portrait
on it. Warburg: "Mr. Chancellor, may I ask you to read, if you can, the
inscription on this stamp?" Stresemann, with a smile: "Johann Wolfgang Goethe." Warburg: "With due respect, Mr. Chancellor, this is
wrong. What you see here is Joh dot, Wolfg dot, Goethe. This is the
main problem of the Weimar Republic: Everything is abbreviated and
therefore everything is too short."[11]

In comparison with the GDR, Goethe was certainly "abbreviated"
in the Federal Republic of Germany. This abbreviation did not mean,
however, that democracy fell short in the West.

8

German Reunification: The Failure of the Interpreting Class

Cultural Guardians

After the Second World War, culture served as an emotional refuge in Germany, a divided country in danger of never becoming a political subject again. After the founding of two separate German states in 1949, the cultural unity of the German nation was seen as a consolation for political partition, in the West as well as in the East. Invoking the survival of the cultural nation compensated for the lack of a long-term policy directed toward reunification. Even the *Ostpolitik* of Willy Brandt in the early 1970s aimed at improving relations between the two German states without really anticipating the restoration of German unity. When the Berlin Wall tumbled down in 1989, it turned out that the federal government in Bonn—regardless of the parties forming it— was unprepared for the challenge reunification brought with it. It must also be remembered that a tacit understanding had been almost unanimously shared outside Germany: to split the country that had produced the Nazi regime was a good thing.

It was even more understandable, therefore, that in the two German states poets, writers, and artists saw themselves as guardians of the *Kulturnation* in times of political conflict. Culture had to bridge a political gap that was growing bigger during the cold war. In 1949, when Thomas Mann gave his speech in honor of Goethe's two hundredth birthday not only in West but also in East Germany—not only in Frankfurt but also in Weimar—he thereby made a political statement: the cultural nation was undivided. Nineteen forty-nine had been the year that sealed the separation of the two German states and prepared the entry of the Federal Republic into the Western European Union and NATO. The cold war turned into an ice-cold conflict. In 1945 Buchenwald had become a concentration camp again under Soviet occupation. In 1950, in a letter to a Swedish journalist, Thomas Mann welcomed the reactivation of the camp since other attempts to reeducate the Germans had failed. The uproar his letter caused in West Germany let Mann distance himself from what he had written. The camp was dissolved in the same year. In 1955, 150 years after Schiller's death, Mann was invited to give a speech in honor of the poet—in both West and East. In the Federal Republic, Mann was attacked for his intention to pay tribute to the dictatorship of a mock state that called itself, preposterously, the German Democratic Republic. Mann hesitated for a while over his decision to visit the GDR, since his hope for a period of détente had not been fulfilled. The new political tensions between East and West had caught him by surprise. In the end, however, he decided to repeat in honor of Schiller what he had done already in honor of Goethe in 1949. He would speak not only in Stuttgart but also in Weimar. Furthermore, this would be a good occasion to pick up the honorary degree that the University of Jena had bestowed upon him, the university where Friedrich Schiller had taught as a professor of history. Mann was especially relieved when Theodor Heuss, the first president of the Federal Republic, supported his plan to speak in both cities. Mann held the liberal Heuss in high esteem and vigorously disliked Konrad Adenauer, the first West German chancellor. "Adenauer's Germany," as Mann contemptuously called it, remained a cultural desert for him.

The solemn remembrance of three poets was especially important for the survival of one and only one German cultural nation: Goethe, Lessing, and Schiller. Goethe was such a towering figure that it would have been ridiculous if one German state claimed him solely for itself. He remained the undisputed symbol of Germany's cultural unity. Lessing had advanced the unification of the German states by creating a national theater. After 1945 he became a symbol of how culture could serve even remote political ends. Schiller had been hailed as a national hero across Germany in 1859, the year of his hundredth birthday. In 1955 he was recalled as a German patriot and as a cosmopolitan who had fought for the unification of all mankind.

Thomas Mann's attitude while speaking in honor of Goethe and Schiller in East and West Germany was anything but modest. He behaved like a literary statesman. Pride turned into near arrogance when Mann became convinced that an all-German production of a film based on his early novel *Buddenbrooks* could serve as the best symbol of culture's victory over politics in the midst of the cold war. Such a film had been proposed in 1954 by the East German film company DEFA, which had already turned Heinrich Mann's novel *Der Untertan* (*Man of Straw*) into a movie in 1951.

Thomas Mann's *Königliche Hoheit* (The beloved returns) had been adapted for the screen in West Germany in 1953.[1] West German producers, however, refused to cooperate with the East German DEFA on the *Buddenbrooks* project for political reasons. When they offered Thomas Mann forty thousand dollars for the rights to do their own movie adaptation, Mann became furious. He could not be bribed. He did not want to see his novel turned into a movie that would be regarded as a product of "Adenauer's Germany." In the end, the project was abandoned. One year after Thomas Mann's death in 1958, however, a West German *Buddenbrooks* film was made; Erika, Mann's daughter, coauthored the script. As far as one can tell, the movie neither helped nor hindered history's decision to reunite the two Germanys in the long run.

Intellectual Disaster in the East

While the Federal Republic was westernized, the German Democratic Republic did not undergo a comparable process of "Russification." Although broken English soon became the lingua franca for West German tourists, for example, most East Germans simply refused to learn Russian. The West was internationalized, while the East remained a province where the *International* hymn had to be sung daily. Censorship took its toll. In the East, the years from 1933 to 1989 belong to a single epoch conspicuously lacking in cultural modernity. In the first German state of workers and peasants, it was impossible for a literary scholar to read and teach Franz Kafka, for a philosopher to read and teach Wittgenstein, for a sociologist to read and teach Max Weber, for an economist to read and teach Keynes, and for a psychologist to read and teach Sigmund Freud in an unbiased way—if the works of these authors could be read at all. This complaint was voiced by a philosopher from Leipzig in 1987 at a meeting of historians and social scientists from the GDR and the Federal Republic in East Berlin. The chairman of the meeting, a philosopher-apparatchik and member of the Academy of Sciences of the GDR, tried to silence his colleague. When the West Germans threatened to leave the meeting, the courageous philosopher from Leipzig was able to continue. He was an exception. A continuity of moral cowardice was painfully apparent: the absence of civil disobedience, the lack of empathy with the oppressed, the tricks of adjustment and of self-deception, and the flight into inner emigration were characteristic of intellectual life in the east of Germany during the long period from 1933 all the way through 1989.

In the West, the moral failure to confront the Nazi past proved to be of considerable intellectual advantage. In East Germany, good moral intentions eventually turned into an intellectual disaster. Heinrich Mann was elected first president of the newly founded Academy of Arts in East Berlin and received the National Prize of the GDR, the country's highest civilian honor. Only his death in 1950 in Santa Monica, California, prevented him from returning to East Germany for good and becoming a citizen of the GDR. His presence there, together with writers like Anna Seghers and Stefan Heym, would have given considerable cultural legitimacy to the first socialist German state. Communists who had survived Nazi persecution and Russian exile tried to make "denazification" work in East Germany. But culture soon became politically correct, and also, to a large degree, boring and repetitive. Debates among the intelligentsia dealt with minor corrections of the established cultural canon; rarely did they question the canon itself. Once seen as stimulating within the intellectual microclimate of the GDR, these debates have today been rightly forgotten. Bertolt Brecht was something of an exception, but even he turned more and more into a director who was, above all, interested in the survival of his company and much less in the afterlife of an aesthetic program. The communist émigrés first helped the GDR win moral recognition. The regime used their bona fide antifascism to paint the GDR as the better Germany—with the additional profit that it never assumed any responsibility for the crimes of Nazi Germany and took the liberty of siding with the Arab world in criticizing the politics of Israel without restraint. This moral recognition withered away with the fall of communism. When the archives of the Communist Party in Moscow were opened, it became evident what an ignominious role many heroes of German emigration to the east—and also West German politicians, like the Social Democrat Herbert Wehner—had played during the Soviet purges and political trials of the thirties. These émigrés had left one totalitarian regime, only to succumb to another.

What the majority of cultural elite of the GDR learned better than anything was the art of being ruled, as Wyndham Lewis had called it. In East Germany, whose political leadership would later claim a Prussian past, one legacy of Germany survived especially well: professors of philosophy and Protestant pastors gave advice on how to lead the life of a vassal and feel free at the same time.[2] With notable exceptions like the physicist Robert Havemann, the philosopher Rudolf Bahro, and the writer Erich Loest, dissident intellectuals did not become martyrs in the GDR. Intellectuals who spent many years in jail, like Walter Janka and Wolfgang Harich, did not wish to be regarded as dissidents, but saw themselves as opponents within the Communist Party system. East Germany had also its Samizdat and catacomb culture, but their political impact was not comparable to those in Poland or Czechoslovakia. More important, the GDR did not—and could not—produce groups of engaged émigrés who became a political force to reckon with. A Czech writer who fled to Paris or London thereby became an alienated speaker, thus viewing his country from the outside. A writer from Leipzig who went to Munich or Berlin was still writing in Germany. He remained a native speaker. Uwe Johnson, arguably the most important of the literary émigrés from the GDR, who had great difficulties feeling at home in the West, insisted that he had not moved from one German state to another, but had only changed his zip code.

Most authors who stayed in the GDR found ways and means to come to an arrangement with political reality, that is, the *nomenklatura*. Not all intellectuals became fellow travelers, to be sure, but a great many of them enjoyed the security and subsidies accorded to the cultural elite by a communist regime that leveled, but never equalized. This is one reason why the ratio of poets and novelists to the total population was seven times higher in the GDR than in the Federal Republic of Germany. Many of them had to live on modest means, but none of them starved. An inner protest of the mind shaped their mental outlook, but their working conditions were not characterized by poverty.

When Thomas Carlyle spoke of the man of letters as a modern priest and of the "Priesthood of the Writers of Books" that had become so influential in modern times, he was not speaking merely metaphorically. It was obvious to him that "to give our Men of Letters stipends, endowments and all furtherance of cash" would do little to improve their true business.[3] Literary men who wanted to fulfill their mission ought to be poor. They had to form a mendicant order. Communist regimes in Central and Eastern Europe probably committed their worst mistake in forcing members of the cultural elite to either collaborate or join the lower classes. Many intellectuals had to work as furnace stokers and road sweepers, as cabdrivers and handymen. Thus they became mendicant friars indeed. The communist regimes in the East were dealt a deadly blow by an intellectual proletariat they themselves had created. The situation in the GDR was different, though there were writers and artists who suffered as much as their colleagues in other countries of the communist bloc. When the cultural elite of the GDR were put to the test with the breakdown of the regime, their failure became obvious. It was the failure of the interpreting class.

Intellectual Tragicomedy

The performance of intellectuals in East Germany in the period of reunification resembles a tragicomedy in five acts—the five days in which they were able to act as heroes indeed. Thereafter, a myth of missed opportunities was born. It was a myth that glorified the five days from November 4, 1989—when a mass demonstration of close to a million people in East Berlin, planned by the opposition group Neues Forum and organized by artists and writers, announced the fall of the ancien régime—through November 9, when the disorderly and unplanned opening of the Berlin Wall inevitably led to the collapse of the GDR. Among those who spoke at the demonstration on November 4 were party members like Markus Wolf, Gregor Gysi, and Günter Schabowski and writers like Christoph Hein, Christa Wolf, and Heiner Müller. On this day, the East German intelligentsia behaved like a collective of modern Emile Zolas. But these intellectuals resembled a Zola who cast his *J'Accuse* into the public arena after Captain Dreyfus had already been rehabilitated and inducted into the Legion of Honor by the authorities of the Third Republic. After November 9, intellectuals complained that anarchy and chaos should have been prevented. Such restraints might have enabled them to build up a "true" socialist regime in the East. The avant-garde turned out to be a group of latecomers. Not all were tarnished, however. The group of intellectuals cultivating the myth of the five *glorieuses* included members of the Socialist Unity Party who were honest proponents of a radically ascetic socialism, because they were young enough to have remained outside the corrupt party establishment. For these members of the artistic and literary intelligentsia, an inner-worldly socialism linked—as demonstrated in the outward appearance, rhetoric, and habitus of its believers—communist atheists with members of oppositional groups like the Neues Forum that had their stronghold in the Protestant Church.

To explain the role of the East German intelligentsia, one has to remember the way political change was brought about in the GDR. The first successful German revolution was a true and spontaneous *levée en masse*, supported by the very visible hand of Mikhail Gorbachev. It was neither the result of a long and open struggle against communist rule, like the fight of solidarity in Poland, nor the final triumph of twenty years of resistance, as in the underground of Prague, nor the outcome of shrewd piecemeal reform, as in Budapest. The East German workers' revolt of June 1953, crushed by Soviet tanks, had remained only an episode. The German November revolution in 1989 was neither led by a workers' union nor designed by intellectuals. Its heroes were hundreds and thousands of ordinary people who, with very mixed motives, seized the opportunity to leave a dictatorial regime by fleeing into the West German embassies of Prague and Budapest. Its heroes were thousands and hundreds of thousands who courageously took to the streets of Leipzig and of Dresden and of other cities in the East. Therefore it was only appropriate that the population of the GDR called Leipzig, where the street demonstrations had been especially risky but also most effective, *Heldenstadt*, "city of heroes."

In this peaceful revolution, the intellectuals were with the crowd, not of it. The heroes of this revolution were not intellectuals, with a few exceptions like Kurt Masur, the conductor of the Gewandhaus orchestra in Leipzig. In contrast to the velvet revolution in Czechoslovakia, artists and students were not spearheads of the German revolt. *Wir sind das Volk* (We are the people) was a most appropriate slogan indeed. It parodied the Marxist mottoes, and it was, at the same time, an illustration of Emile Zola's remark that a well-crafted sentence is already a political act. With their exit and their voice, ordinary people with admirable courage created the revolution in East Germany.[4]

Intellectuals liked the slogan "We are the people"—and misunderstood it completely. What they read into it was the wish to realize a socialist dream, while in truth the slogan expressed the people's farewell to any socialist utopia. This misunderstanding remained hidden from November 4 through November 9. During these five days it seemed as if ordinary people and intellectuals were speaking the same language. In December 1989, the slogan was slightly changed on the streets of Leipzig. The masses no longer chanted "We are the people" but "We are one people" (*Wir sind ein Volk*).[5] This minor change of just one word, however, revealed the true intentions of the crowd: what it wanted, above all, was to join the capitalist West. This alteration of one word eventually led to a break between the masses and those who had regarded themselves as their intellectual leaders, but who had been unable to read the public mood.

It was painful for intellectuals to recognize their error. They had misunderstood the semantics of the four magic words: *Wir sind ein Volk*. To make matters worse: intellectuals had failed on their own ground. They had neither misjudged a political power structure nor given too little attention to the economy: they had misunderstood the meaning of words. The failure of the East German intellectuals was neither the misfortune of amateur politicians nor the ignorance of would-be economists: it was the failure of the interpreting class. This failure turned into a disaster when a group of well-known artists, musicians and writers, with Stefan Heym as their leader, published a manifesto with the grand title *Für unser Land* (For our country). It was not only an appeal to preserve the cultural identity and the political sovereignty of the GDR vis-à-vis West Germany. It was at the same time a denunciation of the so-called consumerism of the vast majority of the inhabitants of East Germany who, for reasons of their personal well-being, were striving for an immediate unification of the two Germanys. Once again, the interpreting class failed on its home turf: having first not understood what people said, it subsequently misjudged what people wanted to hear. The copy-rights of authors who were propelled into politics quickly turned into copy-wrongs.[6]

The intellectual was not born in the times of Dreyfus; yet the social role of the intellectual and his important function in modern politics and modern art became an issue for public debate in the course of the "immortal affair," as Marcel Proust called it. The personal and collective significance for those who lived through it consisted above all in the necessity to make a choice. Looking back at the Dreyfus Affair, the seventy-year-old Julien Benda wrote that it had been a fortunate episode for the men of his generation. They were given the rare opportunity to make a clear-cut choice, at the threshold of life, between two fundamental ethics. Thus they were able to learn who they were. Intellectuals who remained in the GDR were living in a culture with blurred moral alternatives. This is one reason why the revolution in the GDR did not give rise to intellectual heroes.

After 1989 the intellectual climate and scholarly life in the former GDR became characterized by the high degree of illegitimacy of the former elite and by the conspicuous absence of alternatives. Scientists, writers, and artists alike tried to adjust as smoothly as possible to the new cultural context of a united Germany. They did so for economic as well as for intellectual reasons—considerably "helped" by West German arrogance and openly displayed feelings of Western superiority toward the East. The reunited Germany experienced another round of reeducation. Germany thus did not enjoy the invaluable advantage of having different elites compete for the shaping of public discourse in the same cultural context. As a result, a kind of spiritual *Anschluss* took place, whereby Eastern overadjustment and Western complacency complemented each other. Culture is about interpretation and making sense. In Germany, cultural elites, both in the West and in the East, had great difficulty making sense of reunification.

In his attack on German philosophical egotism, George Santayana wrote, "just as in pantheism God is naturalized into a cosmic force, so in German philosophy the Biblical piety of the earlier Protestants is secularized into social and patriotic zeal."[7] Political opposition in the GDR was, to a considerable extent, propelled by Protestant zeal. The Lutheran Church knew how to get along with the socialist state, but at the same time it was able to resist and to contradict the Socialist Party, often at great personal sacrifice for individual members. In this context, the vote of the opposition group Neues Forum was especially important. In this group, scientists like Jens Reich played a central role. Unfortunately, the admirable moral stance of the protestors never developed into a coherent and effective political strategy. What they were interested in, above all, was the strengthening of the individual soul, not the weakening of the authoritarian state. The moralization of politics led to a mentality of "all or nothing" that, in the end, desecrated for all time the concept of politics, at least in the sense of party politics, and the medium of exchange, compromise, that arguably is the most important political currency in a democracy.

I vividly recall a meeting of a group of former East German dissidents with Senator Edward Kennedy and Willy Brandt shortly after the fall of the Wall in Berlin. The German dissidents, stubborn and sticking to their principles, and the American senator, willing to listen and obviously trying to promote pragmatism, had nothing to say to each other. It was especially sad that Willy Brandt, the émigré, was not able to translate between the two "camps" and said almost nothing throughout the entire meeting. As it turned out much later, some participants in the meeting, for instance Ibrahim Boehme, the chairman of the newly founded East German Social Democratic Party (SDP), had worked as informants for the Stasi, the secret service of the GDR.

After the end of the Second World War, the confrontation of different political moralities, the coexistence of fellow travelers and refugees, of victims and perpetrators, of internal exiles and émigrés had created a cultural milieu full of creative tension in a defeated Germany, notably in the West. Nothing comparable happened after 1989. The moral alternatives confronting each other were murky. There were no real émigrés and only a few dissidents. Most important, perhaps, was another difference: though many of the émigrés who returned after 1945 nostalgically represented the best of Germany's cultural past, they were also carriers of new ideas, whereas the East German dissidents were molded by a milieu conspicuously lacking in cultural modernity. After 1945, pragmatism and a culture of compromise entered Germany for the first time. After 1989, idealism and inwardness were coming back. Even after the dissidents had won their freedom of political expression, their fundamental contempt for politics and the procedural intricacies of democracy remained: "We had hoped for justice, and all we got was the rule of the law," one of them, Bärbel Bohley, quipped. Most of the dissidents rejected the idea of forming a party, and when parties were formed, it happened with great inner resistance indeed.

As an unintended consequence, the antipolitics of the East German protest movement created a political vacuum that helped the resurgence of the Communist Party in the East, under a new name but with the old slogans. With few exceptions, East German dissident intellectuals remained without influence in the West, because they did not see compromise as a political value. One was reminded of Helmuth Plessner's 1924 characterization of the German spirit as one who "instead of closing the inner gap between being bound to ideals and being responsible to reality . . . constantly expands such a gap."[8] Culture, with "a voice as tender and as powerful as religion itself," claimed once again to be the better politics.[9] At the same time, the antipolitical attitude of dissidents from the East made it easier for the West to escape an evaluation of its own political routine. Exceptional political talents like Jens Reich and Richard Schröder, who had lived a courageous life in the former GDR, were thus refused access to well-deserved higher political office in a united Germany. The arrogance of the political establishment in the West kept them out.

When the first all-German parliament after reunification assembled in Berlin in 1994, the opening session was presided over by Stefan Heym, the oldest member of the Bundestag. Stefan Heym was a Jew whose family members had perished in the Nazi death camps, a communist who had become an American citizen, and—a writer. A writer as president of parliament was a symbol of the possible reunification of politics and culture in Germany. After only one year, the East German Stefan Heym resigned his seat in the Bundestag in protest.

9

Culture as Camouflage: The End of Central Europe

Europe: Dream and Bureaucracy

In the last speech he gave in Germany before he went, unknowingly, into exile, Thomas Mann insisted on the modernity of Richard Wagner's Germanness, which was "broken down and disintegrating, . . . decorative, analytical, intellectual; and hence its fascination, its inborn capacity for cosmopolitan, for world-wide effectiveness."[1] Before he composed the most German of all operas, *The Mastersingers of Nuremberg*, Wagner had already been a democrat and a European. His nationalism was steeped in European art; Germanness and Europeanism no longer excluded each other. Speaking about Wagner, Mann was also talking to himself. He had always wanted to be a great German and hence a great European writer. This ambition could no longer be fulfilled in his fatherland, where the Nazis had replaced the intellectual's dream of a European Germany with the dreadful reality of a German Europe. During the First World War, Thomas Mann had somewhat coquettishly painted himself as an unpolitical man; now, in the ominous year 1933, he quoted Wagner's sentence, "Whoever tries to get away from the political deceives himself," and called it a very un-German view indeed, yet one that would have to be adopted by the Germans in the future. In 1918 Thomas Mann had attacked his brother for his cosmopolitanism and outrageous ambition to be a German *homme de lettres*; thirteen years later, he called Heinrich Mann "a classical representative of the Germanic-Mediterranean artistic genius" and bade farewell to the isolationist tendencies of German culture. Europe would grow together and Germany would be a part of it. This prophecy has been fulfilled. The process of European integration—fueled, at the beginning, more by coal and steel than by culture and science—has reintroduced Germany into Europe.

Levis, argutus, inventor; versatile, shrewd, inventive—these were the characteristics a great European, the Swedish naturalist Carolus Linnaeus, used in the eighteenth century to describe what he regarded as the highest form of *homo sapiens*, the *homo europaeus*. Seen as an ideal type, the European was a scientist, a researcher, a scholar, an author— a man of culture rather than a man of politics. *Levis, argutus, inventor*— after the fall of communism in 1989, it seemed as if no one had come closer to the flattering description of Linnaeus than the cultural intelligentsia of Central and Eastern Europe.

A unified Europe was always a dream. As a dream it aroused an enthusiasm that could not possibly be evoked by the Brussels bureaucracy when the European Union eventually became a reality. In 1796 Edmund Burke had written that no European could be a complete exile in any part of Europe. He was right—not because Europe was a political reality, but because Europe was a politically extremely influential idea. After 1989, Burke's much-quoted sentence no longer served as an *idée directrice* in the countries of the Common Market, but was just a legal claim. Europe did not grow into a sacred union, as the historian Leopold von Ranke had once foreseen, but became the profit-oriented communal economy that a manager and politician, Walther Rathenau, had already predicted at the end of the First World War. The utopian European visions of authors like Romain Rolland and Hugo von Hofmannsthal, of Heinrich and Thomas Mann, seemed to be gone forever. To the dismay of many intellectuals in the West, the realization of the European dream turned into a process of disenchantment. One was reminded of William Butler Yeats: "In dreams begins responsibility."

After the First World War, Julien Benda, who had always urged the "clerks" to stay aloof from politics, complained that few intellectuals had fought for the League of Nations. Once it had become a full-fledged organization, however, the United Nations no longer needed intellectuals, but had to seek the services of loyal civil servants and able administrators. The fight for human rights must be a concern for intellectuals; the adjustment of the value-added tax is, as a rule, none of their business. Inevitably Brussels, the capital of the European Common Market, became the European symbol of bureaucracy. The Common Market featured the Europe of the expert, not the Europe of the intellectual. Intellectuals retaliated by blaming the failures and shortcomings of the European unification process on the minimal role that matters of culture had been given in this process. Over and over again, Jean Monnet, the visionary architect of the European Union, was quoted as saying that he would start with culture, and not with coal and steel, if he had to rethink the European Union. That Monnet had never said this gave his alleged quotation the monumentality and indisputable truth of an antique omen.

As far back as the eighteenth century, both Rousseau and Herder had written that there were no Germans and French anymore, but only Europeans. As a rule, their words were read as the joyous anticipation of a truly united Europe. In truth, Rousseau and Herder had asked a fearful question: might not Europe, in the process of its political and economic unification, lose its greatest asset, its cultural diversity? This fear remained especially alive across the Channel and among the smaller European nations, as I realized in 1989 in the Dutch city of Groningen. In a street, I saw a poster with a portrait and an inscription. The inscription read: "The United States of Europe? It was *his* idea!" The portrait was, unmistakably, that of Adolf Hitler. The ongoing process of European integration in the West was not regarded by all as the fulfillment of a dream that the intellectuals of the Continent had been dreaming for a long time. Not everyone had forgotten that even before the times of Hitler and Napoleon, the idea of a unified Europe often served purposes of expansion and colonization.

A Victory of Culture over Power

After the fall of communism, a truly united Europe seemed to become a viable political option for the near future. All of a sudden, the European idea regained its splendor and caused new excitement—at least for a moment, before economic fears and political animosities again got the upper hand. The new excitement was fueled in part by the fact that men of culture assumed political responsibilities in many countries of Central and Eastern Europe. One had to go back to the end of the nineteenth century and to the Dreyfus Affair to recover a constellation of public issues and private concerns in which intellectuals played a role similar to the one György Konrad, Václav Havel, Bronisław Geremek, Milan Kundera, and Czesław Miłosz were playing in Central and Eastern Europe. It seemed as if Tocqueville's prophecy had become reality: men of letters took charge in Europe.

One reason for the spiritual and political success of the dissident intellectuals was their rejection of the term "Eastern Europe" as a political or geographical label that had been attached to them from the outside. Using the notion of "Central Europe" (Mitteleuropa) instead, intellectuals were able to gradually turn a semantic opposition into a political fight. The vagueness of the term *Mitteleuropa*, which sounds like the name of a utopian novel, was therefore of considerable advantage.[2] It was much less the name of a geographical region than the abbreviation of a cultural vision. It was a political idea in constant need of interpretation. The never-ending necessity of this hermeneutical task explains why poets, essayists, novelists, artists, and historians were leading the spiritual and political opposition in countries like Poland, Hungary, and Czechoslovakia. Unlike in the GDR, it was the interpreting class of these countries that changed the course of history, at least for some time.

Central Europe consists of small nations. The change of hegemonic powers has been the only constant element in their history. This is one reason why irony and utopian thinking became such important features of the Central European mind. People had no choice: they had to believe in ideas and suspect reality. Novels and poetry were a part of everyday life. Visions and prophecies were not condemned as a flight from reality, because they were only utopias *ad interim*. They reflected a melancholic, yet in the end successful, desire to change the world. At the beginning of the nineteenth century, Fichte, in his utopia of the closed commercial state (*Der geschlossene Handelsstaat*), described the basic presumption of all totalitarian regimes: "As long as no one complains, it can be assumed that everything is taking its due course." Montesquieu, in contrast, surmised that freedom was absent from a state where the noise of quarrel and complaint could not be heard. Many intellectuals in Central Europe traveled a long road—from Fichte back to Montesquieu. Sacrificing careers and giving up opportunities, they created a culture of quarrel and complaint that finally became strong enough to overthrow the old regimes. Their fight for human rights, the classic ideal of the modern European intellectual, endowed intellectuals in Central and Eastern Europe with certain unalienable rights and with positions of political power that intellectuals in the West had not been able to acquire. Exceptions were countries like Spain, Portugal, and Greece, where the memory of dictatorship and military regimes remained alive for quite a while and influenced who gained political office.

Amos Elon has described how the revolutions in the East, and above all the Prague Autumn, led to a victory of culture over power: "The only meaningful opposition came from a handful of prominent writers, philosophers and jazz musicians—jazz was a form of protest in Czechoslovakia and was considered heresy—and from the young students to whom only culture gave a sense of a better life in a better world. In Czechoslovakia, where the struggle between reformation and counter-reformation had prevented the emergence of a national church, the world of culture had often been a breeding ground for liberal revolt—from the time of Magister Jan Hus down to the days of Professor Tomás Masaryk in this century. A great book could be written on how, in our time, the Havels, Seiferts, Kunderas, Kohouts, Hrabals, and Vaculíks were able to survive the age of darkness in a Czechoslovakia where Kafka was banned for years because his nightmares recalled everyday life. When all other points of moral reference were failing, culture alone—the novelists, playwrights, actors, philosophers, poets, filmmakers, artists, musicians—retained a measure of moral credibility, dignity, and ability to inspire the young. To think that it all started right under Kafka's window on Staromestké námesti (the Old Town Square)! The Prague Autumn of 1989 was a victory of culture over power."[3] It was, one might add, a wonderful example of how aesthetics, as if this were the most natural thing in the world, encapsulated morality.

The rapid transformation of cultural reputation into political influence became a common feature of the developments in Central and Eastern Europe after 1989. Many intellectuals were promoted to high political office. The basis for their promotion was less political experience or economic expertise than artistic sincerity and moral probity. Václav Havel, the playwright and president, was only the most conspicuous example. To their own surprise, Europeans applauded the return of a *persona*, an actor, who seemed to have disappeared altogether from the stage of world history: the modern hero. Carlyle's prophecy had come true: "I prophesy that the world will once more become *sincere*; a believing world: with *many* heroes in it, a heroic world!" In premodern times, the hero appeared on the stage of history as divinity and as prophet, as poet, priest, and king. One of the main forms of heroism for all future ages, however, was a product of modernity: the hero as man of letters. "Endeavouring to speak-forth the inspiration that was in him by Printed Books, and find place and subsistence by what the world would please to give him," the man of letters had to be regarded as "our most important modern person" indeed, wrote Carlyle.[4] In Poland, a worker, Lech Wałesa, and a union, Solidarity, were the key actors in overthrowing the communist regime—at the same time, however, it seemed as if writers whom the Poles had buried like kings, like Adam Mickiewicz and Julius Słowacki, had come back, bestowed with the honorary title of "seer."

Trying to explain why the heroic man of letters had such an enormous impact on the course of modern history, Carlyle asserted that the spiritual always determines the material—as if he were writing expressly to refute future Marxist views. Ironically enough, socialism was dealt its deadly blow not least with the help of the modern man of letters—who became a "hero" partly because his attitude was, as a rule, rather unheroic and full of self-doubt and irony. For Carlyle there was sacredness to be found in these true literary men; they were the light of the world, the world's modern priests. Coleridge's vision of the clerisy as a kind of worldly church, an *enclesia* that was opposed to the traditional *ecclesia*, belongs in the same context of argumentation as does Julien Benda's "treason of the intellectuals." Without using the word, Carlyle was already talking about the intellectual as the hero of the modern age.

The twentieth century had seen the decline of the intellectual. The treason that fascist and Stalinist intellectuals committed in the age of totalitarianism seemed to have destroyed the moral claim of this social actor forever. At the end of the century, however, one could realize, with the fall of the communist regimes in Eastern Europe, a rehabilitation of intellectuals. They made a heroic comeback to the political stage. Writing and democracy were, for an author like Thomas Carlyle, linked to each other—"Invent writing, Democracy is inevitable."[5] Literature was a spiritual parliament. In the twentieth century, artists and poets, essay-ists and novelists were instrumental in bringing parliamentary democ-racy to Central and Eastern Europe. As a consequence, one could imag-ine in Europe, after the fall of communism, the clash of two political cultures: on the side of the economic have-nots, intellectuals with high moral credit but without expertise; on the side of the economic haves, professionals with great expertise but without much moral concern. As Alexander Solzhenitsyn had done much earlier, notably in his famous speech at Harvard University in June 1978, politicians like Václav Havel and, above all, the Polish pope urged the nations of Central and Eastern Europe not to imitate the expert cultures of the West. Instead they should try to preserve their own, distinct cultures of freedom, where the public moralist would continue to play an essential role. In the case of John Paul II, this plea was accompanied by the wish for a Christian, if not altogether Catholic, *reconquista* of Europe. The clash between experts and moralists indeed took place—but it did not turn into an ongoing battle. It remained an episode.

In his testimony before the U.S. Senate Foreign Relations Commit-tee on January 17, 1989, where he underscored the need to design a new European security framework, George F. Kennan said: "First, and for the short term, I suggest that we should press for an internationally accepted and binding moratorium of at least three years' duration on basic changes in the two alliance structures—to give all of us time to prepare in a careful and deliberate manner and by wide international discussion and agreement, a new European security structure." An in-tellectual was speaking before the committee—and what he was asking for was only one thing: time for thinking. The rush of politics was threatening the true business of the intellectual. The indispensable lei-sure for the working of the theory class was becoming more and more jeopardized. Timeless thought had to give way to timely political advice. It seemed long ago that Julien Benda, the incarnation of the modern *clerc*, could call the noncurrent his true domain. He said so in a letter written to André Gide in 1941, when France was occupied by German troops. In the same year, François Mauriac signed a contract with his publisher, Flammarion, to write "quatre livres inactuels," four books without any actual relevance. For Benda, the remark in his letter to Gide was anything but casual. Avoiding being up-to-date was the main virtue of the intellectual, a virtue that had almost been destroyed in the Dreyfus Affair and its aftermath. The treason of the intellectuals consisted in their attempt to enter politics and thereby exert an influence on the issues of the day.

The events of 1989 created a unique moment: all of a sudden, the intellectual could assume political responsibilities and become a modern hero—yet he did not have to betray his genuine mission. Aesthetic convictions shaped political programs. Culture defeated power. But it was an episode only. The routinization of charisma took its toll, and many heroes, to adopt Werner Sombart's distinction, realized that they were in danger of disappearing from the political stage if they did not change into shopkeepers as quickly as possible. In the second round of free elections, the former communists returned to power almost everywhere in Central and Eastern Europe. The heroes who refused to become shopkeepers became marginalized. Public moralists turned into public servants. At the same time, the specter of the old and aggressive nation-state was haunting Europe again, anti-Semitism and xenophobia grew stronger, ethnic cleansings started, and then, unbelievably, a new European war broke out in the Balkans; Sarajevo again became a symbol of death and destruction. To accelerate the enlargement of Europe was seen as the only strategy to prevent the Continent from falling back into its usual strife and struggles.

Cultural policy played an ambivalent part in this process. This ambivalence had to do with the dilemma between a rhetoric that invited more countries of the Continent to join the European Union and the harsh economic reality that led the haves, who wanted to become the have-even-mores, to protect themselves against the have-nots. Readers of Franz Kafka, of whom there are quite a few in Central Europe, were reminded of one of his short, fragmentary texts that he left untitled: "We are five friends, one day we came out of a house one after the other, first one came and placed himself beside the gate, then the second came, or rather he glided through the gate like a little ball of quicksilver, and placed himself near the first one, then came the third, then the fourth, then the fifth. Finally we all stood in a row. People began to notice us, they pointed at us and said: Those five just came out of that house. Since then we have been living together; it would be a peaceful life if it weren't for a sixth one continually trying to interfere. He doesn't do us any harm, but he annoys us, and that is harm enough; why does he intrude where he is not wanted? We don't know him and don't want him to join us. There was a time, of course, when the five of us did not know one another, either; and it could be said that we still don't know one another, but what is possible and can be tolerated by the five of us is not possible and cannot be tolerated with this sixth one. In any case, we are five and don't want to be six. And what is the point of this continual being together anyhow? It is also pointless for the five of us, but here we are together and will remain together; a new combination, however, we do not want, just because of our experiences. But how is one to make all this clear to the sixth one? Long explanations would almost amount to accepting him in our circle, so we prefer not to explain and not to accept him. No matter how he pouts his lips we push him away with our elbows, but however much we push him away, back he comes."[6]

The rebels of Central and Eastern Europe had won their freedom and paid a price for it: almost overnight they became the poor relatives for whom the West now had to assume responsibility. It had been exciting for the spectators in the West to watch the revolutions in the East unfold; it became a nuisance for them to enter the long and bureaucratic procedures by which the new democracies would eventually be invited to join the European Union. Before 1989, poems, novels, and plays had to be read in order to understand what was going on behind the Iron Curtain. Now the some eighty thousand pages of a document called the *acquis communautaire*, which all prospective members of the European Union must abide by, would become required reading in East and West.[7]

Overemphasizing the role of culture became a strategy of the European Union to deal with its bad conscience. While the countries of Eastern Europe were still denied entrance into the Common Market, they were invited to join NATO and were, above all, commended for their cultural achievements. The military and cultural invitations had to make up for economic discrimination. Western cultural policy thus acquired a rather bad name in the East. It was seen as an escape and as a cheap excuse. Instructive in this context was the survival of the notion of "Central Europe" (Mitteleuropa) in Western discourse. "Central Europe" was a political idea hidden behind a cultural mask. Pursuing an ideal with this name was of great political significance—until 1989. After the fall of communism, however, it lost its function and its appeal. Politics no longer needed cultural camouflage. When the rhetoric of "Central Europe" was resuscitated in the West, it was used as a trick: cultural benevolence had to provide cover for political indolence.

Among the first to develop the utopian vision of a unified "Central Europe" was Friedrich Naumann, whose book *Mitteleuropa* had been published in 1915, in the midst of the First World War. He was convinced that "economic considerations, however serious they may be, will not of themselves suffice to arouse the necessary enthusiasm" for the idea of Central Europe. For its realization it also needed "thinkers and poets." Yet Naumann was never in danger of substituting culture for politics. His basic aim was "to make of 'Central Europe' a largely self-sufficing and an effectively united economic idea." When, after the founding of the European Union, this utopian economic vision was no longer a viable option, the reduction of "Central Europe" to a cultural label became even more pointless and politically dangerous.[8]

With the enlargement of the European Union, the clash between culture and politics seems to be over. Yet one should hesitate to accept this happy judgment all too quickly. The history of the past decades has taught us how difficult it is to distinguish between epochs and episodes, between deep historical change and mere hiccups of history. It was not a European cultural hero but an American politician who made the best prediction of what would happen in Central and Eastern Europe after 1989. Vice President Dan Quayle, whose linguistic blunder proved to be more correct than most of the carefully crafted blueprints of experts on foreign policy, pronounced that the "recent developments in Central and Eastern Europe are irreversible," adding, "but this may change any minute."

Irony and Politics: Cultural Patriotism in Europe and the United States

An American Patriot from Europe

Thomas Mann not only wished to become an American citizen, he also wanted to be seen as an American patriot. This, however, was easier said than done. In September 1941 Mann had distanced himself from an old-fashioned American patriotism whose motto "America first" reminded him of the fateful *Deutschland, Deutschland über alles*. He was reacting against the National Committee of America First that also called itself "the party of non-intervention" and had been founded in 1940 in Chicago by General Robert Wood, the chairman of Sears Roebuck. The committee claimed some eighty thousand members—among them Henry Ford, Henry Cabot Lodge, and Charles Lindbergh—the "real" Lindbergh, as one must specify after Philip Roth published his novel *The Plot against America* in 2004. Retreating to a cheap and irresponsible isolationism, charged Thomas Mann, the United States would disclaim its most noble ideals. Three months later came Pearl Harbor, the United States entered the Second World War, the National Committee of America First was dissolved, and Thomas Mann no longer had to worry about an old-fashioned, isolation-prone American patriotism.

Mann's restored confidence became apparent in a letter Thomas Mann wrote to his friend Agnes Meyer shortly before dinner guests arrived on Christmas Eve 1942 in his home in Pacific Palisades. Mann wished her well and thanked her for all she had done for him in a country that was his home now and yet would remain forever foreign to him. He praised Meyer for her enthusiastic, matter-of-fact patriotism; in the meantime, he had become an American patriot of sorts himself. In a speech written for the Nobel Prize dinner in New York on December 10, which his daughter Erika read aloud because he could not be present in person, he expressed his wish that the world would rather sooner than later become "Americanized"—"in a certain fundamental moral sense," he added—and that "the Peace of Washington" would prevail. As an antidote to the moral confusion that had driven the nations of the old continent over the brink to disaster, nothing would be more salutary than a worldwide victory of the clear rules of moral conduct upon which the founding fathers had built the Union.

These words, as befitted a European, were spoken with a touch of irony, as Mann made clear. His irony, though, was lost on another Nobel Prize laureate and speaker at the dinner. Pearl Buck reacted to his speech, in the eyes of the perplexed Mann, more like a Chinese than like an American patriot. She was shocked by the word "Americanization" and predicted that it would be misused as a linguistic shield for an American imperialism that pursued not just economic but also political goals, notably in Asia. An editorial in the *New York Times* confronted Mann's and Buck's differing views. Mann declined an invitation to repeat what he had said in an article to be entitled "The Americanization of the World." When the editors of the *New York Times* felt insulted by his refusal, Mann got angry. Why was he asked to defend a term like "Americanization" that he had been careless enough to use in a public speech? Why did he have to get involved in politics at all? In another letter to Agnes Meyer, he wrote how much he longed for peace and the restitution of nice monarchies and Catholic, semifascist regimes all over Europe as dreamed about by the State Department. Thinking of Buck's reaction, Mann added: "I fear that you might take seriously what I just said."[1] Irony seemed to be a European good that did not travel easily.

Not least due to his admiration for Franklin D. Roosevelt, Thomas Mann had become an American citizen and an American patriot. Yet his feelings for the United States remained ambivalent. He had never given up the idea of returning to Europe after the end of the war. When a German friend wrote to him in 1951 that he was eager to leave the Continent, where the rearmament of Germany was well under way, Mann voiced sympathy for his wish—but spoke of his own longing to come back to Europe. This crossover of pro- and anti-American sentiments was the perfect illustration of the anecdote Mann loved to tell: two immigrants meet in the midst of the Atlantic, one of them sailing to Europe, the other to America, both shouting at each other the same question: "Are you crazy?" To return to Germany was out of the question. Political correctness would have required him to take up residence in England—but to live in a country with not only a bad climate but also bad food was *un poco troppo*, as Mann remarked. In June 1952 Katia and Thomas Mann left the United States, a "land of gangsters" and an "air-conditioned nightmare," as he called it all of a sudden, for good and settled in Switzerland.

In 1953 the French magazine with the telling title *Comprendre* (To understand) asked Mann to explain why he had returned to Europe. He began his reply, published under the title "Retour d'Amérique" (Return from America), with warm words of gratitude for the country that had welcomed the refugee from Hitler's Germany, offered him its citizenship, and always honored his literary work. And yet, Mann wrote, the longer he lived in America, the more he felt that he was a European and had to return there, even in old age, whenever this would be possible again. And so he once more changed the basis of his life. He was seventy-eight years old. Politics had forced him to leave Germany, and therefore Europe, in 1933; politics caused him to leave America in 1952. America's rise to unprecedented power was worrisome. He was scared by Europe's military pact with the United States. McCarthyism also took its toll. Although anticipating McCarthy's fall from grace that announced itself in 1953 and happened a year later, the refugee from Nazi Germany felt inhibited by an atmosphere of censorship and denunciation. A misleading semantics allowed aggressive conformism to hide behind the overused and therefore abused word "loyalty." Scholarship and research were in jeopardy. Thomas Mann, who had defended the composer Hanns Eisler before a congressional investigation, feared he might be hunted as a fellow traveler before long. He bitterly remarked that an essay about the use of the semicolon in Schopenhauer's philosophy was the utmost one could still dare to publish. For him, freedom was doomed to perish in the Land of the Free. Europe, not America, was home to the idea of freedom—and freedom, Mann was convinced, would be better preserved by courageous self-restraint than by military force. He dreamed of Europe as a third power, a mediator in the upcoming fight between America and the Soviet Union, between capitalism and communism.[2]

Thomas Mann's postemigration skepticism toward the United States came as a surprise for many, but not for all. In 1942 Reinhold Niebuhr, the American theologian of German origin, published a review of *Order of the Day*, the collection of Mann's "political essays and speeches of two decades" that contained the expurgated version of the 1922 speech in defense of the German Republic. Niebuhr, his praise notwithstanding, called the political essays a "handsome penance" for the author's earlier indifference to politics. He expressed an almost prophetic lack of confidence in the emphasis with which Thomas Mann had paired Novalis and Walt Whitman in his attempt to win German youth over to the cause of democracy: "What would have become of democracy in the non-German world," Niebuhr asked, "if only Rousseau and not [also] John Locke had informed our tradition? It is significant that even after Mann espouses democracy he makes much of the similarity between the thought of the German romantic, Novalis, and our own romantic, Walt Whitman. Rousseau, Novalis, and Whitman may persuade us to love the people en masse, but more is required to save the people from themselves and each other."[3] Niebuhr, the theologian, mistrusted Mann's democratic conversion. He spoke of Mann's tragic inability to cut his ties with German romanticism, which had been an inspiration for Nazi ideology. Somewhat surprisingly, Thomas Mann, not given to great tolerance when criticized, found the review "unusually beautiful and intelligent." But he had not been tragically unable to separate himself from German romanticism—he had been deliberately unwilling to do so.

Thomas Mann, the American citizen, not only accepted but even supported European criticism of American politics. Yet he rejected the view—shared, among others, by Theodor Adorno—that capitalist America was heading toward a fascist society. The foundations of American democracy were unshaken; it was ludicrous to compare a country, whose sacrifice had made Hitler's defeat possible, to Nazi Germany. Still, politics was not the field where the United States could be thoroughly defended. Mann, the newborn European, delivered a eulogy on American culture instead. America's big cities were home to magnificent art collections; Boston, New York, and Philadelphia had the best orchestras in the world; American radio stations ensured that classical and modern music could be listened to each evening and everywhere; lecture halls were filled not by hundreds only, as in Europe, but by thousands; the social novel had reached new heights in America; and the elegance and sensibility of American literary criticism often measured up to the French. Yet American culture was not for the elite only—a large public was served by it as well, not least in institutions like the museum of natural history in Chicago, which Mann never failed to visit whenever he was in town.

After the First World War, American democracy, as seen by an American romantic, had helped Thomas Mann to praise the German Republic; after the Second World War, the German, romantic view of culture helped him to compensate for his critique of American politics. In the end, what Thomas Mann was left with to admire in the United States was not so much the country's democratic traditions and institutions as its orchestras and libraries, its literature, its criticism, and its museums. The Met that (almost) never closed: culture.[4]

Hamlet and Fortinbras

In 1949 Oxford University invited Thomas Mann to speak on the occasion of the two hundredth anniversary of Goethe's birth. Mann accepted and delivered his speech not only at Oxford but also in the United States and in various European countries, Germany among them, as we have seen. The prelude was his talk "Goethe and Democracy," which he gave on May 2, 1949, at the Library of Congress. It was also a speech on Europe and America as representations of two different political temperaments. The United States had always fascinated Goethe, for whom the American War of Independence had been a "relief for humanity." More than once, he speculated on what would have become of him, had he not known Kant and the whole ballast of European history and culture and had sailed to America as a young man. Goethe called the United States a wonderful country, whose spiritual and economic growth knew no limits. At the end of his life, he wished for nothing more than to be able to follow the exciting developments in the New World. Yet he knew that he would not live long enough to rejoice, for instance, at the opening of the Panama Canal, a project with great consequences for the civilized as well as for the "uncivilized" world.

In Goethe's novel *Wilhelm Meister's Travels*, America was hailed as the antidote to European misery. In verses dedicated "To the United States," Goethe envied America not only for its lack of ruined castles but also for the absence of useless memories and fruitless brooding over its own identity that haunted Europe. It was a distinctly German mind-set that Goethe applied to the whole of Europe. Thomas Mann, writing two hundred years later, said as much: Europe suffered from a chronic illness, a self-inflicted headache. The Europeans were constantly thinking: What did it mean to be a European? Where did Europe come from? Where was it heading and where did it end? Pondering these unanswerable questions made Europe unfit for political action, while American influence in the world grew stronger and stronger. Goethe was the principal witness for anyone who believed that Europe, for its rejuvenation, would have to look to America.

Far from being a short-lived intellectual caprice, Goethe's enthusiasm for the United States was grounded in firm political beliefs that one would not have expected from a minister at the Weimar court. To appreciate this enthusiasm, Mann wrote, one had to understand that Goethe's maxim "to make a success of things," which sounded American, was the expression of a democratic pragmatism that was born more out of common sense than out of ideology. Somewhat surprisingly, Mann asserted that a democratic Europe could count on Goethe, who had understood the global consequences of America's fight for freedom. Eventually this fight would lead to the worldwide victory of democracy. The democratic ideal was the bond that tied the Old Continent and the New World together. Thus the "West" was born.

Yet political and cultural differences between America and Europe would not completely disappear, Mann said. A total amalgamation was even more unlikely since Europe and America represented two different political temperaments. At the time of the First World War, Paul Valéry had already spoken of Europe as Hamlet's continent. Thomas Mann went even further: "The future belongs to the man of the day, whose mind and 'common sense' are directed toward the nearest, most useful matters; it belongs to him whose energy is not tainted by the pallor of thought. Not only Germany, all of Europe is Hamlet, and Fortinbras is America."[5] Hamlet, the Danish prince, is the doubter and brooder who fails to act when it is necessary and therefore is later forced to commit deeds that make bad things worse. Fortinbras, the young son of the Norwegian king, however, is not at all tainted by the "pallor of thought." He acts forcefully and swiftly, convinced that perhaps not always the law, but certainly the law of the strongest, will be on his side. It was Jacques Delors who took up the Hamlet metaphor when he complained about the European *repli sur soi*, the constant brooding and hesitation that prevented the European Union from becoming a forceful actor on the stage of world politics. America did not run the danger of slipping into the role of Hamlet; Europe, though, desperately needed to learn how to act like Fortinbras.

In 1992 Patrick Buchanan ran a surprisingly strong campaign in the Republican presidential primaries with an explicitly anti-imperialist platform whose motto was also the title of a book: *A Republic, Not an Empire*. In this book, Buchanan called the United States of America the Fortinbras who, in the end, always had to intervene in European and Asian family feuds while other nations, cowardly, preferred to play Hamlet. Although a Buchananite foreign policy did not prevail, it became part of the self-understanding of many American and also a few European politicians to identify America with Fortinbras and Europe with Hamlet. At the end of Shakespeare's *Hamlet*, Fortinbras declares: "I have some rights of memory in this kingdom, / Which now to claim my vantage does invite me." Interestingly, the word "memory" is lacking in Schlegel and Tieck's German translation of this scene: "Ich habe alte Recht' an dieses Reich, / Die anzusprechen mich mein Vorteil heißt." It is not possible, however, to understand American politics without seeing how much those politics, as far as they are directed toward Europe, are a politics of memory. Americans have not forgotten—and are eager to remind their friends and allies—how often they had to come to the help of Europe in the twentieth century. America is not least Fortinbras because Europe is still Hamlet.

Confronting America = Fortinbras with Europe = Hamlet easily led to the temptation to confront, somewhat simplistically, politics and culture as the realm of action and the realm of thought, respectively. At the end of *Wilhelm Meister's Travels*, the novel in which America was praised as the antidote to European misery, Goethe, as if to remind himself of his spiritual origins, comes to a forceful defense of European culture, this "priceless culture that, for several thousand years arose, grew, spread, was suppressed, oppressed, never quite extinguished, re-vivified, revitalized, continues to emerge in never ending activity."[6] Being able to admire America and remaining proud of Europe were signs of unmatched spiritual independence and great personal freedom. Thomas Mann, so often a wanderer in Goethe's footsteps, showed a similar independence when he refused to join the chorus of Europeans who looked with condescension at what they ridiculed as "so-called American culture." Neither Goethe nor Mann succumbed to a cultural patriotism that tried to elevate Europe at the expense of America.

After the shock of September 11, 2001, it seemed for a moment as if the differences between an American and a European view of the world were disappearing and as if, under the same threat, the West would be reborn. In December 2001 Don DeLillo published an essay in *Harper's Magazine* with the title "In the Ruins of the Future." The essay was an attempt to come to terms with the shock of 9/11—by admitting that such a coming to terms was impossible. DeLillo insisted that neither modernity nor the West had been the terrorists' target. The target had been America: "It is America that drew their fury. It is the high gloss of our modernity. It is the thrust of our technology. It is our perceived godlessness. It is the blunt force of our foreign policy. It is the power of American culture to penetrate every wall, home, life, and mind."[7] Most democratic nations, however, insisted on having been attacked together with the United States. If 9/11 was an attack on America, then the West was nothing but America. *Nous sommes tous des Américains*, as the French newspaper *Le Monde* famously headlined. The attacks of 9/11 were an attack on Western civilization.

This claim did not survive the decision of the Bush administration to wage a "War against Terror" and, allegedly as a part of this war, to invade Iraq. With the unfolding of the invasion, American-European differences of judgment and opinion were once more portrayed, on both sides of the Atlantic, as a clash of civilizations. This clash made Europeans who became fierce critics of the United States almost forget that the first European Union had been founded, two hundred years ago, across the Atlantic, in America. At the same time Americans were asked by members of the Bush administration to distance themselves from their European heritage. It remained obvious, though, that America, to a considerable degree, was still Europe in disguise—and vice versa. The missionary faith of Americans in the superiority of their civilization is old. Faced with the question of whether their own values should be imposed on others by force or implanted in them by persuasion, the early American settlers opted for what they called a "new diplomacy" that would distinguish itself from the bellicose policies of the European monarchs. While still serving as secretary of state under President James Monroe, John Quincy Adams, the future president, spoke on the Fourth of July in 1821: "[The true America] goes not abroad in search of monsters to destroy. . . . She well knows that by once enlisting under other banners than her own, were they even the banners of foreign independence, she would involve herself, beyond the powers of extrication, in all the wars of interest and intrigue, of individual avarice, envy, and ambition which assume the colors and usurp the standard of freedom . . . She might [then] become the dictatress of the world; she would no longer be the ruler of her own spirit." That civic persuasion had to reign over military force was an early American creed.[8]

At the same time it was not the Americans, but the French who first came to the conclusion that progress, liberty, and civilization must, if necessary, be implemented with force at home and abroad. After 1792, a missionary fury took hold of the French revolutionaries, who were willing to fight beyond their borders not just to defend themselves but to spread civilization and republican ideals. In *The Closing of the American Mind*, Allan Bloom had written "when we Americans speak seriously about politics, we mean that our principles of freedom and equality and the rights based on them are rational and everywhere applicable" and concluded that it was only legitimate "to force those who did not accept these principles to do so."[9] But the idea that the world, in the long run, will be secure and stable only when democracy and human rights have been exported everywhere, if necessary by force, is a genuinely French idea and one that did not fail to influence American politics.

During the debates over a possible invasion of Iraq, a curious crossover could be observed in the meetings of the Security Council at the United Nations. The Americans were fuming over the French unwillingness to give up diplomacy too early—a position reminiscent of the policies of the first Americans and their soft diplomacy of persuasion.

The French, in contrast, were repudiating the American attempt to spread liberty and civilization by force—a truly French idea that any government in Paris would like to pursue even today, if only Saint-Just or Napoleon were still around. When France and the United States attacked each other, they were striking at their own past. With this retrospective insight, fights between the United States and "Old Europe"—aggravated on the one side by the undiplomatic clumsiness of American politicians like Dick Cheney and Donald Rumsfeld and on the other by the illusionary power dreams of European statesmen like France's President Jacques Chirac—often resembled more a soap opera than a genuine political conflict.

European Pygmies and the American Giant

In the political and cultural clash with the United States, Europeans were reminded of a powerful weapon: irony. In the debates over the necessity and justification of the war against Iraq, the term "pygmies" entered the political vocabulary. American officials first called France and Germany "moral pygmies"—as a punishment for their cowardice. Then by extension all Europeans, with the exception of the British and the mighty Spanish and Poles, were called "pygmies" across the Atlantic—whereupon Lord Robertson, secretary-general of NATO, dutifully promised a dramatic increase in European defense spending so that nobody would speak of the Europeans as "military pygmies" anymore. Europeans were indebted to an American author, Robert Kagan, for drawing their attention, though inadvertently perhaps, to an early use of the term "pygmies" in political-philosophical discourse. In his much-quoted book *Of Paradise and Power*, Kagan poked fun at the Europeans, who allegedly came from Venus, whereas the Americans had descended from Mars. This distinction was simplistic, but useful in a sense Kagan had perhaps not anticipated. The polemic split he posited between the Hobbesian world of the Americans, a world of eternal war and conflict, and the Kantian world of the Europeans, a world of perpetual peace, made a rereading of Hobbes and Kant mandatory for Kagan's more skeptical observers, notably Europeans.

As had been known before to some and as it turned out for many after the reading, Kant's tract on perpetual peace was anything but a starry-eyed vision of paradise. It was almost the contrary, an early and powerful plea for *Realpolitik* and its limits. There was much more skepticism in Kant than Kagan had ever dreamed of. "Perpetual Peace," to begin with, was a deeply ironic title, taken from the "satirical inscription on a Dutch innkeeper's sign upon which a burial ground was painted." Perpetual peace was for the dead, not for the living. It was a regulative idea, not an idealist misconception of harsh reality. In Kant's view, the boundless hope that we might place in the unfolding of history finds its limits in humanity, the crooked timber, out of which no straight thing can ever be made. In times of war, Immanuel Kant was asked by his publisher to update one of his popular essays, "Idea for a Universal History from a Cosmopolitan Point of View." The philosopher flatly refused. When the world powers were raging, Kant wrote to his publisher, it was much better for "the pygmies" to keep quiet and not try to meddle in the business of the mightiest powers in the world. As Robert Burton, author of the *Anatomy of Melancholy*, had written in the seventeenth century, "pygmies placed on the shoulders of giants see more than the giants themselves." A Europe that did not sever its ties with the United States could be a farseeing dwarf on the shoulders of the American giant. Irony, not cynicism or *Schadenfreude*, could legitimately be used as a weapon against political hubris and economic aggression. The Europeans had to be indebted to an American author for having unearthed, in Kant, a master of "political irony."

The Irony of American History

Finding a master of political irony in Kant had been Thomas Mann's comfort when he was about to finish the *Reflections of a Nonpolitical Man* and came to realize that it would not be possible much longer to stick to an anti-European, nondemocratic posture like the one he had assumed throughout the First World War and throughout the writing of his book. There were other ironists, Adam Müller, Friedrich Gentz, Heine, Nietzsche, and Ibsen among them, but there was above all Kant: "Irony. It is possible that I see it where other people do not see it; but it just seems to me that one cannot grasp this concept comprehensively enough, that it should never be taken too ethically and too politically.

When Kant, after a terrible and only too successful epistemological campaign, reintroduced everything again under the name of 'Postulates of *Practical* Reason', and made possible again what he had just critically crushed . . . , then I see political irony in this."[10] Another example of political irony was given by Adam Müller, who defined politics or state-craft, in contrast to justice, as a principle "that teaches us 'to be some-what indulgent' in the administration of positive-historical and absolute justice, to reconcile it with conscience, common sense, the present and the future, and with utility."

Given Mann's somewhat melancholic delight in political irony, it was perhaps no coincidence that an American author of German origin, impressed by Mann's ability to produce "a perfect piece of irony," Rein-hold Niebuhr, later wrote a book with the title *The Irony of American History*.[11] The irony of American history was caused by the necessity for the greatest power in the world to use power in global terms: "Our idealists are divided between those who would renounce the responsibil-ities of power for the sake of preserving the purity of our soul and those who are ready to cover every ambiguity of good and evil in our actions by the frantic insistence that any measure taken in a good cause must be unequivocally virtuous."[12] It was the predicament of American his-tory and, consequentially, also of American politics to be torn between too-easy escape from responsibility and too-great confidence in its own virtue. Reading Niebuhr's book, published in 1952, today makes one immediately understand why it could be called the best book on the war against terror and the second Iraq war. More than fifty years ago, Niebuhr quoted a European statesman as saying that "American power in the service of American idealism could create a situation in which we would be too impotent to correct you when you are wrong and you would be too idealistic to correct yourself." To avoid the danger of over-estimating the purity of one's own wisdom one had to understand "the ironic tendency of virtues to turn into vices when too complacently relied upon."[13]

The American-European clash was not confined to the political sphere or to the current administrations on both sides of the Atlantic. It did not leave the realm of culture untouched or unharmed. Two book reviews, written in November and December 2003, can be read as signs of a cultural divide between America and Europe that runs deeper than disagreements between "Old Europe" and the New World about the future of NATO or the role of the UN. They reflect George Steiner's sad and devastating statement that "the isolation, the hounding, the social and political humiliation of the Jew has been integral to the Christian presence, which has been axiomatic, in Europe's grandeur and abjection."[14]

In November 2003, Cynthia Ozick wrote a review of John Updike's *Early Stories* for the *New York Times Book Review*. In Updike's novel *Rabbit Is Rich*, Harry Angstrom called the United States "the happiest fucking country the world has ever seen," and in one of his 1972 stories Updike characterized America as "a vast conspiracy to make you happy." Sentences like these led Ozick to write: "It may be that the absence of a brooding and burdensome history in these stories accounts for the luxuriance of their lyrical andantes. Here are lives essentially tranquil, unhurried by turmoil and threat beyond the extrusions of plaintively aspiring passions. There may be local and topical distractions, but by and large Updike's scenes and characters express a propitious America, mottled only by metaphysical ruminations." This unabashed pursuit of happiness, though it did not always indeed result in happiness, at least not for Updike's characters, acquired dignity and moral power by distancing itself from European doubts and self-inflicted uneasiness: "If, as Adorno tells us, there can be no poetry after Auschwitz, possibly the converse is true: poetry belongs to the trustful calm that is the negation of Auschwitz—and that, at its bountiful heart, is Updike's witty and incandescent America." Only by looking at what had happened in Europe could Updike's America appear as a "mostly untrammeled land."[15]

In December of the same year, Martin Amis paid tribute to Saul Bellow when a collection of Bellow's novels was published in the Library of America and a Fiftieth Anniversary Edition of *Augie March* came out from Viking at the same time. For Amis, Saul Bellow's preeminence did not rest on sales figures and honorary degrees, not on rosettes and sashes, but on incontestable legitimacy. "Compared with him, the rest of us are only fitfully sentient," Amis wrote. He saw only two writers in a position strong enough to rival Bellow: Philip Roth and John Updike. In words strikingly similar to the description Cynthia Ozick gave of John Updike's work, Amis reminded his readers that Saul Bellow had once called the United States "the land of historical redress." This characteristic also acquired its moral weight through a comparison with Europe. With "cold simplicity," Bellow spoke of America as a place where "the Jews could not be put to death."[16]

Philip Roth challenged Bellow's "cold simplicity" with his novel *The Plot against America*.[17] Reminiscent of Sinclair Lewis's novel *It Can't Happen Here*, written two years after Hitler had come to power in Germany, Philip Roth seemed to ask: "Could it have happened here?" by imagining an anti-Semitic Charles Lindbergh defeating Roosevelt in the 1940 election and becoming president of the United States. *The Plot against America* must be read as the first true post–9/11 novel. Unlike Bellow and Updike, Philip Roth no longer looked back at "Europe's grandeur and abjection" to take America's goodness for granted. The tone of "fear, perpetual fear" in which the novel is written reflects uneasiness about itself that America has to live with after the fall of the Twin Towers. Throughout most of the novel, Roth, with his mastery of the craft of writing and his trust in storytelling, is able to demonstrate that the counternarrative that seemed to have become impossible after 9/11 can still be told.[18] At the end, however, the compelling force of the narrative fades away and history must come to the author's rescue. After Pearl Harbor, Roosevelt returns to Washington, and the specter of a fascist America under Lindbergh disappears. The future may be uncertain, but history can be trusted. It did *not* happen here. America is still the place where "the Jews could not be put to death." In the end, though with considerable self-doubt, Philip Roth joins Saul Bellow and John Updike in a writer's pride that seems, in an unintentional yet forceful way, to give America's will to power a hidden and forceful legitimacy.

11

Germany after Reunification: In Search of a Moral Masterpiece

Culture and Realpolitik

Among the first German professors who were ousted from their university chairs in 1933 was the economist Wilhelm Röpke, who had uncompromisingly opposed the Nazi regime. He first emigrated to Istanbul and then, in 1937, to Geneva. In 1945 Röpke addressed the question of how Germany could be admitted again to the community of nations after the crimes of the Nazi regime. In his book *Die deutsche Frage* (The German question) he outlined four conditions: Germany would have to renounce its Prussian heritage, join the West, become a federal state—and remain divided. In the nineteenth century, the Spanish thinker Donoso Cortés had called the prospect of a unified Germany an idea that was equally condemned by reason and by history—*una idea condemnada justamente per la razon y per la historia*. After Auschwitz, his verdict sounded like a prophecy.

By fiat of the Allies, Prussia ceased to exist in 1947; two years later the Federal Republic was founded and not only joined the West but became, together with France, the driving force toward the unification of the Continent. Germany, however, remained divided. Röpke's four conditions were fulfilled. In the German body politic, two wounds remained open: the indelible remembrance of Auschwitz and the prospect of unending partition. German politics had to live with these two wounds and was quite successful at it. To see the partition of Germany as penance became part of the political consensus in the Federal Republic. Konrad Adenauer, a Rhenish Catholic, insisted on penance, that is, *Wiedergutmachung*, instead of mere repentance. Deeds mattered more than thought. At the beginning of the sixties, Adenauer and David Ben-Gurion agreed upon large-scale reparations for victims of the Holocaust and their families. Later, diplomatic relations between the Jewish state, Israel, and the Federal Republic were established. Seeking to repair the unrepairable, Germans could see all this as a decisive step toward regaining a good conscience, as the term *Wiedergutmachung* made clear. At the same time, the partition of Germany had apparent advantages: the Federal Republic profited first from the Marshall Plan and then from the swift gliding into the economic and political union that was developing between the democratic European nations. The partition of Germany was seen as a punishment for the Holocaust, but it was a punishment to be endured more and more easily. Lamenting the divided country became a routine in West German political rhetoric. Reunification seemed impossible—at least in the foreseeable future.

In their "inability to mourn," most Germans, after 1945, wanted above all to rebuild their cities and to return to a normal life.[1] In the Federal Republic, normality meant to become part of the political and the economic West, that is, to join NATO and the European Community that began to take shape. West Germans were forced into a cosmopolitanism they accepted ever more eagerly as the economic recovery of their country made dramatic progress. The economic miracle (*Wirtschaftswunder*), whose architect was Ludwig Erhard, minister for economic affairs and father of the "social market economy" (*Soziale Marktwirtschaft*), became a prerequisite for the political miracle: the Federal Republic quickly achieved a stability that the Weimar Republic had never been able to enjoy. This security also meant that the clash between high, often lofty cultural aspirations and the necessities and compromises of daily *Realpolitik*, which had been a constant feature of German public discourse in the past, became less and less vivid.

Harmony between politics and culture, however, did not reign supreme. In Adenauer's Germany—Thomas Mann's "cultural desert"— both the chancellor and Ludwig Erhard were attacked by the literary intelligentsia and vigorously hit back, Erhard by infamously calling left-wing intellectuals "pinschers," unsympathetic small dogs. Peter Weiss turned his dramatization of the Auschwitz trial in Frankfurt into a reckoning with fellow travelers of the Nazi regime who had joined the ranks of the German political establishment again. The revelations of the author Rolf Hochhuth caused the Christian Democrat Hans Filbinger to resign as premier of Baden-Württemberg, because, as a Third Reich naval judge, he took part in trials of deserters who were sentenced to death in the last days of the Second World War. The year 1968 saw a coalition between rebelling students and writers and artists that not only tried to undermine the capitalist basis of the country's economy but also attempted to delegitimize the existing parliamentary system. All this was exciting or alarming, depending on one's own political standpoint—but it was normal in the sense that developments in West Germany did not differ from those in other Western countries.

Culture did not play a bigger role in West German politics than in any other Western democracy. No other text better illustrates the normalization in the relationship between German culture and politics than the *Diary of a Snail* by Günter Grass, published in 1972. In it, Grass looked back at the 1969 election campaign, which brought the Social Democrats to power for the first time, under the leadership of Willy Brandt. Grass gave almost one hundred speeches in support of the Social Democrats and Brandt. Absorbed by the daily chores of a campaign that made him travel all over the Republic, Grass showed a political attitude that hitherto had been unknown in Germany: the writer or poet no longer claimed the grave role of a seer or prophet who delivered the truth to the world of politics. Rather, the writer-citizen showed pride and pleasure in acting as a political worker and handyman. He just wanted to be "a little quicker than the snail," suggested the party use as its campaign flower light-gray skepticism, "which blooms all year round," and said a main purpose of his grass-roots engagement was "to pull the weeds of German idealism, which spring up again as inexorably as rib grass."[2] Looking back at the Prussian wars of liberation, the historian Friedrich Meinecke had once spoken of the spirit that "descended" to politics. Now the spirit did not have to descend to politics but could join it easily, since Willy Brandt the émigré was able to combine political realism with the grand moral gesture, unforgettably in his genuflection in 1970 at the memorial to the Warsaw ghetto. Once the grand gesture had become part of democratic politics, writers and artists could work for democracy in a sober and matter-of-fact way. Culture was no longer a penthouse from which the basement of everyday politics was looked upon with a certain disdain and arrogance.

Solving Political Problems in the Field of Culture

The partition of Germany had been seen as the price for the unforgettable and unpardonable crimes of the Nazi era. The theological undertones of this view were obvious. After the Holocaust, merely considering German unity a viable political option had to be regarded as nothing less than a revolt against divine justice. In the framework of this "political theology," crime and punishment, penance, and predestination all had a role to play. The "economic miracle," however, was always put in quotation marks; it was the secular compensation for the true miracle, the miracle of political unification that was unlikely to happen in the foreseeable future. When the two Germanys were reunited, the incredible revision of German partition came to be regarded as an instance of divine grace. In a political-theological context, reunification was almost unanimously described as a true "miracle" indeed.

Yet there remained an unbeliever, a lone voice that spoke out against reunification: Günter Grass. Grass had always preferred Herder's "cultural nation" to the Reich that had been forced upon the Germans by Bismarck. For Grass, reunification was neither morally justified nor politically desirable. He sought a federation of the two German states in the European house instead. A unified Germany, Grass argued, would run the danger of again developing the nationalistic attitude that had caused Europe and the world so much harm in the past. Since Auschwitz could not be undone, Germany had to remain divided: "The crime of genocide, summed up in the image of Auschwitz, inexcusable from whatever angle you view it, weighs on the conscience of this unified state." As Goethe and Herder had done in the eighteenth and nineteenth centuries, Grass implored the Germans to happily resign themselves to exist as a cultural nation in a political confederation: "It implies a modern, broader concept of culture, and embraces the multiplicity of German culture without needing to assert unity in the sense of a nation-state." It was only this plea for political restraint, I believe, that made it possible for Grass to tell, in an exemplary fashion, the "repressed story" of German suffering during the Second World War. His novel *Crabwalk* dealt with the sinking of the *Wilhelm Gustloff*, a cruise ship turned into German refugee carrier that was attacked by a Russian submarine on January 30, 1945, the anniversary of Hitler's coming to power, and went down in the Baltic Sea with nine thousand people aboard, four thousand children and youth among them.[3]

Grass now assumed the voice of the seer and the prophet: "I fear a Germany simplified from two states into one."[4] Yet Günter Grass was not the only poet who claimed greater political wisdom than the political class or the majority of the population. Martin Walser, a writer of equally high reputation, did the same and, in regard to German reunification, came to a view that was diametrically opposed to that of Günter Grass. Given the realistic assumption that the reunification of the two German states was not even a remote prospect, those who believed not only in the desirability but also in the possibility of reunification had been regarded as daydreamers. Among those "daydreamers" was Martin Walser, who, with considerable stubbornness and for decades, criticized German politicians in both East and West for not seriously aiming at reunification. His position was even more provocative since he did not accept as a consolation what he regarded as the much-used but cheap argument that the unity of the cultural nation had been preserved after the political nation had been divided.

When Walser received the prestigious German Peace Prize in the Paulskirche in Frankfurt on October 11, 1998, he asked that the remembrance of the Holocaust be reduced if not outright terminated. Walser criticized a moral overreach in the German public sphere that had led the majority of German citizens not to compassion but to indifference. Whereas Grass claimed that Auschwitz made it forever impossible to overcome the political partition of Germany, Walser argued that, with the miracle of German reunification, the moment had finally come to correct the moral overreach. The debate that ensued after Walser's speech was one of the most heavily publicized in the history of the Federal Republic, reinforced by the fact that Ignaz Bubis, head of the Jewish Community in Germany, was appalled by Walser's speech and left the Paulskirche while Walser was applauded by the audience, including Roman Herzog, the president of the Republic.

In a later statement, Walser named two witnesses to support his rejection of the moral overreach that, in his view, the German Republic had imposed upon its citizens. These witnesses were Hannah Arendt, the author of *Eichmann in Jerusalem*, and Thomas Mann who, in desperate irony, had once spoken of Hitler as his "brother."[5] Walser's principal witness, though, should have been another Thomas Mann—the Mann who had written, in 1941, that a decent Germany would again have the right to distance itself from Western values and to attack Western rationalism. For Walser, Germany obviously had become a decent nation again with reunification. Its moral self-castigation had to come to an end. More for its tone than its content, Walser's speech in the Paulskirche was scandalous, but it was not foolish. It pointed to the seemingly irresistible German urge to solve a political problem in the field of culture.

In official remembrance of the Holocaust, buildings since 1989 have become a political and moral battleground in Germany. The powerful architecture of Daniel Libeskind turned the new Jewish Museum in Berlin, which recalls a broken Star of David, into a deliberately depressing monument. The interior division of the rooms oppresses the visitor as much as do the façade's cuts and breaks. As it has turned out, it is very difficult, if not impossible, to mount an exhibition in this building that does not show Jewish-German history to be a one-way road that inevitably led to the Holocaust. The constant attempt of the museum curators to overcome this architectonic barrier is therefore even more to be commended. The all-too-strong meaningfulness of the building is a statement in the field of culture that cannot easily be contradicted on the political level. Libeskind's construction became a problem above all for a colleague, the architect Peter Eisenman. As decided by the German parliament, Eisenman was to build the Memorial for the Murdered European Jews, a huge field of 1,500 rectangular concrete steles in the center of reunified Berlin, near the Brandenburg Gate. The 1990s saw seemingly endless and heated debates about this memorial, especially regarding its size and monumentality. No agreement was reached, either in parliament or in public debate, on whether it would have been more adequate to erect a memorial on this spot for all the victims of the Nazi dictatorship. Nor was the conflict between aesthetics and didactics resolved: while one group of critics demanded that the memorial should be effective through its aesthetic power alone, others demanded that an information center be appended to the memorial. An information center was ultimately added.

Just as Libeskind's architecture created a problem for Eisenman—wasn't there already a memorial that, strangely enough, was called a museum?—Eisenman's memorial created a problem for the so-called Topography of Terror. This name was given to the former prison in the Prince Albrecht Palace, with its subterranean caverns where the Gestapo had tortured and murdered its prisoners. In great part through the efforts of the Berlin historian Reinhard Rürup, the Topography of Terror had become an institution in which, penetratingly and precisely, information on the Third Reich and its murder machinery was conveyed at one of the "scenes of the crime." Its provisional and rather shabby appearance contributed to a feeling of authenticity. Wishing for a more impressive memorial, the Berlin Senate asked the Swiss architect Peter Zumthor to erect a spectacular building above the caverns. As it turned out, however, his design was much too complicated and too costly to build and had to be abandoned—a decision reached not least because, in close vicinity to the Topography of Terror, Peter Eisenman was already building his massive memorial for the murdered Jews of Europe.

The creation of the various Berlin memorials has occupied a large place in German public debates since the fall of the Wall. During these debates it became obvious that one main problem in erecting the memorials was the preponderance given to aesthetic considerations. This is also a consequence of the "monumentalization" of the Nazi crimes: their remembrance, so it seems, can best be served in the sphere of culture, where monumentality plays a much less precarious role than in politics.

The monumentality of the central Berlin Holocaust memorial, which was inaugurated in May 2005, is based on the unspoken, politically motivated premise that the biggest crime must necessarily be represented and remembered by the biggest memorial. Such monumentality, however, might lead to a disastrous interpretation of the history of Nazi Germany. It could support the view that an impervious and unassailable power structure planned and ordered unimaginable crimes from on high. Only a few Germans seemingly became accomplices of these crimes—out of fear and coercion. Precisely because the crime was so immense and unimaginable, the majority of Germans could not possibly know anything about it. They were ignorant of their guilt, and therefore—as a paradoxical consequence of misguided monumental-ity—they will be asked to remember a void.

The "monumentalization" of Nazi crimes runs the danger of conceal-ing the deep moral problem represented by the Germans' daily conduct during the Third Reich. Most Germans are credible when they insist they knew nothing, or at least not much, about the concentration camps. But hardly anyone can deny having known that a Jewish neigh-bor had disappeared, that a synagogue had burned, or that a friend had been forced to leave the country or divorce his wife. The Germans had become masters of "subtle silence."[6] That the overwhelming major-ity of Germans remained silent and were too scared to inquire about the fate of their fellow human beings—this is the core problem of German history from 1933 to 1945. The accelerating disappearance of decency in everyday life is the problem Germans must be concerned with above all.

There is a moving document that describes the gradual loss of human decency in the Third Reich with a saddening irony and in painstaking detail: Victor Klemperer's diaries with the titles *I Shall Bear Witness* (1933–1941) and *To the Bitter End* (1942–1945). Klemperer was Jewish, a well-known professor of Romance languages in Dresden who had served as a volunteer in the First World War, which at the time he called the only catharsis available to a man of culture. In 1935 he was no longer allowed to teach. Klemperer notes in his diary: "Not one of my colleagues came to see me. For them, I have become a victim of the plague." The first to understand the importance and the far-reaching impact of these diaries was Martin Walser, who read Klemperer's manu-scripts and made sure that they were published. Walser rightly insisted that Klemperer's greatest and most admirable asset was his precision as an observer and as a writer.[7] Reading Klemperer's diaries one could argue indeed, with the term Hannah Arendt used, that the core moral problem of German history in the twentieth century was not the monu-mentality of the Nazi crimes, but the everyday banality with which ordinary citizens abandoned decency. For its remembrance and repre-sentation, this banality requires above all precision—and least of all monumentality. In this respect, Walser and Grass were of the same opinion. *The Diary of a Snail*, Grass's diary while campaigning for Willy Brandt, had to be read as a document of the newly won normality of German politics. It was a normality whose undercurrent consisted in the remembrance of a monstrous abnormality, the Holocaust. Writing a diary for his children, Grass impressively combined two narrative strands: his actual political errands were interspersed with the story of the persecution of the Jews of Danzig, his childhood city. For Grass, remembering the Holocaust did not so much mean remembering a big, state-ordered crime as mourning the daily loss of decency by ordinary citizens under a dictatorial regime.

In Berlin, the city of monuments, many small memorials can be found that reflect the same attitude as that of Grass's diary and the diaries of Victor von Klemperer. They recall the Nazi period and the persecution of the Jews as a daily ordeal. In Bebel Square, for example, near the State Opera, a stroller suddenly encounters, without any warning, a glass window in the pavement of the parking lot. Through it she sees a series of empty, white bookshelves: Micha Ullman's "Sunken Library," which commemorates the Nazi book burning of May 10, 1933. In the Bavarian Quarter, where the number of Jewish residents was once especially high—Gottfried Benn established his medical practice in this quarter after 1945—passersby are shocked by dozens of posters with the Nazis' anti-Semitic regulations: "Jews are forbidden to be members in the German Singing Association," "Jews are no longer allowed to buy groceries except between 4:00 and 5:00 P.M." If you begin your vacation, as many Berliners do, on the car-transport train from Grunewald station, you cannot fail to see abandoned rotten rails that recall the first deportations from Berlin to the concentration and death camps. And on Hermann Ehlers Square in Berlin-Steglitz, a mirrored wall reports on the deportation that sent Jewish fellow citizens from the neighborhood to their deaths. The passerby looks into a mirror and sees himself: *Tua res agitur*—this too is your concern.

These small memorials—there are others—disturbingly recall that the Nazis could commit their heinous crimes only because normal Germans showed too little civil courage in their daily affairs. Such remembrances hold up a mirror to each citizen. They remind us that human decency begins in everyday life. In comparison with these small memorials, the great monuments have been given too much attention.

They convey another message: the crimes committed were so big that they are beyond reach and understanding. Memory politics thus runs the danger of creating an unbridgeable distance between itself and the citizen by retreating into awe-inspiring aesthetics. The plea for decency is neglected in favor of monumental but distant and abstract guilt. Once more, politics finds its welcome substitute in culture: the moral masterpiece.

NOTES

Notes to Introduction

1. Sebald, *On the Natural History of Destruction*, 43.

2. This connection is, of course, not confined to Germany. From June 1944 on, for instance, the French Resistance knew that the Allied invasion was about to begin when the lines "Les sanglots longs / des violons de l'automne" from Paul Verlaine's poem *Chanson d'automne* could be heard over Allied radio. When the two lines "Blessent mon cœur / d'une langueur monotone" followed, the invasion was to be expected in the next forty-eight hours. These lines were aired on June 5, 1944, at 9:15 P.M. The invasion (D-Day) began the next morning. German counterespionage was informed about this "plot," but the German military command refused to believe that the Allied leadership would use poetry for a military purpose. All of this belongs in a context that Paul Fussell has called "the curious literariness of Real Life," with special emphasis on the "unparalleled literariness of all ranks who fought the Great War," that is, the First World War. See Fussell, *The Great War and Modern Memory*, ix, 156.

3. See Fest, *Inside Hitler's Bunker*, viii. The Labor Front was the union the Nazis created in 1933, after having abolished the traditional unions.

4. Joseph Goebbels, diary entry, April 27, 1942: *The Goebbels Diaries, 1942–1943*, 189.

5. See Backes, *Hitler und die bildenden Künste*, 116–117. Such priorities are appalling. Yet they are not confined to authoritarian regimes. "Big Boy," as the second atomic bomb was called by the American military, was originally to be dropped on Kyoto in August 1945. J. Robert Oppenheimer intervened by pointing out the architectural treasures and the spiritual significance of the city. Only then was Nagasaki chosen as the alternate site.

6. Thomas Mann in a letter to Agnes E. Meyer from Pacific Palisades, Calif., May 5, 1942, in Mann and Meyer, *Briefwechsel 1937–1955*, 394.

7. Buruma, "The Destruction of Germany," 12.

8. Elias, *The Germans*, 126–127.

9. Elias, *The Civilizing Process*, 4. It is difficult for a non-German to talk about "Kultur," this inflated German term, without resorting to irony. An example can be found at the beginning of Sinclair Lewis's *Main Street*, where he

says of the heroine, Carl Kennicott, "She played tennis, gave chafing-dish parties, took a graduate seminar in the drama, went 'twosing,' and joined half a
dozen societies for the practice of the arts or the tense stalking of a thing called
General Culture." Lewis, *Main Street and Babbitt*, 6. Lewis used capital letters
in his ironic expression; H. L. Mencken preferred italics. In his attack on
"national letters," he spoke of "the dwindling survivors of New England *Kultur*" and in "The Calamity of Appomattox" (1930) he called "Ku Kluxry, political ecclesiasticism, nigger-baiting, and the more homicidal variety of wow-
serism" the chief contribution of the Confederates "*to American Kultur.*" See
Mencken, "The National Letters" (1920), in *The Vintage Mencken*, 92, 199.

   10. Elias, *The Germans*, 127.

   11. I should report one instance, however, when the term was used without
irony, and by an unlikely author at that. In 1961, at Hyannis, John F. Kennedy
asked Gore Vidal, "How do you explain how a sort of backwoods country like
this, with only three million people, could have produced the three great ge-
niuses of the eighteenth century—Franklin, Jefferson, and Hamilton?" Vidal
remarked that the American Constitution and laws were grounded in England
and "Anglo-Saxon attitudes"—an answer the Irish-Catholic president grudgingly approved of. I mention this episode also because the term "Anglo-Saxon
attitudes" basically referred to "culture," as Vidal made clear when explaining
the greatness of Franklin, Jefferson, and Hamilton: "Time. They had more of
it. . . . They stayed home on the farm in winter. They read. Wrote letters.
Apparently, thought, something no longer done—in public life." See Vidal,
Inventing a Nation, 187–188.

Notes to Chapter 1: Culture

   1. In 1987, however, as Declan Kiberd notes, Roy Foster published an essay
in which he claimed that "far from abating, political campaigns [in Ireland] in
the 1890s simply found other forms, leading (for instance) to a revitalization
of local government across the countryside. [Foster] served warning that he
was not to be beguiled by poetic Yeatsian versions of history when intrepid
archival research might yield a different story." Kiberd, "At Full Speed," 3.
Kiberd was reviewing R. F. Foster's book *W. B. Yeats: A Life*, vol. 2, *The Arch-
Poet, 1915–1939* (Oxford: Oxford University Press, 2003).

   2. I am alluding to publications by David Blackbourn, John Breuilly, Geoff
Eley, Harold James, Charles Maier, Arno J. Mayer, and Jim Sheehan.

   3. Mayer, *The Persistence of the Old Regime*, 5.

4. It was the German historian Ernst Nolte who insisted on the reactive character of National Socialism. The French historian François Furet expressed some agreement with Nolte's views, but reminded him at the same time that there is a difference between chronology and causality. See Furet, *Le passé d'une illusion*, and the exchange between Furet and Nolte: "Sur le fascisme, le communisme et l'histoire du XXe siècle."

5. Dewey, *German Philosophy and Politics*, 69. There is a strange similarity between Dewey's view and Charles Maurras's claim that barbarism could find its exact formula in "Kant's mathematical head." Maurras, *Réflexions sur la révolution de 1789*, 14.

6. Santayana, *Egotism in German Philosophy*, 21.

7. Oswald Spengler, *Jahre der Entscheidung: Deutschland und die weltgeschichtliche Entwicklung* (Munich: Beck, 1933), 3, 5. Only one year later, an American edition was published: *The Hour of Decision: Germany and World-Historical Evolution*, trans. Charles Francis Atkinson (New York: Knopf, 1934). I am providing my own translation of Spengler's terms.

8. Santayana, *Egotism*, 141. Thorstein Veblen's book *Imperial Germany and the Industrial Revolution*, originally published in 1915, was also reprinted in 1939.

9. Santayana, *Egotism*, viii.

10. Dewey, *German Philosophy and Politics*, 15. The claim of causality was formulated, most clearly, by Peter Viereck, who set himself the task to "explain crucial parts of the causal chain leading from the German past to the Hitler cult of 1941." See Viereck, *Metapolitics*, ix.

11. Gooch et al., *The German Mind and Outlook*, viii.

12. Arnold, *Culture and Anarchy*.

13. Ibid., 87–88.

14. Ibid., 117.

15. Ibid., 161–162. Joseph Coulthard, the first translator of Wilhelm von Humboldt's essay, somewhat misleadingly rendered the title *Ideen zu einem Versuch, die Grenzen der Wirksamkeit des Staates zu bestimmen* (1791–92). It would have been much more appropriate to translate it, as J. W. Burrow later did, as *The Limits of State Action*. In the context of my argument here, it might be useful to mention that Humboldt was twenty-four years old when he published his essay, after having "just resigned his first minor post in the Prussian administration, having found administration, as he said, 'geistlos' [dull]." Burrow, "Editor's Introduction," in Humboldt, *The Limits of State Action*, ix.

16. Arnold, *Culture and Anarchy*, 117, 113.

17. Thomas Mann, "Lessing," in *Past Masters*, 119.

18. Mosse, *The Crisis of German Ideology*, 2–3.

19. Richard Wagner, "Deutsche Kunst und deutsche Politik" [1867–68], in Wagner, *Dichtungen und Schriften*, 8:261.

20. Thomas Mann, "The Sufferings and Greatness of Richard Wagner," in *Past Masters*, 86. In a similar vein, Ernst Troeltsch had spoken of the *Mastersingers* as the most German work of Wagner, who was much more a modern than a German composer. See Troeltsch, "Der metaphysische und religiöse Geist der deutschen Kultur" [1916], in Troeltsch, *Deutscher Geist und Westeuropa*, 68.

21. See Fritz Stern's early books *The Politics of Cultural Despair: A Study in the Rise of the Germanic Ideology* (1961; Berkeley: University of California Press, 1974) and *The Failure of Illiberalism* (New York: Alfred A. Knopf, 1972).

22. Gooch et al., *The German Mind and Outlook*, viii.

23. See Sherry, *The Great War and the Language of Modernism*.

24. On the origin of and the reactions to the manifesto, see vom Brocke, " 'Wissenschaft und Militarismus,' " 649–719. For an English version of this manifesto and similar texts, see Chapman, *Deutschland über Alles or Germany Speaks*. The English title of the manifesto blurs the distinction between culture and civilization that was so important for the Germans. Thomas Mann's manifesto against Hitler, written between November 19 and November 24, 1938, in Princeton, was called "An die Gesittete Welt" and translated as "To the Civilized World." It is unclear whether Mann was deliberately alluding to the manifesto of the ninety-three from 1914. See Mann, "An die Gesittete Welt," in *Essays*, 5:28–35.

25. T. S. Eliot to his brother Henry Eliot, September 8, 1914, in *The Letters of T. S. Eliot*, 1:56.

26. Valéry, "Une conquête méthodique" [1897], in *Œvres*, 1:971–987.

27. Nietzsche, *Briefe* (April 1869–Mai 1872), in *Kritische Gesamtausgabe*, II:1, pp. 130, 131, 164.

28. See the second chapter in Iggers, *The German Conception of History*, 29.

29. Trevor-Roper, "Jacob Burckhardt," 360–361, 370–373.

30. Nietzsche, "David Strauss, the Confessor and the Writer," in *Untimely Meditations*, 3.

31. Nietzsche, *Twilight of the Idols*, 43 ("What the Germans are missing"). For a comparison of Rembrandt and Bismarck, see Langbehn, *Rembrandt als Erzieher* [1888], 188. For the development of the Bismarck myth that praised the chancellor as an artist-politician, see Parr, *"Zwei Seelen wohnen, ach! in meiner Brust."*

32. Weber, "National Character and the Junkers" [1917–1921], 390.

33. Nietzsche, *Twilight of the Idols*, 45–46.

34. Ralph Waldo Emerson, "Goethe; or, the Writer" [1850], in *Essays and Lectures*, 751, 757.

35. Nietzsche, *Human, All Too Human*, vol. 1, no. 465 ("Resurrection of the Spirit"), 169.

36. Ibid., vol. 2, p. 258.

37. Walther Rathenau, "Staat und Vaterland: Der letzte Aufsatz vor der Revolution," in *Gesammelte Schriften*, 6:254–255.

38. Ernst Troeltsch, "Die Ideen von 1914" [1916], in *Deutscher Geist und Westeuropa*, 31–32, 38.

39. Meinecke, *The Age of German Liberation, 1795–1815*, 3. Emphasis added. (The German original, *Das Zeitalter der deutschen Erhebung*, was first published in 1906.)

40. Ibid., 18–24.

41. Meinecke, *Cosmopolitanism and the National State*, 42, 46. Meinecke's book *Weltbürgertum und Nationalstaat* was first published in 1907.

42. This equation has been vigorously corrected by Theodore Ziolkowski, *German Romanticism and Its Institutions*.

43. See Pois, *Friedrich Meinecke and German Politics in the Twentieth Century*, 32.

44. Gay, *Weimar Culture*, 1–2.

Notes to Chapter 2: From the Republic into Exile

1. *Letters of Heinrich and Thomas Mann, 1900–1949*, 120.

2. Thomas Mann, *Reflections of a Nonpolitical Man*, 16–17.

3. Ibid., 183.

4. Ibid., 171. See also Thomas Mann, "An einen Opern-Spielleiter" (November 15, 1927), in *Wagner und unsere Zeit*, 52.

5. Thomas Mann, "Germany and the Germans" [May 29, 1945], in *Thomas Mann's Addresses*, 64.

6. It was a sign of political perspicacity and courage that Heinrich Mann published chapters of his novel *Der Untertan* as early as 1911–12 in the magazine *Simplicissimus*.

7. "Literary Prophet of Civilization" is the translation of "Zivilisationsliterat" in Erika and Klaus Mann's "Portrait of Our Father," in their *Escape to Life*, 95. I prefer it to the term "civilization's literary man" that Walter D. Morris uses in his translation of the *Reflections*.

8. Thomas Mann, *Reflections*, 430.

9. "A Soldier, and Brave" is the title of the last section in chapter 6 of Thomas Mann's novel *The Magic Mountain*.

10. Thomas Mann, *Reflections*, 430.

11. Erika and Klaus Mann, "Portrait of Our Father," 95.

12. Thomas Mann, "On the Theory of Spengler" [1924], in *Past Masters*, 226.

13. Thomas Mann wrote this in a letter to Ernst Bertram of March 16, 1920, in which he responded to his friend's description of the French occupation policy in the Rhineland. *Thomas Mann an Ernst Bertram*, 89–90.

14. Thomas Mann, "Foreword," in *Order of the Day*, ix.

15. Thomas Mann himself was well aware of this: "Did it, think you, escape me, that this book [*Reflections of a Nonpolitical Man*] is worth far more, artistically speaking, as a literary performance, with all the melancholy of its mood, than the fatherly admonishment to a republic with which a few years later the author surprised refractory youth?" Mann, "Culture and Socialism," in *Past Masters*, 202–203.

16. In 1925, Thomas Mann wrote these sentences in a review of Heinrich Mann's novel *Der Kopf*. See *Letters of Heinrich and Thomas Mann, 1900–1949*, 273.

17. Thomas Mann, "On the Profession of the German Writer in Our Time: Address in Honor of a Brother," ibid., 282.

18. Thomas Mann, "An Appeal to Reason," in *Order of the Day*, 47–55.

19. Ibid., 52.

20. See Hugo Preuß's book *Das deutsche Volk und die Politik* (Jena: Eugen Diederichs, 1915), 186.

21. Thomas Mann, "Culture and Socialism," in *Past Masters*, 207.

22. Ibid., 213–214.

23. Thomas Mann, "The Sufferings and Greatness of Richard Wagner," in *Past Masters*, 86.

24. Spotts, *Hitler and the Power of Aesthetics*, 133, 86. It was Henriette von Schirach who told of Hitler's promise. Churchill, however, was thinking about a larger time span than that of being a painter in Hitler's Thousand-Year Reich. As Churchill's daughter, Lady Soames, recalled on the occasion of the meeting of the International Churchill Societies in 1988, her father once wrote, "When I get to heaven I mean to spend a considerable portion of my first million years in painting and so get to the bottom of the subject."

25. Armand Crommelin, "Goethe und Bismarck, die Staatskünstler," in *Bayreuther Blätter* 42 (1919): 11, as quoted in Parr, *"Zwei Seelen wohnen, ach! in meiner Brust,"* 27.

26. *The Goebbels Diaries, 1942–1943*, 370 (May 10, 1943).

27. Ziegler, *Adolf Hitler aus dem Erleben dargestellt*, 50.

28. Thompson, "The Problem Child of Europe," 391.

29. *The Goebbels Diaries, 1942–1943*, 160–161 (April 5, 1942).

30. Heller, *Europa und der Faschismus*, 54.

31. Kessler, *In the Twenties*, 470–471.

32. Troeltsch, *Das Wesen des Deutschen*, 7.

33. Walther Rathenau, "An Deutschlands Jugend" (July 1918), in *Gesammelte Schriften*, 6:171.

34. Spotts, *Hitler and the Power of Aesthetics*, 54.

35. Jünger and Schmitt, *Briefe 1930–1983*, 15.

36. Thomas Mann to Franz Werfel, May 26, 1939, in *Letters of Thomas Mann, 1889–1955*, 303.

37. Peter Paret has given a detailed account of the ambivalence characteristic of the relation between artistic modernism and authoritarian politics in his book *An Artist against the Third Reich: Ernst Barlach, 1933–1938*.

38. One hesitates to use a term with a positive connotation like "style" in this context. It caused quite a stir in Germany, therefore, when one of the better-known critics and literary theorists of the Federal Republic, Karl-Heinz Bohrer, deplored the absence of form in German politics and claimed that the Nazi regime had been the last style-conscious movement in recent German history. See Bohrer, "Stil oder 'maniera.' "

39. Henderson, *Failure of a Mission*, 66–67.

40. Lewis, *The Hitler Cult* [1939], 47.

41. Brasillach, *Œuvres complètes*, 6:241. See Tucker, "Politics and Aesthetics," 608.

42. Pierre Drieu la Rochelle, "Hypothèse sur le Duce" (May 20, 1938), in *Chronique politique 1934–1942*, 126.

43. *The Goebbels Diaries, 1942–1943*, 71.

44. See Bardèche, *Qu'est-ce que le fascisme?* Bardèche was the brother-in-law of Robert Brasillach, with whom, in 1939, he had jointly published a history of the Spanish Civil War.

45. Chateaubriant, *La gerbe des forces (nouvelle Allemagne)*, 69.

46. Robert Brasillach published his review on July 8, 1937, in *Action Française*. See Hamilton, *The Appeal of Fascism*, 211–212.

47. It is this far-reaching aesthetic underpinning of National Socialist politics that does not allow one to make light of the films of Leni Riefenstahl or of an author like Paul de Man's predilections for German "aesthetic nationalism," to see them as expressions of a merely peripheral and hence morally defensible sympathy for Nazism. They point to the heart of the matter. Nevertheless, I agree with the conclusion drawn by Peter Schjeldahl after his visit to

New York's Jewish Museum's controversial exhibition "Mirroring Evil: Nazi Imagery / Recent Art" that opened on March 17, 2002: "I think that we could save ourselves a great deal of intellectual backing and filling by accepting Nazism—along with everything else that it was—as one of the twentieth century's major stylistic movements. Leni Riefenstahl's films, Albert Speer's architecture, the choreographed rallies, those uniforms, and the Nazi flag were creative feasts. Why pretend otherwise? Giving the Devil his due is an intelligent way for defeating him. . . . The more conscious we are of the limited but potent attraction of Nazi culture, the less its redolence will strike third-rate artists as a surefire ticket to sensation." Schjeldahl, "The Hitler Show," 87.

48. Mann, "Foreword," in *Order of the Day*, xiii–xiv.

49. Ibid., 156–157. In *Esquire* 11 (1939) the essay had the title "That Man Is My Brother." It was republished in *Order of the Day* with the title "A Brother." I am quoting it from the latter volume but retain the title from *Esquire*. The German essay was first published in Paris in the German refugee paper *Das Neue Tagebuch* on March 25, 1939. In a challenging and original essay in *Critical Inquiry*, Otto K. Werckmeister has described how much resentment he produced by looking at "Hitler, the Artist" from a somewhat unconventional point of view. See Werckmeister, "Hitler, the Artist." I disagree with Werckmeister's view, though, that Thomas Mann had been "unwilling or unable to recognize that Hitler was neither fake nor an aberration, that his politicization of art had been for real." Ibid., 297.

50. See Thomas Mann, "In Defense of Wagner." This essay is Mann's reply to Peter Viereck's article "Hitler and Richard Wagner," *Common Sense*, November 1939, 3–6.

51. Pachter, "On Being an Exile," 16.

52. Henry James, "The New Novel," in *Literary Criticism*, 124. (James's essay was first published under the title "The Younger Generation" in the *Times Literary Supplement* of March 19 and April 2, 1914.) See Harrison, *The Reactionaries*, 26.

53. In October 1932, Theodor Litt, rector of Leipzig University, suggested that the faculty speak out against the agitation of the Nazi student groups on campus. Eduard Spranger disagreed: he believed that the sincerity of the students was obvious and to be commended, and only the way in which they behaved should be criticized. See Spranger: "Mein Konflikt mit der nationalsozialistischen Regierung 1933."

54. Quoted in Reinhard Paul Becker, "Introduction," in Benn, *Prose, Essays, Poems*, xxviii.

55. I have not used the term "theater state" because Clifford Geertz wrote "the expressive nature of the Balinese state . . . was always pointed not toward

tyranny," and that in Bali "power served pomp, not pomp power." This qualification precludes the borrowing of the original term. See Geertz, *Negara*, 13.

56. Benn, *Prose, Essays, Poems*, xxix. The poetess Ina Seidel, who had penned an ode for the Führer's fiftieth birthday, had become as disenchanted with the Nazi movement as Benn—and for the same, largely aesthetic, reasons.

57. See Hébey, *La NRF des années sombres, Juin 1940–Juin 1941*.

58. Thomas Mann, March 15, 1933, in *Diaries, 1918–1939*, 127.

59. Thomas Mann, "The Theme of the Joseph Novels" [address delivered in the Coolidge Auditorium of the Library of Congress, November 17, 1942], in *Thomas Mann's Addresses*, 9.

60. Erika and Klaus Mann, "Compromise Fails," in *Escape to Life*, 47.

61. Thomas Mann, November 20, 1933, in *Tagebücher 1933–1934*, 14.

62. These are the words of Serenus Zeitblom, the narrator, in Thomas Mann's novel *Doctor Faustus* (1947). See Mann, *Doctor Faustus*, 175.

63. Thomas Mann, *Tagebücher 1933–1934*, 502.

64. Thomas Mann, *Diaries, 1918–1939*, 170–171 (September 8, 1933).

65. Thomas Mann, *Diaries, 1918–1939*, 200 (March 14, 1934).

66. See Gottfried Benn, letter to Hans Paeschke, March 19, 1949, in Benn, *Briefwechsel mit dem 'Merkur' 1948–1956*, 22–23. Hans Paeschke and Joachim Moras, Benn's correspondents, were the editors of *Merkur*, arguably the most important German cultural magazine after the Second World War.

67. Thomas Mann quotes Goethe, "the greatest unpatriot of them all," *Past Masters*, 86. It is one of those references that remind the reader that Mann had once said: "I am no Goethe; yet a little, afar off, somehow or other, as Adalbert Stifter put it, I 'belong to his family.'" Mann, "The German Republic," in *Order of the Day*, 8.

Notes to Chapter 3: Novalis and Walt Whitman

1. Picker, *Hitlers Tischgespräche im Führerhauptquartier*, 59–61 (July 21 and July 22, 1941).

2. Hitler, *Monologe im Führerhauptquartier*, 184. I quote the English translation from Spotts, *Hitler and the Power of Aesthetics*, 107.

3. Picker, *Hitlers Tischgespräche im Führerhauptquartier*, 231.

4. *The Goebbels Diaries, 1942–1943*, 180–181.

5. The only occasions for which the Met—before September 11, 2001—has ever closed were John F. Kennedy's assassination, the death of a singer during the opening night of Leos Janacek's opera *The Makropulos Case*, and a blackout in the city caused by a snowstorm. In 1942 there were opera houses

in Cincinnati, San Francisco, Chicago, Denver, Milwaukee, Pittsburgh, Hartford, Miami, Charleston, and other American cities. John Church, information service director at OPERA America, who was kind enough to provide this information, became quite angry when asked about Goebbels's allegation and closed his rejoinder as follows: "In fact, opera was alive and well in America going back as far as the American Revolution. . . . There are several books on the market that list American Opera Houses and the dates of their founding. . . . Many were established in the 1880s. Sorry, but Mr. Goebbels was a jackass. And misinformed."

6. Ellison, "The Little Man at Chehaw Station," 45, 48.

7. Thomas Mann, *Reflections*, 320.

8. Thomas Mann, "Goethe's Career as a Man of Letters," in *Essays*, trans. Lowe-Porter, 71.

9. In truth, things were a bit more complicated. On May 15, 1937, Agnes Meyer wrote Thomas Mann that the fight for democracy was acute. It would matter a great deal if a creative mind like his would form the first line of defense. To this, she added a postscript: "I realize the contradiction in my letters. In the last one I recognized your influence as that of a Kulturmensch contrasted to that of a politician, and yet I am doing my best to draw you into the political arena." Mann and Meyer, *Briefwechsel 1937–1955*, 79–80.

10. Thomas Mann to Agnes E. Meyer, January 24, 1941, in *Letters of Thomas Mann, 1889–1955*, 354. As a warrior for true German culture, Thomas Mann was seen as a representative of the "good" Germany fighting the "bad" one. When he gave his talk on "War and Democracy" at the University of Georgia on January 17, 1941, he was introduced by William C. Jones, the editor of the *Atlanta Journal*, as "a man self-exiled from the tyranny which also would have banished Goethe and Schiller and Beethoven." Mann and Meyer, *Briefwechsel, 1937–1955*, 904n1.

11. Meyer, *Out of These Roots*, 184.

12. Quoted from chapter 10 ("A Turn in the Wheel of Fortune") in Agnes Meyer's unpublished memoir, "Life as Chance and Destiny," in Mann and Meyer, *Briefwechsel, 1937–1955*, 811.

13. Thomas Mann, "The Theme of the Joseph Novels," 10. This affinity between the Old World and the New may also have helped to promote the book, of which a million copies were sold through the Book-of-the-Month Club.

14. Ibid., 9.

15. Thomas Mann, "Germany and the Germans," in *Thomas Mann's Addresses*, 47

16. Thomas Mann, *Reflections*, 31.

17. Thomas Mann, "The German Republic," in *Order of the Day*, 10, 20.

18. Ibid., 11.

19. See Thomas Mann, "Hans Reisigers Whitman-Werk," in Mann, *Gesammelte Werke in zwölf Bänden*, vol. 10 (Reden und Aufsätze 2), 626–627. As early as 1868, Ferdinand Freiligrath translated ten poems by Walt Whitman in the *Augsburger Allgemeine*. Freiligrath (1810–1876), a collaborator of Karl Marx, was called "The Trumpeter of the Revolution" of 1848.

20. Thomas Mann, "The German Republic," 26.

21. See Wisskirchen, "Republikanischer Eros," 17–40.

22. Walt Whitman, *Democratic Vistas*, in *Complete Poetry and Collected Prose*, 981.

23. It is therefore an underestimation of Whitman's influence on Thomas Mann to marvel only at the bringing together of Whitman's humanism with the *humanitas* of Novalis. See Leslie A. Fiedler, "Images of Walt Whitman," in Hindus, ed., *Leaves of Grass One Hundred Years After*.

24. Gore Vidal, "The Romance of Sinclair Lewis," in *The Last Empire*, 63.

25. David Fernbach, "Translator's Note," in Maar, *Bluebeard's Chamber*, 111. In the preceding passage, I have relied on Fernbach's comments and have quoted his translation—the first—of the omitted passages from Mann's speech. Mann's letter to Agnes Meyer in Mann and Meyer, *Briefwechsel, 1937–1955*, 402. In September 1943, Agnes Meyer was not only Thomas Mann's censor in erotic matters. She also refused to translate a passage by Thomas Mann on communism, "for it would be fatal to you to use them." Ibid., 513. It is even more telling, therefore, that neither Agnes Meyer nor Thomas Mann saw a problem in confronting the American public with two passages in which Mann had assured his German audience in 1922 that the Republic should not be regarded as the domain of "keen-witted" or "sharp-witted Jews." Mann, "The German Republic," 18, 33.

26. I quote the first of Walt Whitman's "Inscriptions," in Whitman, *Complete Poetry and Collected Prose*, 165.

27. Thomas Mann, "The German Republic," 34.

28. Ibid., 37–38.

29. Whitman, "Preface" to *Leaves of Grass*, in *Complete Poetry and Collected Prose*, 8.

30. Whitman, "To the States," ibid., 172.

31. Whitman, *Democratic Vistas*, ibid., 939. It is no coincidence therefore, I think, that Gore Vidal, one of the fiercest critics of the American Republic turned into Empire, chose "Democratic Vistas" as the title of one of his polemics. See Vidal, "Democratic Vistas," *The Nation*, January 8–15, 2001, in *The Last Empire*, 444–447.

32. Whitman, *Democratic Vistas*, in *Complete Poetry and Collected Prose*, 974.

33. Whitman, "Letter to Ralph Waldo Emerson" (Brooklyn, August 1856), in Whitman, *Complete Poetry and Collected Prose*, 1328–1329.

34. Ibid., 1328, 1330.

35. Whitman, "A Visit, at the Last, to R. W. Emerson," in *Complete Poetry and Collected Prose*, 913.

36. Ralph Waldo Emerson, "The American Scholar," in Emerson, *Essays and Lectures*, 53, 71. In his own Phi Beta Kappa address, given on March 29, 1941, at Berkeley, Thomas Mann spoke about the necessity of bringing life and thought together. He amused his audience by claiming that Nietzsche, were he still alive, would have emigrated to the United States and would probably have been admitted to Phi Beta Kappa—his romantic sins notwithstanding.

37. William Carlos Williams, "The American Background" (1934), in *Selected Essays of William Carlos Williams*, 144.

38. Thoreau, *Journal*, 3:179.

39. George Ripley to James Marsh, February 23, 1837, in Duffy, ed., *Coleridge's American Disciples*, 192–193.

40. See Gay, *Weimar Culture*, 67.

41. Emerson, *The Journals and Miscellaneous Notebooks*, 7:198. Bettina von Arnim was a writer and friend of Goethe.

42. I am quoting Henry James who is quoting James Elliot Cabot's "Memoir of Ralph Waldo Emerson," which he reviewed in December 1887 in *Macmillan's Magazine*, in James, *Literary Criticism*, 265.

43. Parker, "German Literature."

44. Emerson, *The Journals*, 7:124.

45. H. L. Mencken, "The National Letters" [1920], in *The Vintage Mencken*, 89, 86.

46. Ellison, "The Little Man at Chehaw Station," 37.

Notes to Chapter 4: German Culture Abroad

1. Bloom, *The Closing of the American Mind*, 141–142.

2. Benda, *The Treason of the Intellectuals*, 101.

3. See Eliza Marian Butler, *The Tyranny of Greece over Germany; A Study of the Influence Exercised by Greek Art and Poetry over the Great German Writers of the Eighteenth, Nineteenth, and Twentieth Centuries* (New York: Macmillan, 1935).

4. Wharton, *A Backward Glance*, 147. The episode was obviously very important for Edith Wharton. She had already recounted it in *French Ways and Their Meaning* [1919], 65.

5. Bloom, *The Closing of the American Mind*, 147.

6. Ibid., 153.

7. Ibid., 237. See *The Republic of Plato*. Trans., with notes and an interpretive essay by Allan Bloom (New York: Basic Books, 1968).

8. Thomas Mann, "The German Republic," in *Order of the Day*, 41.

9. Ellison, "The Little Man at Chehaw Station," 30.

10. Emerson, *The Journals and Miscellaneous Notebooks*, 14:151.

11. "Dickens said, I will outamerica America," in Emerson, *The Journals and Miscellaneous Notebooks*, 14:147. Thomas Mann, "I Am an American," in Mann, *Essays*, vol. 5 (Deutschland und die Deutschen 1938–1945), 132–135.

12. Curtius, *Deutscher Geist in Gefahr*, 12. Curtius was quoting the Anglicist Herbert Schöffler's book *England in der deutschen Bildung*, which had been published in 1929.

13. Curtius, *Deutscher Geist in Gefar*, 127.

14. Thomas Mann quotes Goethe in his address "Goethe and Democracy," delivered at the Library of Congress on May 2, 1949, in *Thomas Mann's Addresses*, 128–129. Harvard, however, did not become a Goethe headquarters in the United States. The first professor of German whom Harvard appointed was Karl Follen, who had been a member of the rebellious German student union and saw Goethe as a lackey of aristocracy and a sworn enemy of democracy. Only later, propelled above all by the so-called St. Louis movement, did Goethe become a cult figure in the United States. The second part of *Faust* was read as an American book and Faust was seen as the incorporation of the American myth. See Walter Hinderer, "Goethe and America," in Hinderer, ed., *Goethe und das Zeitalter der Romantik*, 489–505.

15. Parker, "German Literature," 327.

16. Lionel Trilling, "The Situation of the American Intellectual at the Present Time" [1952–53], in *A Gathering of Fugitives*, 78.

17. Ibid., 74.

18. Trilling, "Dr. Leavis and the Moral Tradition" [1949], in *A Gathering of Fugitives*, 112.

19. Lionel Trilling, "Edmund Wilson: A Backward Glance" [1952], in *A Gathering of Fugitives*, 54.

20. Emerson, "Goethe; or, the Writer," in *Essays and Lectures*, 750.

21. Wharton, *The Age of Innocence* [1920], in *Novels*, 1191, 1069, 1096, and Wharton, *A Backward Glance*, 144.

22. Drury, *Leo Strauss and the American Right*, 3.

23. Lilla, "The Closing of the Straussian Mind," 54.

24. Strauss, *Natural Right and History*, 2.

25. Bloom, *The Closing of the American Mind*, 153.

Notes to Chapter 5: French-German Culture Wars

1. See Brooks, "Gallic Invasion." This article is a review of François Cusset's book *French Theory: Foucault, Derrida, Deleuze & cie et les mutations de la vie intellectuelle aux Etats-Unis* (Paris: La Découverte, 2004).

2. Rohden, "Deutscher und Französischer Konservatismus," 98.

3. Theodor W. Adorno, "Die auferstandene Kultur," in *Gesammelte Schriften*, vol. 20.2, 453–464.

4. Friedrich Schlegel, Athenäums-Fragment 216, "Charakteristiken und Kritiken I (1796–1801)," in *Kritische Friedrich-Schlegel-Ausgabe*, 2:198–199. Fichte, whose nationalist fervor was born out of hatred of Napoleon, of course enraged the French. Charles Maurras called Fichte a poet lost in ontology; he was appalled at Fichte's contempt for the Latin spirit and the Latin languages. See Maurras, *Quand les Français ne s'aimaient pas* [1916].

5. Friedrich Schlegel, Athenäumsfragment 424, in *Charakteristiken und Kritiken*, 1:248. For both aphorisms I have, if only partially, used the translations by Ernst Behler and Roman Struc in Novalis, Schlegel, Schleiermacher, and others, *German Romantic Criticism*, ed. A. Leslie Willson, The German Library, vol. 21 (New York: Continuum, 1982), 129, 133.

6. Goethe, *Conversations of Goethe with Eckermann and Soret*, trans. John Oxenford (London: Smith, Elder & Co., 1850), 2:290–291. In the quotations from this edition, I have kept the spelling Geoffrey de Saint Hilaire.

7. Ibid., 292. Goethe's judgment, however, that Geoffroy Saint-Hilaire had won the duel against Cuvier was a bit premature. Today it is still difficult to decide who was the winner in this immortal controversy: "If Cuvier was wrong to be right, Geoffroy Saint-Hilaire was right to be wrong. A century and a half later, which is the more enviable situation?" See Le Guyader, *Geoffroy Saint-Hilaire, 1772–1844*, 254.

8. Landauer, "Goethes Politik: Eine Ankündigung" [1918/1921], in *Goethe im Urteil seiner Kritiker*, 3:477–486.

9. *Conversations of Goethe*, 402–403.

10. Goethe's attack on the French language must not be overestimated, though he was among the first to challenge its universal presumptions. When he attacked Sulzer's *Aesthetics*, in 1770, Goethe could find no harsher criticism

for it than the malicious remark that the book read as if it had been translated from the French. In 1808, however, he made sure that the troupe of the famous actor Talma, who was accompanying Napoleon, could perform the tragedies of Voltaire and Corneille at Weimar—and in French. Only the supernumeraries were played by German actors. Goethe was not enough of a nationalist and despised the romantics too much to join their anti-French propaganda efforts. For a nostalgic yet persuasive tale of how the French language shaped European consciousness and European mores, see Fumaroli, *Quand l'Europe parlait français.*

11. Valéry, "Address in Honor of Goethe," in *The Collected Works of Paul Valéry,* 9:147.

12. Ibid., 173.

13. Emerson, "Goethe; or, the Writer," in *Essays and Lectures,* 750–751; Valéry, "Address in Honor of Goethe," 170, 171.

14. Valéry, "Address in Honor of Goethe," 156, 161.

15. Ibid., 175. In 1948 Carl Jacob Burckhardt visited the cemetery in Sète where Valéry had written his poem "Le cimetière marin" and where he had been laid to rest. The gardener approached him: *M. Valéry venait composer ici—* "That's where M. Valéry composed. . . ." See Carl J. Burckhardt/Max Rychner, *Briefe 1926–1965* (Frankfurt am Main: Fischer, 1987), 123.

16. It is telling, therefore, that in 1808, the year he met Napoleon in Erfurt, Goethe compared the French emperor to a conductor, a *Konzertmeister.* See *Goethes Gespräche,* 2:352.

17. Emerson, "Goethe; or, the Writer," 751. Maurice Barrès had called Goethe's drama *Iphigenie* "a civilizing work which 'defends the rights of society against the arrogance of the spirit' "—a rejection of the German overestimation of culture and the spirit if there ever was one. I quote Barrès from Thomas Mann's speech "Goethe and Democracy," which he delivered in the Library of Congress on May 2, 1949. It seems to me that this speech, in which Mann mentions the Sorbonne address of 1932, is an implicit answer to Paul Valéry— and full of complicity.

18. Valéry, "Address in Honor of Goethe," 174, 175.

19. Benda, *The Treason of the Intellectuals,* 20. See Julien Benda, *La trahison des clercs* (Paris: Grasset, 1975), 118.

20. Kolb, *Versuch über Briand,* 10. Annette Kolb is referring to Alessandro Manzoni's novel *I Promessi Sposi* (The betrothed) from 1827.

21. Guizot, "La France et la Prusse responsables devant l'Europe."

22. Troubat, *Souvenirs du dernier secrétaire de Sainte-Beuve,* 319–320.

23. It was a small triumph for the secretary Troubat, though, that he was able to secure Sainte-Beuve's wine cellar from the Prussians.

24. Nietzsche, *Twilight of the Idols*, 46.

25. Hugh Trevor-Roper even spoke of a "Macedonian theory." See his essay "Jacob Burckhardt," 377.

26. See Caro, "La morale de la guerre." 577–594. The philosopher Elme-Marie Caro had published a book on Goethe's philosophy. I take his article as a *pars pro toto* example of the many attempts to separate a "good" from a "bad" Germany.

27. Maurras, *Réflexions sur la révolution de 1789*, 14.

28. Parker, "German Literature," 318.

29. The first to address the problem of Durkheim's and Weber's "mutual unawareness" was Edward A. Tiryakian: "A Problem for the Sociology of Knowledge: The Mutual Unawareness of Emile Durkheim and Max Weber," *European Journal of Sociology* 7 (1965): 330–336.

30. Marcel Mauss, "Note de méthode sur l'extension de la sociologie, énoncé de quelques principes à propos d'un livre récent" [1927], in *Œuvres*, ed. Victor Karady (Paris: Les Editions de Minuit, 1969), 3:291. The "recent book" that Mauss was reviewing was *The History and Prospect of the Social Sciences*, edited by H. E. Barnes in 1925.

31. Aron, *Memoirs*, 45.

32. Marcel Mauss in a letter to the Danish sociologist Sven Ranulf on November 6, 1936. With the permission of Marcel Mauss, Ranulf included this letter in his article "Scholarly Forerunners of Fascism," *Ethics* 50 (1939): 16–34. Ranulf attacked sociologists and intellectuals who endangered the survival of democratic societies by imposing Gemeinschaft-like norms and ideals upon them. This had been the prerogative of German scholars. Unwittingly, the "French" school of sociology had followed in their footsteps.

33. Maurice Halbwachs, "Une expulsion," Manuscript, Institut Mémoires de l'Edition Contemporaine (IMEC) Paris; Fonds Halbwachs 021/ H 37. 7 pp.

34. Bourdieu, "L'assassinat de Maurice Halbwachs."

35. Semprun, *Literature or Life*, 42.

36. See Becker, *Maurice Halbwachs*.

37. Rosenberg, "Das Ende der Französischen Revolution."

38. Gustave Flaubert to George Sand, November 27, 1870, in Flaubert and Sand, *Correspondance*, 319.

39. See Drieu la Rochelle, *Chronique politique 1934–1942*, 63.

40. Maurras, *Réflexions sur la révolution de 1789*, 157, 158. One cannot quote Maurras without mentioning that he got many things wrong, especially in regard to the mutual influences between France and Germany. For an authoritarian thinker like him, for instance, even "democracy" rhymed with "Ger-

many"—and for the anti-Semite, the French Revolution was nothing but the expression of a "Jewish-Germanic principle."

41. Bloch, *Strange Defeat*, 161.

42. Heinrich Heine, *Religion and Philosophy in Germany: A Fragment* [1833–34], 158–160. Henry Morgenthau saw in Heine's "remarkably accurate prophecy" a description of the German national character and a proof of Germany's "will to try it again." See Morgenthau, *Germany Is Our Problem*, 106.

43. Parker, "German Literature," 325.

44. Bloch, *Strange Defeat*, 151. Although they would make strange bedfellows, there is a similarity here between Bloch and Charles Maurras, who had called the defeat of 1870 a sensible image of France's obvious loss of spirit. See Maurras, *Quand les Français ne s'aimaient pas*, 31.

45. The book I am referring to is Albert Hirschman, *Getting Ahead Collectively: Grassroots Experiences in Latin America* (New York: Pergamon Press, 1984). For Hirschman's collaboration with Varian Fry, see Fry, *Surrender on Demand* [1945], and Hirschman, *A Propensity to Self-Subversion*.

46. See Curtius, *Der Syndikalismus der Geistesarbeiter in Frankreich*, 29–33.

47. Bloch, *Strange Defeat*, 172.

48. Canguilhem, *Vie et mort de Jean Cavaillès*, 23.

49. Namer, "Halbwachs," 11.

50. Canguilhem, *Vie et mort de Jean Cavaillès*, 32.

51. Bourdieu, "L'assassinat de Maurice Halbwachs," 163.

52. Thomas Mann, *Reflections of a Nonpolitical Man*, 365.

53. Ibid., 427.

54. Eliot, *Christianity and Culture*, 15.

55. Benda, *The Treason of the Intellectuals*, 159–160. The notion of the "socially unattached intelligentsia" (*sozial freischwebende Intelligenz*) goes back to Alfred Weber. But Karl Mannheim made it notorious. It is remarkable that in Mannheim's works neither Maurras's *L'avenir de l'intelligence* nor Maurice Barrès's novel *Les déracinés* is mentioned.

56. In Germany itself, the battle over the claims and limits of a sociology of knowledge, in which Mannheim and the literary critic Ernst Robert Curtius confronted each other, was fought with a constant attempt to compare French and German social thought.

57. Benda, *Treason of the Intellectuals*, 58.

58. This is how Karl Jaspers saw him at the "Rencontres Internationales de Genève" in 1946. See Karl Jaspers's letter to Hannah Arendt, September 18, 1946, in Arendt and Jaspers, *Correspondence, 1926–1969*, 57.

59. An attempt at a "reconciliation of cultures" was on the agenda when Hitler and Count Ciano, the Italian foreign minister and Mussolini's son-in-

law, met on the Obersalzberg in Berchtesgaden in October 1936. See Anfuso, *Rom-Berlin in diplomatischem Spiegel*, 37–38. Mussolini may have told his son-in-law that in 1922 an Italian diplomat who was visiting Germany had written to him that Adolf Hitler, the leader of the German fascists, was "a young man, whose temperament, voice and gestures are more Latin than German." See Rosen, "Mussolini und Deutschland 1922–1923," 23. Marc Bloch would later call Hitler "a brown-haired *Homo alpinus* of middle height, with a little red-headed cripple as his chief spokesman." Bloch, *Strange Defeat*, 151.

60. Arendt, "The Aftermath of Nazi Rule," 349.

61. Arthur Miller, "Uneasy about the Germans: After the Wall," in *Echoes down the Corridor*, 222–229.

Notes to Chapter 6: German Culture at Home

1. Hannah Arendt to Karl Jaspers, August 17, 1946, in Arendt and Jaspers, *Correspondence, 1926–1969*, 54.

2. Letters by Heinrich Blücher to Hannah Arendt, July 15 and 16, 1946, in Arendt and Blücher, *Within Four Walls*, 84–87.

3. Jaspers mentions Blücher's self-reproach in a letter to Hannah Arendt on December 13, 1963. Arendt and Jaspers, *Correspondence, 1926–1969*, 542.

4. Karl Jaspers to Hannah Arendt, October 19, 1946, ibid., 62.

5. Mary McCarthy, "General Macbeth," in *The Writing on the Wall and Other Literary Essays*, 14.

6. Podhoretz, "Hannah Arendt on Eichmann," 201. For a resumé of the debate, see Anson Rabinbach, "Eichmann in New York."

7. Abel, "The Aesthetics of Evil." Mary McCarthy responded to Abel's attack on her friend Hannah Arendt with her essay "The Hue and the Cry," in *The Writing on the Wall*, 54–71. For her, neither Macbeth nor Eichmann were "monsters." See *Between Friends: The Correspondence of Hannah Arendt and Mary McCarthy, 1949–1975*, 145ff. The "theatricality" of the Eichmann trial has remained a topic of debate. In a review of Hanna Yablonka's book *The State of Israel vs. Adolf Eichmann*, the author was commended for having shown that Moshe Landau, the presiding judge, "never permitted the theatrics of the proceeding to overwhelm its legal character." See Douglas, "A Nation's Trial."

8. In his memoirs, Meinecke admitted having been a harsh anti-Semite from his student years into the 1890s. Even as a professor in Straßburg, where he had been appointed in 1901, he did not lose his feeling of antipathy toward

his Jewish colleagues. See Meinecke, *Straßburg/Freiburg/Berlin 1901–1919*, 26–30.

9. Weber, "National Character and the Junkers," in *From Max Weber: Essays in Sociology*, 393–394.

10. Meinecke, *The German Catastrophe*, 117.

11. Ibid., 120–121. In his book *Friedrich Meinecke and German Politics in the Twentieth Century*, Robert A. Pois uses the terms "Goethe study groups" and "Goethe circles." It is important, though, to translate *Goethe-Gemeinden* as "Goethe communities," since the term carries the well-established opposition of German *Gemeinschaft* against Western *Gesellschaft*.

12. Meinecke, *The German Catastrophe*, 119.

13. Riefenstahl, "Interview with Hilmar Hoffmann." After the war, this issue became a topic of debate in the German Democratic Republic. The DEFA, the official East German film producer, had inherited the bulk of movies that had been produced by the UFA during the Third Reich. East German television was showing most of these movies because they were deemed "apolitical." A debate ensued over whether a socialist state could show movies that had been made under the Nazi regime. The movies continued to be shown, though, not only because they were very popular with East German viewers, but not least because they created one of the rare occasions when many West Germans tuned in to East German television.

14. Meinecke, *The German Catastrophe*, 117, 119.

15. Hughes, *Consciousness and Society*, 246. I agree with Hughes, though, that, asked to choose between Weimar and Potsdam, Meinecke would have chosen—Königsberg, Kant's city. For a positive view of Meinecke's alleged return to cosmopolitanism, see also Hofer, *Geschichtsschreibung und Weltanschauung*, and Sterling, *Ethics in a World of Power*.

16. See Berg, *Der Holocaust und die westdeutschen Historiker*. See also Hughes, *Consciousness and Society*, 245.

17. Theodor W. Adorno, "Scientific Experiences of a European Scholar in America," in Fleming and Bailyn, eds., *The Intellectual Migration*, 367.

18. Adorno and Mann, *Briefwechsel 1943–1955*, 44–54.

19. Karl Jaspers to Hannah Arendt, September 18, 1946, in *Correspondence, 1926–1969*, 59.

20. Hannah Arendt to Karl Jaspers, November 11, 1946, ibid., 64. "Unblessed memory" made Hannah Arendt also nostalgically remember Martin Heidegger, for her a "poetic thinker" like Benjamin and Broch, as the leader of an "apolitical revolution" in the twenties, her Marburg years. See Wolin, *Heidegger's Children*.

21. Hannah Arendt to Karl Jaspers, January 28, 1949, in *Correspondence, 1926–1969*, 129.

22. Pachter, "On Being an Exile," 18.

23. Arendt, "The Aftermath of Nazi Rule," 353.

24. Karl Jaspers to Hannah Arendt, April 19, 1947, in *Correspondence, 1926–1969*, 81.

25. Theodor W. Adorno, letter to Thomas Mann, December 28, 1949, in *Briefwechsel, 1943–1955*, 48. It is hard to understand how Adorno could think that this remark could please Thomas Mann, who had, in 1941, written that he had read Niemöller's last sermons "with an emotion for which sympathy is a very weak word." Mann, "Niemöller," in *Order of the Day*, 276.

26. In his letter to Hannah Arendt of March 19, 1947, Jaspers spoke of a "Gesinnungsgemeinschaft" between them, a community created by fate. In the English translation, the emotional weight of the word has been lost with its rendering as the rather banal "similarity of outlook." *Correspondence, 1926–1969*, 75.

27. Rychner, " 'Auferstehung der Kultur in Deutschland.' "

28. See Grosser, ed., *Die große Kontroverse: Ein Briefwechsel um Deutschland*.

29. "The Germans should not utter the word '*Gemüt*' for a span of thirty years and then '*Gemüt*' would gradually be forthcoming again; now it only signifies condoning our own and other people's foibles." Goethe, *Maxims and Reflections* (no. 340), 40.

30. Thomas Mann to Agnes Meyer, September 21, 1941, in *Briefwechsel, 1937–1955*, 315.

31. Thomas Mann, "Germany and the Germans," in *Thomas Mann's Addresses*, 5–6.

32. These are the last sentences in the devastating rejection of *Doctor Faustus* in Walter Boehlich's essay "Thomas Manns Doktor Faustus."

33. Pachter, "On Being an Exile," 14.

34. Gottfried Benn, "Letter from Berlin, July 1948," trans. Ernst Kaiser and Eithne Wilkins, in Benn, *Prose, Essays, Poems*, 80. Klement Gottwald became the communist prime minister of Czechoslovakia in 1946.

35. Quoted from Reinhard Paul Becker, "Introduction," ibid., xix.

36. This was at least Benn's view. Allan Bloom insists, in his interpretation of the *Republic*, that Socrates did not wish to entirely banish poetry from the city but rather wanted to reform it. *The Republic of Plato*, translated with notes and an interpretive essay by Allan Bloom, 426–434. See also Strauss, *The City and Man*.

37. The allusion, of course, is to Clifford Geertz's "Blurred Genres: The Refiguration of Social Thought," *American Scholar* 49 (1980): 165–179.

38. Quoted from E. B. Ashton, "Foreword," in Benn, *Prose, Essays, Poems*, xiii.

39. Lionel Gossman, "Burckhardt and Ranke: Basel und Berlin," in *Basel in the Age of Burckhardt*, 450. See also Gilbert, *Politics or Culture?*

40. Due to restrictions of copyright, the letters between Adorno and Gehlen cannot (yet) be quoted or published. Thanks to the permission of Arnold Gehlen's daughter, I was able to reprint and to comment upon one letter from 1962 between the two unlikely correspondents: "Arnold Gehlen and Theodor W. Adorno," *Süddeutsche Zeitung* 86 (2003): 19.

41. Hannah Arendt had made a similar observation, not just in regard to the student population but in regard to German attitudes in general: "The old virtue of seeking excellence in the finished product, no matter what the working conditions, has yielded to a mere blind need to keep busy, a greedy craving for something to do every moment of the day." Arendt, "The Aftermath of Nazi Rule," 345.

42. Klemperer, *Curriculum Vitae*, 2:687.

43. Goltz, *Die Deutschen*, 4, 7. I quote the English translation from Harold James, *A German Identity, 1770–1990*, 14.

44. Theodor W. Adorno, letter to Thomas Mann, December 28, 1949, in Adorno and Mann, *Briefwechsel, 1943–1955*, 46.

45. Steiner, "Zion's Shadows, 3. Steiner's essay is a review of Pierre Bouretz, *Témoins du Futur: Philosophie et messianisme* (Paris: Gallimard, 2004).

46. Thomas Mann, diary entry, July 29, 1934, in *Tagebücher 1933–1934*, 486.

47. *Thomas Mann an Ernst Bertram*, 185. In all likelihood, Adorno did not know of this letter.

48. Thomas Mann, *Reflections*, 175–176. The italics are Mann's.

49. Thomas Mann, *Tagebücher 1933–1934*, 473–474. Theodor Lessing had left Germany one month after the Nazis came to power and had moved to Czechoslovakia. He was murdered by Nazi death squads on August 30, 1933, in Marienbad. Lessing had attacked the Nazis in Germany and he continued with his anti-Nazi polemics in articles for the *Prager Tageblatt*.

50. Thompson, "The Problem Child of Europe," 399.

51. Hannah Arendt to Karl Jaspers, October 31, 1948, in *Correspondence, 1926–1969*, 118.

52. Hannah Arendt to Karl Jaspers, September 7, 1952, ibid., 198.

53. Thomas Mann, "Warum braucht das Jüdische Volk nicht zu verzweifeln?" [1936], in *An die gesittete Welt*, 852. This volume contains a whole section with the title "Zur Jüdischen Frage" (The Jewish question), 829–891.

54. Thomas Mann, "Germany and the Germans," 19. Goethe made his remark to Chancellor von Müller on December 14, 1808, in *Goethes Gespräche*, 2:393. Goethe's remark to Wilhelm von Humboldt is quoted by Humboldt in a letter to his wife on November 19, 1808. Ibid., 383.

55. Goethe in the presence of Christine von Reinhard, June 1, 1807, in *Goethes Gespräche*, 2:229: "Die Deutschen würden *wie die Juden* sich überall unterdrücken lassen, aber *unvertilgbar* sein wie *diese*, und wenn sie kein Vaterland mehr haben, erst recht zusammenhalten." Goethe to Riemer on March 15, 1808: "Deutsche gehen nicht zu Grunde, so wenig wie die Juden, weil es Individuen sind." Ibid., 293.

56. See Morgenthau, *Germany Is Our Problem*, 104.

57. Andrei Pleşu, who was kind enough to read this passage, reminded me that Jews and Germans share the same archangel: Michael.

Notes to Chapter 7: The Survival of the Typical German

1. *Demoskopie und Kulturgeschichte* (Allensbach: Institut für Demoskopie, 1999).

2. Thomas Mann could not know, while writing *Doctor Faustus*, that one of the murderous doctors at Auschwitz was a Dr. Faust.

3. For the writing of this chapter, I have especially profited from the following publications: *Weimarer Klassik in der Ära Ulbricht*, ed. Lothar Ehrlich and Gunther Mai (Weimar: Böhlau, 2001); *Das Dritte Weimar: Klassik und Kultur im Nationalsozialismus*, ed. Lothar Ehrlich, Jürgen John, and Justus H. Ulbricht (Cologne: Böhlau, 1999); and Karl Robert Mandelkow, *Goethe in Deutschland: Rezeptionsgeschichte eines Klassikers*, 2 vols. (Munich: Beck, 1980–1989).

4. Thomas Mann, "Goethe's Career as a Man of Letters," in *Essays*, 71.

5. Nietzsche, *Human, All Too Human*, vol. 2, pt. 2 ("The Wanderer and His Shadow," no. 125: "Is there such a thing as a 'German classic'?"), 340. The italics are Nietzsche's.

6. As proof that Goethe had remained alive and well among German youth after the end of the war, a volume was published in which young authors described how important Goethe was to them. See Wilhelm Stutz, ed., *Goethe in unserem Leben: Niederschriften junger Menschen 1942–46*, (Willsbach: Scherer, 1947).

7. See Semprun, *What a Beautiful Sunday!* and Rost, *Goethe in Dachau*. (Hamburg: Konkret Literatur Verlag, 1981).

8. Martin Walser, "Das Prinzip Genauigkeit: Über Victor Klemperer," in *Deutsche Sorgen*, 570.

9. Dieckmann, "Die Frage Mephisto: Klassik-Bilder in der frühen DDR," 560.

10. See Grimm and Hermand, eds., *Die Klassik-Legende*.

11. Berger, "Erinnerungen an Aby Warburg," 52–53.

Notes to Chapter 8: German Reunification

1. The leading female actress in this film was Ruth Leuwerik, who was later honored in 2004 with an exhibition in the Berlin Film Museum: "The Ideal Woman: Ruth Leuwerik and the Cinema of the Fifties." Arguably, Leuwerik was the ideal *German* woman. As Queen Luise of Prussia in a movie with this title in 1957, she reminded the Germans of the Prussian wars of liberation, a political past of which they were proud.

2. See Niekisch, *Die Dritte Imperiale Figur*, 62.

3. Carlyle, *Sartor Resartus / On Heroes and Hero Worship* [1841], 394.

4. See Albert O. Hirschman's brilliant interpretation of the collapse of the German Democratic Republic: "Exit, Voice, and the Fate of the German Democratic Republic," in *A Propensity to Self-Subversion*, 9–44.

5. Not many of them may have known or have wished to remember that Otto Grotewohl, the first prime minister of the GDR, had, in April 1955, given a speech on Friedrich Schiller with the title "Wir sind ein Volk!"

6. The juxtaposition of copy-rights and copy-wrongs is to be found in Carlyle's *On Heroes and Hero-Worship*, 383.

7. Santayana, *Egotism in German Philosophy*, 12.

8. Plessner, *The Limits of Community*, 57. The German original, *Grenzen der Gemeinschaft*, was published in 1924.

9. Stern, *The Failure of Illiberalism*, 5. The chapter in Stern's book from which I quote this passage is called "The Political Consequences of the Unpolitical German."

Notes to Chapter 9: Culture as Camouflage

1. Thomas Mann, "The Sufferings and Greatness of Richard Wagner," in *Past Masters*, 92.

2. In 1969, the Austrian writer Oswald Wiener published a novel with the title *Die Verbesserung von Mitteleuropa* (The betterment of Central Europe).

3. Elon, "A Reporter at Large: Prague Autumn," 132.

4. Carlyle, *On Heroes and Hero-Worship*, 403–404, 384.

5. Ibid., 392.

6. Franz Kafka, "Fellowship," in *Description of a Struggle*, 217–218. For the German original—in which no title for the text is given—see Kafka, *Nachgelassene Schriften und Fragmente*, ed. Jost Schillemeit (Frankfurt am Main: S. Fischer, 1992), 2:313–314.

7. See Smolar, "1989—Geschichte und Gedächtnis."

8. See Friedrich Naumann, *Central Europe*, 34, x, 41.

Notes to Chapter 10: Irony and Politics

1. Thomas Mann to Agnes Meyer, January 23, 1943, in *Briefwechsel 1937–1955*, 459.

2. For a detailed overview of Thomas Mann's political statements after the end of the Second World War, see Stachorski, ed., *Fragile Republik*.

3. Niebuhr, "Mann's Political Essays," 584. Norman Podhoretz tells about another confrontation of John Locke with German culture: "[The] persistent belief in the superiority of German culture, despite Nazism but also in a certain sense because of it, did not apply to America alone. One night Hannah [Arendt] came to our apartment for a small dinner party at which the only other guest was a fellow German Jewish intellectual who had found refuge in England and was now visiting New York from London. At a certain moment in the conversation, when the name of John Locke came up, Hannah turned to him and said, 'Ach, these English, they think they have philosophers,' and the two of them shared a chuckle of amusement at the thought. What, after all, was Locke compared with the like of Heidegger? It did not seem to occur to either of them that there might be some relevance in the fact that Locke and his successors had laid the philosophical basis for a free society while Heidegger had found it consistent with his philosophy to support the Nazis." Norman Podhoretz, "Hannah Arendt's Jewish Problem—And Mine," in Podhoretz, *Ex-Friends*, 172n.

4. For a succinct statement on how little American "culture" influenced Thomas Mann and Theodor W. Adorno, see Michael Naumann, "Thomas Mann and Theodor W. Adorno in Exile."

5. Thomas Mann, "Goethe and Democracy" in Thomas Mann's *Addresses*, 130. It is a juxtaposition of two different political temperaments from a Shakespeare play that curiously leaves England, the land of Shakespeare, aside.

6. Goethe, "Wilhelm Meister's Travels," as quoted by Thomas Mann, "Goethe and Democracy," in Mann's *Addresses*, 128.

7. DeLillo, "In the Ruins of the Future," 33.

8. See Gilbert, *To the Farewell Address*, which analyzes the mood of early American diplomacy for which Adams's famous quote is so characteristic.

9. Bloom, *The Closing of the American Mind*, 153.

10. Thomas Mann, *Reflections*, 429.

11. Niebuhr, *The Irony of American History*. Niebuhr had called Thomas Mann's essay "That Man Is My Brother" a "perfect piece of irony." Niebuhr, "Mann's Political Essays," 584.

12. Niebuhr, *The Irony of American History*, 5.

13. Ibid., 132–133.

14. Steiner, *The Idea of Europe*, 33.

15. Ozick, "God Is in the Details," 9. In quoting Ozick's review I am not necessarily agreeing with her glowing assessment of Updike, who, for others like Gore Vidal, is the quintessential "commercial American writer." I am interested in presenting an argument that draws its force from a comparison between Europe and the United States.

16. Amis, "The Supreme American Novelist," 112.

17. Roth, *The Plot against America*.

18. Many reviewers, like Michael Wood in the *London Review of Books*, were impressed by Roth's story, "beautifully, quietly told," and praised "the quiet domesticity of the story and its telling." See Wood, "Just Folks."

Notes to Chapter 11: Germany after Reunification

1. See Mitscherlich and Mitscherlich, *The Inability to Mourn*. The German original, *Die Unfähigkeit zu trauern*, was published in 1967.

2. Grass, *From the Diary of a Snail*, 6, 71, 33.

3. Grass, *Crabwalk*. I see a parallel here with Jörg Friedrich who, before publishing *Der Brand* (*The fire*) had written about the crimes of the Third Reich and reported about neo-Nazi movements in the Federal Republic.

4. Grass, *Two States—One Nation?*, 2, 5–6.

5. Heinar Kipphardt had also tried to bring Arendt and Mann together—in his play *Bruder Eichmann*, which he had begun to write in the sixties and which was first published in 1983.

6. The notion of "subtle silence" that Nietzsche attributed to Goethe had escaped my attention, until I was made aware of it by Fritz Stern. See Nietzsche, *Beyond Good and Evil*, 178, and Stern, *Das feine Schweigen*.

7. In one of the best prose texts he ever wrote, Martin Walser has described how he discovered Klemperer: "Das Prinzip Genauigkeit: Über Victor Klemperer," in *Deutsche Sorgen*, 565–592. See *I Shall Bear Witness: The Diaries of Victor Klemperer, 1933–41*, and *To the Bitter End: The Diaries of Victor Klemperer, 1942–45*.

BIBLIOGRAPHY

Abel, Lionel. "The Aesthetics of Evil: Hannah Arendt on Eichmann and the Jews." *Partisan Review* (Summer 1963): 211–230.

Adorno, Theodor W. *Gesammelte Schriften*. Ed. Rolf Tiedemann. Frankfurt am Main: Suhrkamp, 1986.

Adorno, Theodor W., and Thomas Mann. *Briefwechsel 1943–1955*. Ed. Christoph Gödde and Thomas Sprecher. Frankfurt am Main: Suhrkamp, 2002.

Amis, Martin. "The Supreme American Novelist." *Atlantic Monthly*, December 2003, 111–114.

Anfuso, Filippo. *Rom-Berlin in diplomatischem Spiegel*. Essen: Pohl & Co., 1951.

Arendt, Hannah. "The Aftermath of Nazi Rule: Report from Germany." *Commentary* 10 (1959): 342–353.

Arendt, Hannah, and Heinrich Blücher. *Within Four Walls: The Correspondence between Hannah Arendt and Heinrich Blücher, 1936–1968*. Ed. Lotte Kohler. Trans. Peter Constantine. New York: Harcourt, 2000.

Arendt, Hannah, and Karl Jaspers. *Correspondence, 1926–1969*. Ed. Lotte Kohler and Hans Sahner. Trans. Robert and Rita Kimber. New York: Harcourt Brace Jovanovich, 1992.

Arendt, Hannah, and Mary McCarthy. *Between Friends: The Correspondence of Hannah Arendt and Mary McCarthy, 1949–1975*. Ed. Carol Brightman. New York: Harcourt Brace, 1995.

Arnold, Matthew. *Culture and Anarchy*. In *The Complete Prose Works of Matthew Arnold*, vol. 5, ed. R. H. Super. Ann Arbor: University of Michigan Press, 1980.

Aron, Raymond. *Memoirs: Fifty Years of Political Reflection*. Trans. George Holoch. Foreword by Henry A. Kissinger. New York: Holmes & Meier, 1990.

Backes, Klaus. *Hitler und die bildenden Künste: Kulturverständnis und Kunstpolitik im Dritten Reich*. Cologne: DuMont, 1988.

Bardèche, Maurice. *Qu'est-ce que le fascisme?* Paris: Les Sept Couleurs, 1961.

Becker, Annette. *Maurice Halbwachs: Un intellectuel en guerres mondiales 1914–1945*. Paris: Agnès Viénot Éditions, 2003.

Benda, Julien. *The Treason of the Intellectuals*. New York: W. W. Norton, 1969.

Benn, Gottfried. *Briefwechsel mit dem "Merkur" 1948–1956*. Stuttgart: Klett-Cotta, 2004.

———. *Prose, Essays, Poems*. Ed. Volkmar Sander. New York: Continuum, 1987.

Berg, Nicolas. *Der Holocaust und die westdeutschen Historiker: Erforschung und Erinnerung*. Göttingen: Wallstein, 2003.

Berger, Klaus. "Erinnerungen an Aby Warburg." In *Mnemosyne: Zum 50. Todestag von Aby M. Warburg*, ed. Stephan Füssel. Göttingen: Gratia, 1979.

Bloch, Marc. *Strange Defeat: A Statement of Evidence Written in 1940*. Oxford: Oxford University Press, 1949.

Bloom, Allan. *The Closing of the American Mind*. New York: Simon and Schuster, 1987.

Bloom, Allan, ed. *The Republic of Plato*. New York: Basic Books, 1968.

Boehlich, Walter. "Thomas Manns Doktor Faustus." *Merkur* 2 (1948): 588–603.

Bohrer, Karl-Heinz. "Stil oder 'maniera': Zur Aktualität und Geschichte eines nationalen Unvermögens." *Merkur* 56 (2002): 1057–1069.

Bourdieu, Pierre. "L'assassinat de Maurice Halbwachs." In *Visages de la Résistance* (La Liberté de l'esprit, no. 16), 161–168. Lyon: La Manufacture, 1987.

Brasillach, Robert. *Œuvres complètes*, ed. Maurice Bardèche. Paris: Au Club de l'Honnête Homme, 1964.

Brocke, Bernhard vom. " 'Wissenschaft und Militarismus': Der Aufruf der 93 'An die Kulturwelt!' und der Zusammenbruch der internationalen Gelehrtenrepublik im Ersten Weltkrieg." In *Wilamowitz nach 50 Jahren*, ed. William Calder III, Hellmut Flashar, and Theodor Lindken, 649–719. Darmstadt: Wissenschaftliche Buchgesellschaft, 1985.

Brooks, Peter. "Gallic Invasion." *Times Literary Supplement*, May 28, 2004, 5–6.

Burckhardt, Carl J., and Max Rychner. *Briefe 1926–1965*. Frankfurt am Main: S. Fischer, 1987.

Buruma, Ian. "The Destruction of Germany." *New York Review of Books*, October 21, 2004, 8–12.

Butler, Eliza Marian. *The Tyranny of Greece over Germany; A Study of the Influence Exercised by Greek Art and Poetry over the Great German Writers of the Eighteenth, Nineteenth, and Twentieth Centuries*. New York: Macmillan, 1935.

Canguilhem, Georges. *Vie et mort de Jean Cavaillès*. Paris: Editions Allia, 1996.

Carlyle, Thomas. *Sartor Resartus / On Heroes and Hero Worship*. 1841. London: Everyman's Library, 1973.

Caro, Elme-Marie. "La morale de la guerre: Kant et M. de Bismarck." *Revue des deux mondes* 82 (1870): 577–594.

Chapman, John Jay. *Deutschland über Alles or Germany Speaks*. New York: G. P. Putnam's Sons, 1914.

Chateaubriant, Alphonse de. *La gerbe des forces (nouvelle Allemagne)*. Paris: Bernard Grasset, 1937.

Curtius, Ernst Robert. *Der Syndikalismus der Geistesarbeiter in Frankreich*. Bonn: Cohen, 1921.

———. *Deutscher Geist in Gefahr*. Stuttgart: Deutsche Verlags-Anstalt, 1932.

DeLillo, Don. "In the Ruins of the Future: Reflections on Terror and Loss in the Shadow of September." *Harper's Magazine*, December 2001, 33–41.

Demoskopie und Kulturgeschichte. Allensbach: Institut für Demoskopie, 1999.

Dewey, John. *German Philosophy and Politics*. Freeport, NY: Books for Libraries Press, 1942.

Dieckmann, Friedrich. "Die Frage Mephisto. Klassik-Bilder in der frühen DDR." *Sinn und Form* 53 (2001): 558–565.

Douglas, Lawrence R. "A Nation's Trial." *Times Literary Supplement*, May 28, 2004, 8.

Drieu la Rochelle, Pierre. *Chronique politique 1934–1942*. Paris: Gallimard, 1943.

Drury, Shadia B. *The Political Ideas of Leo Strauss*. London: Macmillan Press, 1988.

———. *Leo Strauss and the American Right*. New York: St. Martin's Press, 1997.

Duffy, John J., ed. *Coleridge's American Disciples: The Selected Correspondence of James Marsh*. Amherst: University of Massachusetts Press, 1973.

Ehrlich, Lothar, Jürgen John, and Justus H. Ulbricht, eds. *Das Dritte Weimar: Klassik und Kultur im Nationalsozialismus*. Cologne: Böhlau, 1999.

Ehrlich, Lothar, and Gunther Mai, eds. *Weimarer Klassik in der Ära Ulbricht*. Weimar: Böhlau, 2001.

Elias, Norbert. *The Civilizing Process: The History of Manners*. Trans. Edmund Jephcott. New York: Urizen Books, 1978.

———. *The Germans: Power Struggles and the Development of Habitus in the Nineteenth and Twentieth Centuries*. Ed. Michael Schröter. Trans. Eric Dunning and Stephen Mennell. New York: Columbia University Press, 1996.

Eliot, T. S. *Christianity and Culture*. New York: Harcourt, Brace & World, 1949.

———. *The Letters of T. S. Eliot*. Vol. 1, *1898–1922*. Ed. Valerie Eliot. London: Faber and Faber, 1988.

Ellison, Ralph. "The Little Man at Chehaw Station: The American Artist and His Audience." *American Scholar*, Winter 1977–78, 25–48.

Elon, Amos. "A Reporter at Large: Prague Autumn." *New Yorker*, January 22, 1990, 125–133.

Emerson, Ralph Waldo. *Essays and Lectures*. New York: Library of America, 1983.

———. *The Journals and Miscellaneous Notebooks*. Vol. 7 (1838–1842), ed. A. W. Plumstead and Harrison Hayford; vol. 14 (1854–1861), ed. Susan Sutton Smith and Harrison Hayford. Cambridge, MA: Harvard University Press, 1969.

Fest, Joachim. *Inside Hitler's Bunker: The Last Days of the Third Reich*. Trans. Margot Bettauer Dembo. New York: Macmillan, 2004.

Flaubert, Gustave, and George Sand. *Correspondance*. Ed. Alphonse Jacobs. Paris: Flammarion, 1981.

Fleming, Donald, and Bernard Bailyn, eds. *The Intellectual Migration: Europe and America, 1930–1960*. Cambridge, MA: Harvard University Press, 1969.

Fry, Varian. *Surrender on Demand*. 1945. Reprint, New York: Johnson Books, 1997.

Fumaroli, Marc. *Quand l'Europe parlait français*. Paris: Editions de Fallois, 2001.

Furet, François. *Le passé d'une illusion. Essai sur l'idée communiste au XXe siècle*. Paris: Robert Laffont / Calmann-Lévy, 1995.

Furet, François, and Ernst Nolte. "Sur le fascisme, le communisme et l'histoire du XXe siècle." *Commentaire* 79 (1997): 559–576.

Fussell, Paul. *The Great War and Modern Memory*. New York: Oxford University Press, 1975.

Gay, Peter. *Weimar Culture: The Outsider as Insider*. New York: Harper & Row, 1968.

Geertz, Clifford. "Blurred Genres: The Refiguration of Social Thought." *American Scholar* 49 (1980): 165–179.

———. *Negara: The Theatre State in Nineteenth-Century Bali*. Princeton, NJ: Princeton University Press, 1980.

Gilbert, Felix. *Politics or Culture? Reflections on Ranke and Burckhardt*. Princeton, NJ: Princeton University Press, 1990.

———. *To the Farewell Address: Ideas of Early American Foreign Policy*. Princeton, N.J.: Princeton University Press, 1961.

Goebbels, Joseph. *The Goebbels Diaries, 1942–1943*. Ed. Louis P. Lochner. Garden City, NY: Doubleday, 1948.

Goethe, Johann Wolfgang von. *Conversations of Goethe with Eckermann and Soret*. Trans. John Oxenford. London: Smith, Elder & Co., 1850.

———. *Goethes Gespräche*. Ed. Wolfgang Herwig. Zurich: Artemis, 1969.

———. *Maxims and Reflections*. Ed. Peter Hutchinson. Trans. Elisabeth Stopp. London: Penguin, 1998.

Goltz, Bogumil. *Die Deutschen: Ethnographische Studie*. Berlin: Otto Janke, 1860.

Gooch, G. P., et al. *The German Mind and Outlook*. London: Chapman & Hall, 1945.

Gossman, Lionel. *Basel in the Age of Burckhardt: A Study in Unseasonable Ideas*. Chicago: University of Chicago Press, 2000.

Grass, Günter. *Crabwalk*. Trans. Krishna Winston. New York: Harcourt, 2002.

———. *From the Diary of a Snail*. Trans. Ralph Manheim. New York: Harcourt Brace Jovanovich, 1973.

———. *Two States—One Nation?* Trans. Krishna Winston with A. S. Wensinger. New York: Harcourt Brace Jovanovich, 1990.

Grimm, Reinhold, and Jost Hermand, eds. *Die Klassik-Legende*. Second Wisconsin Workshop. Frankfurt am Main: Athenäum, 1971.

Grosser, J.F.G., ed. *Die große Kontroverse: Ein Briefwechsel um Deutschland*. Hamburg: Nagel, 1963.

Guizot, François. "La France et la Prusse responsables devant l'Europe." *Revue des deux mondes* 76 (1869): 257–286.

Halbwachs, Maurice. "Une expulsion." Manuscript. Institut Mémoires de l'Edition Contemporaine (IMEC) Paris; Fonds Halbwachs 021/H 37. 7 pp.

Hamilton, Alastair. *The Appeal of Fascism: A Study of Intellectuals and Fascism, 1919–1945*. New York: Avon, 1973.

Harrison, John R. *The Reactionaries*. London: Victor Gollancz, 1966.

Hébey, Pierre. *La NRF des années sombres, Juin 1940–Juin 1941*. Paris: Gallimard, 1992.

Heine, Heinrich. *Religion and Philosophy in Germany: A Fragment*. 1833–34. Albany: State University of New York Press, 1986.

Heller, Hermann. *Europa und der Faschismus*. Berlin: de Gruyter, 1929.

Henderson, Nevile. *Failure of a Mission*. New York: G. P. Putnam's Sons, 1940.

Hinderer, Walter, ed. *Goethe und das Zeitalter der Romantik*. Würzburg: Königshausen & Neumann, 2002.

Hindus, Milton, ed. *Leaves of Grass One Hundred Years After*. Stanford, CA: Stanford University Press, 1955.

Hirschman, Albert O. *A Propensity to Self-Subversion*. Cambridge, MA: Harvard University Press, 1995.

Hitler, Adolf. *Monologe im Führerhauptquartier*. Ed. Werner Jochmann. Munich: Heyne, 1982.

Hofer, Walther. *Geschichtsschreibung und Weltanschauung. Betrachtungen zum Werk Friedrich Meineckes*. Munich: Oldenbourg, 1950.

Hughes, H. Stuart. *Consciousness and Society: The Reorientation of European Social Thought, 1890–1930*. Brighton: Harvester Press, 1979.

Humboldt, Wilhelm von. *The Limits of State Action*. Ed. J. W. Burrow. Cambridge: Cambridge University Press, 1969.

Iggers, Georg G. *The German Conception of History: The National Tradition of Historical Thought from Herder to the Present*. Middletown, CT: Wesleyan University Press, 1986.

James, Harold. *A German Identity, 1770–1990*. London: Weidenfeld & Nicolson, 1989.

James, Henry. *Literary Criticism*. New York: Library of America, 1984.

Jünger, Ernst, and Carl Schmitt. *Briefe 1930–1983*. Ed. Helmuth Kiesel. Stuttgart: Klett-Cotta, 1999.

Kafka, Franz. *Description of a Struggle*. Trans. Tania and James Stern. New York: Schocken, 1958.

Kessler, Harry. *In the Twenties: The Diaries of Harry Kessler*. London: Weidenfeld, 1971.

Kiberd, Declan. "At Full Speed: Inside the Mind of W. B. Yeats—and Outside." *Times Literary Supplement*, September 26, 2003.

Klemperer, Victor. *Curriculum Vitae: Jugend um 1900*. Berlin: Siedler, 1989.

———. *I Shall Bear Witness: The Diaries of Victor Klemperer, 1933–1941*. Trans. Martin Chalmers. London: Weidenfeld & Nicolson, 1998.

———. *To the Bitter End. The Diaries of Victor Klemperer, 1942–1945*. Trans. Martin Chalmers. London: Weidenfeld & Nicolson, 1999.

Kolb, Annette. *Versuch über Briand*. Berlin: Ernst Rowohlt, 1929.

Landauer, Gustav. "Goethes Politik: Eine Ankündigung" [1918–1921]. In *Goethe im Urteil seiner Kritiker: Dokumente zur Wirkungsgeschichte Goethes in Deutschland*, vol. 3, ed. Karl Robert Mandelkow, 477–486. Munich: Beck, 1979.

Langbehn, Julius. *Rembrandt als Erzieher: Von einem Deutschen*. 1888. Reprint, Leipzig: C. L. Hirschfeld, 1922.

Le Guyader, Hervé. *Geoffroy Saint-Hilaire, 1772–1844. A Visionary Naturalist*. Trans. Marjorie Grene. Chicago: University of Chicago Press, 2004.

Lepenies, Wolf. "Arnold Gehlen and Theodor W. Adorno." *Süddeutsche Zeitung* 86 (2003): 19.

———. *Gefährliche Wahlverwandtschaften: Essays zur Wissenschaftsgeschichte*. Stuttgart: Reclam, 1989.

Lewis, Sinclair. *Main Street* [1920]. In *Main Street and Babbitt*. New York: Library of America, 1992.

Lewis, Wyndham. *The Hitler Cult*. 1939. Reprint, New York: Gordon Press, 1972.

Lilla, Mark. "The Closing of the Straussian Mind." *New York Review of Books*, November 4, 2004, 55–59.

Maar, Michael. *Bluebeard's Chamber: Guilt and Confession in Thomas Mann*. Trans. David Fernbach. London: Verso, 2003.

Mandelkow, Karl Robert. *Goethe in Deutschland: Rezeptionsgeschichte eines Klassikers*. 2 vols. Munich: Beck, 1980–1989.

Mann, Klaus, and Erika Mann. *Escape to Life*. Boston: Houghton Mifflin, 1939.

Mann, Thomas. *An die gesittete Welt: Politische Schriften und Reden im Exil*, ed. Hanno Helbling. Frankfurt am Main: S. Fischer, 1986.

———. *Diaries, 1918–1939*. London: André Deutsch, 1983.

———. *Doctor Faustus: The Life of the German Composer Adrian Leverkühn as Told by a Friend*. New York: Alfred A. Knopf, 1948.

———. *Essays*. Trans. H. T. Lowe-Porter. New York: Vintage Books, 1957.

———. *Essays*. Vol. 5, *Deutschland und die Deutschen 1938–1945*. Ed. Hermann Kurzke and Stephan Stachorski. Frankfurt am Main: S. Fischer, 1996.

———. *Gesammelte Werke in zwölf Bänden*. Frankfurt am Main: S. Fischer, 1960.

———. "In Defense of Wagner: A Letter on the German Culture That Produced Both Wagner and Hitler." *Common Sense*, January 1940, 11–14.

———. *Letters of Thomas Mann, 1889–1955*. Trans. Richard Winston and Clara Winston. New York: Alfred A. Knopf, 1971.

———. *Order of the Day: Political Essays and Speeches of Two Decades*. New York: Alfred A. Knopf, 1942.

———. *Past Masters and Other Papers*. New York: Knopf, 1933.

———. *Reflections of a Nonpolitical Man*. Trans. Walter D. Morris. New York: Frederick Ungar, 1983.

———. *Tagebücher 1933–1934*. Ed. Peter de Mendelssohn. Frankfurt am Main: S. Fischer, 1977.

———. *Thomas Mann an Ernst Bertram: Briefe aus den Jahren 1910–1955*. Ed. Inge Jens. Pfullingen: Neske, 1960.

———. *Thomas Mann's Addresses: Delivered at the Library of Congress, 1942–1949*. Washington, DC: Library of Congress, 1963.

———. *Wagner und unsere Zeit: Aufsätze, Betrachtungen, Briefe*. Ed. Erika Mann. Frankfurt am Main: S. Fischer, 1963.

Mann, Thomas, and Heinrich Mann. *Letters of Heinrich and Thomas Mann, 1900–1949*. Ed. Hans Wysling. Berkeley: University of California Press, 1998.

Mann, Thomas, and Agnes Meyer. *Briefwechsel 1937–1955*. Ed. Hans Rudolf Vaget. Frankfurt am Main: S. Fischer, 1992.

Maurras, Charles. *Quand les Français ne s'aimaient pas. Chronique d'une renaissance, 1895–1905*. 1916. Reprint, Paris: Bibliothèque des Oeuvres Politiques, 1928.

———. *Réflexions sur la révolution de 1798*. Paris: Les Iles d'Or, 1948.

Mauss, Marcel. *Œuvres*. Ed. Victor Karady. Paris: Les Editions de Minuit, 1969.

Mayer, Arno J. *The Persistence of the Old Regime: Europe to the Great War*. New York: Pantheon, 1981.

McCarthy, Mary. *The Writing on the Wall and Other Literary Essays*. New York: Harcourt Brace Jovanovich, 1970.

Meinecke, Friedrich. *The Age of German Liberation, 1796–1815*. Ed. Peter Paret. Berkeley: University of California Press, 1977.

———. *Cosmopolitanism and the National State*. Princeton, NJ: Princeton University Press, 1970.

———. *The German Catastrophe: Reflections and Recollections*. Cambridge, MA: Harvard University Press, 1950.

———. *Strassburg/Freiburg/Berlin 1901–1919. Erinnerungen*. Stuttgart: K. F. Koehler, 1949.

Mencken, H. L. *The Vintage Mencken*. Gathered by Alistair Cooke. New York: Vintage Books, 1990.

Meyer, Agnes. *Out of These Roots: The Autobiography of an American Woman*. Boston: Little, Brown and Company, 1953.

Miller, Arthur. *Echoes down the Corridor: Collected Essays I, 1944–2000*. New York: Viking, 2000.

Mitscherlich, Alexander, and Margarete Mitscherlich. *The Inability to Mourn: Principles of Collective Behavior*. New York: Grove Press, 1975.

Morgenthau, Jr., Henry. *Germany Is Our Problem*. New York: Harper & Brothers, 1945.

Mosse, George L. *The Crisis of German Ideology: Intellectual Origins of the Third Reich*. New York: Grosset & Dunlap, 1964.

Namer, Gérard. "Halbwachs." In *Maurice Halbwachs: 1877–1945*. Colloque de la Faculté des Sciences Sociales de Strasbourg (mars 1995). Ed. Christian de Montlibert. Strasbourg: Presses Universitaires de Strasbourg, 1997.

Naumann, Friedrich. *Central Europe*. London: King & Son, 1917.

Naumann, Michael. "Thomas Mann and Theodor W. Adorno in Exile." In *Exiled in Paradise? Exile Literature in California*, 21–28. Leipzig: Villa Aurora Edition, 2004.

Niebuhr, Reinhold. "Mann's Political Essays." *The Nation*, November 29, 1942, 582–584.

———. *The Irony of American History.* New York: Charles Scribner's Sons, 1952.

Niekisch, Ernst. *Die Dritte Imperiale Figur.* Berlin: Widerstands-Verlag, 1935.

Nietzsche, Friedrich. *Beyond Good and Evil. Prelude to a Philosophy of the Future.* Trans. Walter Kaufmann. New York: Vintage Books, 1966.

———. *Briefe* (April 1869–Mai 1872). In *Kritische Gesamtausgabe*, vol. II:1, eds. Giorgio Colli and Mazzino Montinari. Berlin: Walter de Gruyter, 1977.

———. *Human, All Too Human: A Book for Free Spirits.* Trans. R. J. Hollingdale. Cambridge: Cambridge University Press, 1986.

———. *Twilight of the Idols.* Indianapolis: Hackett Publishing Co., 1997.

———. *Untimely Meditations.* Cambridge: Cambridge University Press, 1997.

Ozick, Cynthia. "God Is in the Details." *New York Times Book Review,* November 30, 2003, 8.

Pachter, Henry. "On Being an Exile: An Old-Timer's Personal and Political Memoir." *Salmagundi* 10–11 (1969–70): 12–51.

Paret, Peter. *An Artist against the Third Reich: Ernst Barlach, 1933–1938.* Cambridge: Cambridge University Press, 2003.

Parker, Theodore. "German Literature." *The Dial* 1 (January 1841): 315–339.

Parr, Rolf. *"Zwei Seelen wohnen, ach! in meiner Brust": Strukturen und Funktionen der Mythisierung Bismarcks (1860–1918).* Munich: Fink, 1992.

Picker, Henry. *Hitlers Tischgespräche im Führerhauptquartier.* Stuttgart: Seewald, 1976.

Plessner, Helmuth. *The Limits of Community: A Critique of Social Radicalism.* Trans. Andrew Wallace. Amherst: Humanity Books, 1999.

Podhoretz, Norman. *Ex-Friends.* San Francisco: Encounter Books, 2000.

———. "Hannah Arendt on Eichmann—A Study in the Perversity of Brilliance." *Commentary* 36, no. 3 (1963): 201–208.

Pois, Robert A. *Friedrich Meinecke and German Politics in the Twentieth Century.* Berkeley: University of California Press, 1972.

Preuß, Hugo. *Das deutsche Volk und die Politik.* Jena: Eugen Diederichs, 1915.

Rabinbach, Anson. "Eichmann in New York: The New York Intellectuals and the Hannah Arendt Controversy." *October* 108 (2004): 97–111.

Ranulf, Sven. "Scholarly Forerunners of Fascism." *Ethics* 50 (1939): 16–34.

Rathenau, Walther. *Gesammelte Schriften.* Vol. 6, *Schriften aus Kriegs- und Nachkriegszeit.* Berlin: S. Fischer, 1929.

Riefenstahl, Leni. "Interview with Hilmar Hoffmann," *Die Welt,* January 7, 2002.

Röpke, Wilhelm. *Die deutsche Frage*. Erlenbach-Zurich: E. Rentsch, 1945.

Rohden, Peter Richard. "Deutscher und französischer Konservatismus." *Die Dioskuren: Jahrbuch für Geisteswissenschaften* 3 (1924): 90–138.

Rosen, Edgar R. "Mussolini und Deutschland 1922–1923." *Vierteljahreshefte für Zeitgeschichte* 5 (1957): 17–41.

Rosenberg, Alfred. "Das Ende der Französischen Revolution. Zum Jahrestag am 14. Juli." *Völkischer Beobachter. Kampfblatt der national-sozialistischen Bewegung Großdeutschlands* 53, no. 196 (1940): 1–2.

Rost, Nico. *Goethe in Dachau*. With a foreword by Anna Seghers. Hamburg: Konkret Literatur Verlag, 1981.

Roth, Philip. *The Plot against America*. New York: Houghton Mifflin, 2004.

Rychner, Max. " 'Auferstehung der Kultur in Deutschland.' Zeugnis eines zurückgekehrten Emigranten." *Die Tat* 15 (1950): 11.

———. "Einsames Deutschland." *Neue Zürcher Zeitung*. October 22, 1933.

Santayana, Georges. *Egotism in German Philosophy*. New York: Charles Scribner's Sons, 1940.

Schjeldahl, Peter. "The Hitler Show: The Jewish Museum Revisits the Nazis." *New Yorker*, April 1, 2002, 87.

Schlegel, Friedrich. *Kritische Friedrich-Schlegel-Ausgabe*. Vol. 2. Ed. Ernst Behler. Munich: Schöningh; Zurich: Thomas, 1967.

Sebald, W. G. *On the Natural History of Destruction*. London: Hamish Hamilton, 2003.

Semprun, Jorge. *Literature or Life*. New York: Viking, 1997.

———. *What a Beautiful Sunday*. San Diego: Harcourt Brace Jovanovich, 1982.

Sherry, Vincent B. *The Great War and the Language of Modernism*. Oxford: Oxford University Press, 2003.

Smolar, Aleksander. "1989—Geschichte und Gedächtnis." *Transit. Europäische Revue* 20 (2000–2001): 15–43.

Spengler, Oswald. *The Hour of Decision: Germany and World-Historical Evolution*. Trans. Charles Francis Atkinson. New York: Knopf, 1934.

Spotts, Frederic. *Hitler and the Power of Aesthetics*. Woodstock, NY: Overlook Press, 2002.

Spranger, Eduard. "Mein Konflikt mit der national-sozialistischen Regierung 1933." *Universitas* 10 (1955): 457–473.

Stachorski, Stephan, ed. *Fragile Republik: Thomas Mann und Nachkriegsdeutschland*. Frankfurt am Main: S. Fischer, 1999.

Steiner, George. *The Idea of Europe*. Tilburg: Nexus Library IV, 2004.

———. "Zion's Shadows: The Hidden Thoughts of Philosophers—Including the Guru of Neo-Conservatism." *Times Literary Supplement*, February 27, 2004, 3–5.

Sterling, Richard W. *Ethics in a World of Power: The Political Ideas of Friedrich Meinecke*. Princeton, NJ: Princeton University Press, 1958.

Stern, Fritz. *Das feine Schweigen: Historische Essays*. Munich: Beck, 1999.

———. *The Failure of Illiberalism*. New York: Alfred A. Knopf, 1972.

———. *The Politics of Cultural Despair: A Study in the Rise of the Germanic Ideology*. Berkeley: University of California Press, 1974.

Strauss, Leo. *The City and Man*. Chicago: Rand McNally, 1964.

———. *Natural Right and History*. Chicago: University of Chicago Press, 1971.

Stutz, Wilhelm, ed. *Goethe in unserem Leben. Niederschriften junger Menschen 1942–46*. Willsbach: Scherer, 1947.

Thompson, Dorothy. "The Problem Child of Europe." *Foreign Affairs* 18 (1940): 389–412.

Thoreau, Henry David. *Journal*. Vol. 3 (1848–1851). Princeton, NJ: Princeton University Press, 1990.

Tiryakian, Edward A. "A Problem for the Sociology of Knowledge: The Mutual Unawareness of Emile Durkheim and Max Weber." *European Journal of Sociology* 7 (1965): 330–336.

Tocqueville, Alexis de. *Œuvres, Papiers et Correspondances*. Vol. 1, *De la Démocratie en Amérique*. Ed. J.-P. Mayer. Paris: Gallimard, 1951.

Trevor-Roper, Hugh. "Jacob Burckhardt." *Proceedings of the British Academy* 70 (1984): 359–378.

Trilling, Lionel. *A Gathering of Fugitives*. Oxford: Oxford University Press, 1980.

Troeltsch, Ernst. *Das Wesen des Deutschen*. Heidelberg: Carl Winter, 1915.

———. *Deutscher Geist und Westeuropa. Gesammelte kulturpolitische Aufsätze und Reden*. Ed. Hans Baron. Tübingen: Mohr/Siebeck, 1925.

Troubat, Jules. *Souvenirs du dernier secrétaire de Sainte-Beuve*. Paris: Calmann Lévy, 1890.

Tucker, William R. "Politics and Aesthetics: The Fascism of Robert Brasillach." *Western Political Quarterly* 15 (1962): 608.

Valéry, Paul. *The Collected Works of Paul Valéry*. Ed. Jackson Mathews. Princeton, NJ: Princeton University Press, 1968.

———. *Œuvres*. Paris: Gallimard / Bibliothèque de la Pléiade, 1957.

Vidal, Gore. *Inventing a Nation: Washington, Adams, Jefferson*. New Haven, CT: Yale University Press, 2003.

———. *The Last Empire: Essays, 1992–2000*. New York: Vintage Books, 2002.

Viereck, Peter. "Hitler and Richard Wagner." *Common Sense*, November 1939, 3–6.

———. *Metapolitics: From the Romantics to Hitler*. New York: Knopf, 1941.

Wagner, Richard. *Dichtungen und Schriften*. Jubiläumsausgabe in zehn Bänden. Ed. Dieter Borchmeyer. Frankfurt am Main: Insel, 1983.

Walser, Martin. *Deutsche Sorgen*. Frankfurt am Main: Suhrkamp, 1997.

Weber, Max. "National Character and the Junkers" [1917–1921]. In *From Max Weber: Essays in Sociology*, ed. H. H. Gerth and C. W. Mills, 386–395. New York: Oxford University Press, 1946.

Werckmeister, Otto K. "Hitler, the Artist." *Critical Inquiry* 23 (1997): 270–297.

Wharton, Edith. *Novels*. New York: Library of America, 1984.

———. *A Backward Glance: An Autobiography*. 1933. New York: Simon and Schuster, 1998.

———. *French Ways and Their Meaning*. 1919. Lee, MA: Berkshire House Publishers, 1997.

Whitman, Walt. *Complete Poetry and Collected Prose*. New York: Library of America, 1982.

Wiener, Oswald. *Die Verbesserung von Mitteleuropa*. Reinbek: Rowohlt, 1969.

Williams, William Carlos. *Selected Essays of William Carlos Williams*. New York: Random House, 1954.

Willson, A. Leslie, ed. *German Romantic Criticism*. The German Library, vol. 21. New York: Continuum, 1982.

Wisskirchen, Hans. "Republikanischer Eros: Zu Walt Whitmans und Hans Blühers Rolle in der politischen Publizistik Thomas Manns." In *'Heimsuchung und süßes Gift': Erotik und Poetik bei Thomas Mann*, ed. Gerhard Härle. Frankfurt am Main: S. Fischer, 1992.

Wolin, Richard. *Heidegger's Children: Hannah Arendt, Karl Löwith, Hans Jonas, and Herbert Marcuse*. Princeton, NJ: Princeton University Press, 2001.

Wood, Michael. "Just Folks." *London Review of Books*, November 4, 2004, 3–6.

Ziegler, Hans Severus. *Adolf Hitler aus dem Erleben dargestellt*. Göttingen: K. W. Schütz, 1965.

Ziolkowski, Theodore. *German Romanticism and Its Institutions*. Princeton, NJ: Princeton University Press, 1990.

Zuckmayer, Carl. *Geheimreport*. Munich: Deutscher Taschenbuch Verlag, 2003.

Acknowledgments

This book was written in Berlin and Princeton, where the library staffs of the Wissenschaftskolleg and the Institute for Advanced Study provided invaluable help. I thank Maike Voltmer for her daily support and Mitch Cohen, my English teacher, for his attention and his patience. A grant by the Fritz Thyssen Foundation (Cologne) is gratefully acknowledged.

At Princeton University Press, I profited as much from Brigitta van Rheinberg's enthusiasm and encouragement as from her common sense and critique; I profited from Meera Vaidyanathan's competence and thank her for her patience; to learn about the great craft of copyediting I could not have found a better person than Elizabeth Gilbert. I should also like to thank Lys Ann Weiss for preparing the index and my two anonymous reviewers, whose remarks were very helpful to me.

Index